# To Believe in God?
# To Hope . . . Maybe

# To Believe in God?
# To Hope . . . Maybe

Giorgio Agretti

RESOURCE *Publications* • Eugene, Oregon

TO BELIEVE IN GOD? TO HOPE . . . MAYBE

Copyright © 2021 Giorgio Agretti. All rights reserved. Except for brief quotations in critical publications or reviews, no part of this book may be reproduced in any manner without prior written permission from the publisher. Write: Permissions, Wipf and Stock Publishers, 199 W. 8th Ave., Suite 3, Eugene, OR 97401.

Resource Publications
An Imprint of Wipf and Stock Publishers
199 W. 8th Ave., Suite 3
Eugene, OR 97401

www.wipfandstock.com

PAPERBACK ISBN: 978-1-6667-1234-6
HARDCOVER ISBN: 978-1-6667-1235-3
EBOOK ISBN: 978-1-6667-1236-0

07/27/21

Unless otherwise indicated, all Scripture quotations are taken from the Christian Standard Bible®, Copyright © 2017 by Holman Bible Publishers. Used by permission. Christian Standard Bible® and CSB® are federally registered trademarks of Holman Bible Publishers.

To my wife and my children

# Contents

1. **Spirituality in History** | 1
   Introduction | 1
   Religion in Ancient Europe and the Middle East | 2
     Fertile Crescent Civilizations | 2
     Egyptian Civilization | 5
     Phoenician Civilization | 11
     Greek Civilization | 13
     Etruscan Civilization | 21
     Roman Civilization | 23
     Viking and Germanic Civilizations | 27
   Religion in Ancient Asia | 31
     Confucianism | 32
     Taoism | 35
     Shenism | 39
     Shinto | 39
     Hinduism | 41
     Vedism | 48
     Buddhism | 52
     Jainism | 57
     Zoroastrianism | 58
   Religion in Ancient America | 59
     Native American Civilizations | 59
     Aztec Civilization | 60
     Mayan Civilization | 62
     Inca Civilization | 63
   Religion in Ancient Africa | 64
   Religion in Ancient Oceania | 68
     Aboriginal Civilization | 68
     Maori Civilization | 71

2. **Jewish and Christian Religions** | 73
   Jewish Religion | 73
   Jesus of Nazareth and the Early Stages of Christian Religion | 85
      Early Centers of Christianity | 87
      The Spread of Christianity in the Ancient World | 95
   The Many Gospels and the Controversies about Them | 97
      Before the Canon: A Variety of Writings, Some Long Lost and Recently Found | 97
      Ebionites and Elchasaites | 102
      Nazarenes | 104
      Montanists | 105
      Marcion | 106
      Quartodecimans | 112
   The Need for a Christian Canon and the Threat of Gnosticism | 115
      Irenaeus of Lyon | 115
      Gnosticism and Notable Gnostics | 116
      Irenaeus and the Creation of a Canon against Heresies | 118
      The Christian Canon | 122
   The Growth of Christianity, Further Divisions, and the Struggle for Unity | 125
      Constantine: Religious Peace for Political Peace | 125
      Donatism | 133
      Arianism | 135
      The Defeat of Arianism and the Definition of Catholic Doctrine: The Creed | 139

3. **Faith and Hope** | 146
   The Relationship between Humanity and Religion | 146
   What Is Faith? | 148
   Faith and Reason | 150
      Saint Augustine | 151
      Saint Anselm of Canterbury, Peter Abelard, and William of Ockham | 152
      Saint Thomas Aquinas | 153
      Descartes and Pascal | 155
      The Prevalence of Reason and Its Consequences | 158
      Relativism | 160
      Relativism versus Catholicism | 168
      Political Correctness | 170
      Faith and Reason Today | 173

Hope | 176
   Christian Hope | 178
   The Modernity of Hope: *Spe Salvi* | 180
   Is It Possible to Hope Today? | 187
   Christian Hope as the Ultimate Beacon in Today's World | 191
Conclusion | 195

*Bibliography* | 197

# 1

## Spirituality in History

### Introduction

JOSEPH CAMPBELL,[1] AN EXPERT in mythology, said that the human mind "is the ultimate mythogenetic zone—the creator and the destroyer, the slave and yet the master, of all the gods."[2] This is even more true if one scrolls through the history of mankind, where, from the beginning of time, can be found the will, the desire, the need to pour into unknown entities faculties and capacities that are incomprehensible and unattainable for man's own strength. It can therefore be pointed out that, from the contingency of what exists, arises the need to admit the existence of someone/something on which the contingent depends.

Thus, since the dawn of human history, when survival appears to have been the only purpose of life, we can find something religious: even in the most ancient petroglyphs, among representations of daily life, animals, and hunt scenes, there are some symbolic or fantastic shapes which seem to represent religious rites. On this topic, there are many interesting studies such as evolutionary theories, historical-cultural cycles, functionalism, historicism, and structuralism, which explain, or try to explain, the genesis and evolution of spirituality in the most remote times. Here it is more important to note how such spiritual need already existed over ten thousand years ago. Over the years and in the evolution and progress

---

1. Joseph John Campbell (26 Mar. 1904–30 Oct. 1987) was an American professor of literature at Sarah Lawrence College who worked in comparative mythology and comparative religion.

2. Campbell, *Primitive Mythology*, 472.

1

of humanity, social groupings were formed, which eventually developed into real nations and states with relevant organizational and institutional structures and with their own religious forms and references.

Here begins our story, which, as in an ideal tracking shot through time, will lead us to discover and get to know the religious beliefs and habits of the peoples who have followed one another in the history of humanity.

Let's consider first some of the most ancient civilizations we know, like the Sumerians, Akkadians, Elamites, Amorites, Assyrians, Babylonians, Arameans, Egyptians, and Phoenicians. These civilizations were part of what, in the 1920s, was called by archaeologist James Henry Breasted[3] of the University of Chicago the Fertile Crescent, to indicate that territory which from Egypt goes up to Mesopotamia, having its summit on the borders of Turkey. Each of these civilizations, besides of course the specific traits that distinguished it by state, military, and social organization, also had specific religious beliefs. In this respect, there is a very large historical and literary production of authors of all times and nations, which can be useful for those who may wish to delve deeper into this topic.

Here we will focus on a general information approach.

## Religion in Ancient Europe and the Middle East

### Fertile Crescent Civilizations

The Sumerians, whose civilization developed from 4500 to 2000 BC in Mesopotamia, believed in many gods, just like most major ancient civilizations. In addition, these gods varied according to each different city, where they served as protectors and patrons of cities themselves. Among the main deities worshipped by the Sumerians was *An*, god of creation, to whom the number sixty was sacred (the highest figure of the Mesopotamian sexagesimal system).[4] *Enlil* was the god of wind, air, earth, and

---

3. James Henry Breasted (27 Aug. 1865–2 Dec. 1935) was an American archaeologist, Egyptologist, and historian.

4. Sexagesimal is a numeral system with sixty as its base. It originated with the ancient Sumerians in the 3rd millennium BC, was passed down to the ancient Babylonians, and is still used—in a modified form—for measuring time, angles, and geographic coordinates. The number sixty, a superior highly composite number, has twelve factors, namely one, two, three, four, five, six, ten, twelve, fifteen, twenty, thirty, and sixty, of which two, three, and five are prime numbers. With so many factors, many fractions involving sexagesimal numbers are simplified.

storms. *Enki* was the god of water, knowledge, craftsmanship, sea, lakes, and wisdom. Together with *An* and *Enlil*, he formed the cosmic triad. *Inanna* was the goddess of fruitfulness of beauty and love. The gods, as said, varied from place to place. Studies have counted about six hundred divinities among minor gods and sacred references.

The Akkadis, whose name derives from their capital Akkad, lived in Mesopotamia from about 2350 to 2200 BC. Among their religious traditions, it is particularly worthwhile to mention *Ishafar*, goddess of earth, fruitfulness, love, war, and the evening star, that is, Venus.

The Elamites had settled in a region west of the Tigris River as early as 3400 BC, where they stayed until about 642 BC, when Assurbanipal, king of the Assyrians, destroyed their capital, Susa. Among the gods they worshiped, the most important was the god of Susa named *Inshushinak* (which actually means lord of Susa), as well as his wife *Kiririsha*, and *Nahundi*, god of the sun, besides other ones of Sumerian and Babylonian origin.

Assyrian and Babylonian civilizations had many traits in common, so that we speak generally of Assyrian-Babylonian civilization. Their religions were very similar to each other as well. The Assyrians, before being defeated by the Babylonians, worshiped the god *Assur*, who gave the name to the capital of the empire until the foundation of Nineveh. Assur was the god of war, creator and master of the cosmos, and was represented in a bust of man inside a winged solar disk, as can be seen in the archaeological exhibit in the British Museum of London. The Assyrians called him Assur the Lord, the great Mount, the one who formed himself and the other gods, the one who determines the fate of gods and humans. His bride was *Ninlil*, also called *Assyria*, and his children *Ninurta* and *Zababa*. Other gods were *Adad* (or *Ramman*), god of rain; *Nusku*, god of light and fire; *Amurru*; and *Pazuzu*, who healed diseases.

The history of the Babylonian people began around 2000 BC, and already at its beginning it established a landmark of great importance as Hammurabi who, in addition to expanding the Babylonian influence to all Mesopotamia, drafted a series of laws—among the first mentioned in history—known as the Code of Hammurabi.[5] The Babylonians reached the greatest splendor under Nebuchadnezzar (well-known through the wonderful work of Giuseppe Verdi and its famous chorus), who extended the Babylonian empire by conquering Jerusalem and part of Egypt. His

---

5. The Code of Hammurabi is a well-preserved Babylonian code of law of ancient Mesopotamia. It is one of the oldest deciphered writings of significant length in the world.

figure is also linked to the myth of the tower of Babel, which some scholars believe to be the great sanctuary of Etemenanki,[6] erected probably under Hammurabi but made grandiose by Nebuchadnezzar with a massive tower, called a ziggurat, which precisely recalls the biblical image of the tower of Babel. The Babylonians were defeated by Cyrus, the Persian king, in 530 BC, and their empire ended.

In Babylonian religion, the preeminent god was *Marduk*, whose cult extended to the whole empire. Creator and ruler of the world, he was represented as two-faced to express this duality. His emblem was a dragon with scales or a snake with horns. Other important gods were *Ea*, god of the waters, father of Marduk; *Assur* the warrior god; *Ishtar*, goddess of love and war; *Anu*, supreme god, father of Ishtar; *Enlil*, lord of the air; *Shamash*, god of sun and justice; *Sin*, god of the moon, component of the triad, together with Shamash and Ishtar; *Tammuz*, god of fertility, lover of Ishtar.

The Babylonians, in addition to the Code of Hammurabi, which shows the morality and justice concepts underlying their civilization, also composed a theogonic and cosmogonic poem, the *Enuma Elish*,[7] which depicted the creation of the world with the victory of the youngest gods of heaven over the terrestrial deities: *Tiamat*, goddess of the sea or common mother, representing the female principle, and *Apsu* (fresh water), representing the male principle, were defeated by the other deities, especially by Marduk, who opened in two the shell-shaped body of Tiamat, thus creating the vault of heaven with one half and the earth and the underworld with the other half. Then came the humans, destined to worship the gods as their purpose.

The Arameans were a population who inhabited the Aram region, which included part of northern Mesopotamia and part of Syria. The main god they worshiped was *Hadad*, with his son *ben Hadad*, god of thunderstorm and rain. The female deity was *Atagartis*, goddess of fertility. Worship of the god *Tammuz* was also practiced.

The Amorites were a nomadic population who inhabited from 3000 BC some regions of Mesopotamia: they worshiped the god *Amurru* (or

---

6. Etemenanki (Sumerian: temple of the foundation of heaven and earth) was a ziggurat dedicated to Marduk in the ancient city of Babylon.

7. The Enuma Elish is the Babylonian creation myth. It describes the creation of the world, a battle between gods focused on the supremacy of Marduk, the creation of humans destined for the service of the Mesopotamian deities, and, at the end, a long passage praising Marduk.

*Martu*), described as a shepherd son of *Anu*, god of heaven; they also worshiped *Sin*, god of the moon.

## Egyptian Civilization

The Egyptian civilization, which lasted over three thousand five hundred years, stood out for power, beauty, creation, and elegance, fascinating whomever came in contact with it. The still ongoing research to reveal its mysteries demonstrates its inexhaustible charm.

By Egyptian civilization is meant the one that developed along the Nile River, from south of present-day Sudan to its mouth, in the delta, in the Mediterranean Sea. Several settlements followed one another in the Nile valley during the Predynastic Period, beginning 3900 BC. A first form of state was created, however, from 3100 to 3050 BC with the First Dynasty and the unification of the areas called Upper Egypt (towards the border with Sudan) and Lower Egypt (towards the Nile Delta). They, however, always remained quite distinct from each other, so that Pharaohs were also called, throughout the history of Egypt, Lords of the Two Lands.

As we just mentioned, the history of the Egyptian civilization lasts from 3900 BC (Predynastic Period) to 342 BC (Late Period) and includes, from 3200 BC, thirty archaeo-historically recognized dynasties. On this topic there is immense literature to which I refer those who ae interested in deepening their knowledge; here I summarize only its historical chronology:

- Predynastic Period (3900–3050 BC)
- Archaic Period (c. 3050–2686 BC)
- Ancient Kingdom (2686–2181 BC)
- First Intermediate Period (2181–2050 BC)
- Middle Kingdom (2050–1690 BC)
- Second Intermediate Period (1690–1549 BC) and the Hyksos
- New Kingdom (1549–1069 BC)
- Third Intermediate Period (1069–653 BC)
- Late Period (653–332 BC)
- Ptolemaic Period (332–30 BC)
- Roman Period (30 BC–fourth century AD)

Egyptian society had a great religious sense and participated in manifestations, rites, and religious events; the cult of dead was very strong. The Egyptian religion was polytheistic and animist, driven by the willingness to pay homage and obtain the favor of all those forces that contributed to life, strength, and prosperity of the country. It could be said that the Egyptians had a god for all that happened in the world, so there is a very crowded pantheon,[8] as can be noticed from this list:

- *Anubis*, god of necropolises, embalming, and death; presided over mummification
- *Ra*, god of the sun
- *Horus*, son of Osiris and protector of the pharaoh; god of the sky and the war
- *Nephthys*, goddess of the rivers, daughter of Geb and Nut
- *Amun*, warrior god; the meaning of the name is "hidden"; the priesthood was based in Thebes
- *Ptah*, creator god of the world; he was the god of Memphis
- *Sobek*, god of water; it had a crocodile head
- *Bes*, the dwarf god of sleep and family
- *Hapi*, god of the Nile
- *Apis*, bull, oracle of Ptah
- *Isis*, wife of Osiris and mother of Horus, goddess of magic and fertility
- *Osiris*, god of afterlife, of resurrection and earth
- *Seth*, god of the desert and sandstorms caused by the wind and of all that is evil or unjust
- *Gebka*, one of the deities of the Duat
- *Khnum*, god who created humans using clay
- *Neith*, goddess of hunting and war
- *Nut*, goddess of heaven
- *Geb*, god of the earth

---

8. The word pantheon generally refers to the set of gods belonging to a particular religion, mythology, or tradition. It may refer as well to a commemorative monument and/or burial place.

- *Maat*, wife and daughter of Ra; embodiment of justice, righteousness, and order
- *Aton*, the sun disk, mainly worshiped by Akhenaten
- *Toth*, ibis god protector of scribes and sciences; god of knowledge
- *Hathor*, cow goddess of dance, music, and love, protector of mothers
- *Sekhmet*, lioness goddess of war and bride of Ptah
- *Bast*, cat goddess
- *Tueris*, goddess of women in labor
- *Shu*, god born from the spit of Atum; he was the father of heaven and earth, god of air and wind
- *Aker*, the horizon
- *Imhotep*, architect who built the pyramid of Pharaoh Djoser; he was eventually deified and became god of medicine in the Ptolemaic era
- *Ammit* (better known as the Devourer of the Dead), monster with crocodile head, lion front body and hippopotamus rear body; in case the heart of the deceased had been judged not pure, she would devour it, preventing his survival in the hereafter
- *Renpet*, god of the weather and, above all, the year
- *Menchit*, warrior goddess (originally foreign)
- *Huh*, god of infinity, mainly worshiped in the Old Kingdom
- *Hershef*, one of the many Egyptian creator gods
- *Onuris*, god of hunting
- *Benu*, god who represented the resurrection (like Osiris)
- *Mafdet*, animal goddess who protected against snake bites
- *Min*, an ithyphallic god revered especially in Coptos; in his rituals, a bull and lettuce were sacrificed
- *Mertseger*, goddess whose name means "she who loves silence"
- *Apep*, serpent god of chaos, enemy of Ra
- *Astarte*, goddess linked to fertility
- *Ra-Horakhti*, god born from the syncretism between the god Ra and Horakhti

- *Atum*, like Ptah and Amun, was worshiped as the creator god
- *Pataecus*, deformed god, represented on amulets and necklaces
- *Bat*, bovine goddess, represented the Milky Way
- *Heket*, frog-headed goddess, bride of Khnum (of Antion according to other traditions) and goddess of births
- *Amonet*, female form of the god Amun, named in the texts of the pyramids
- *Anti* (also called the one with the claws), the hawk god of Anteopoli
- *Hu*, personification of the word
- *Heikaib*, god worshiped in Elephantine
- *Anhur*, god who brought the goddess Tefnet back home
- *Iah*, the moon, who challenged Toth in a game similar to chess (probably *senet*), constantly losing
- *Seshat*, wife of Ptah or Toth, goddess of wisdom
- *Horakhti*, a depiction of Ra
- *Hehu*, two deities who helped Shu support Nut
- *Taten*, Memphian deity
- *Khonsu*, son of Amun and Mut
- *Qadesh*, bride of Amurru
- *Nunet*, Nun's female counterpart
- *Kebechet*, helped, along with Anubis, the act of mummifying
- *Serqet*, goddess with a scorpion on her head
- *Big cat of Heliopolis*, cat god who assisted and protected Ra from the attacks by Apep
- *Tait*, protector of royalty
- *Hey*, son of Hator
- *Baba*, baboon god
- *Khentamentyu*, god similar to Anubis; he was considered protector of the dead
- *Hor sa Iset*, god who attended the ritual of opening of the mouth
- *Harmakis*, the sphinx

- *Nepri*, protector of wheat
- *Sokar*, archaic god of Memphis
- *Upuaut*, god of war
- *Nekhbet*, vulture goddess

The Egyptians also had groupings of gods, among which the main ones were:

- *The Ennead*[9]—an extended family of nine deities produced by Atum during the creation of the world. The Ennead consisted of Atum; his twins Shu, god of dry air, and Tefnut, goddess of damp air. From this first couple were derived their children Geb, god of the earth, and Nut, his sister and bride, goddess of heaven; their children Osiris and Isis, as well as Seth, god of the desert, and Nephthys, goddess of the home
- *The four sons of Horus*—four gods who protected the mummified body, especially the interior organs in canopic jars
- *The Ogdoad*[10]—a set of eight deities who personified the chaos that existed before creation. The Ogdoad was made up of Amun, Amunet, Nun, Naunet, Hehu, Hehut, Kekui, and Kekuit.

Among this myriad of gods, preeminent was the god of the sun, called both Ra and Ammon or Atum, who travelled the sky with a daytime boat and at night with a nighttime boat, battling the powers of darkness. The center of his cult was in Heliopolis, from which it spread to many other cities; his symbol was a large obelisk on a pedestal.

Among all the cults and rites that the Egyptians dedicated to their gods, the best known is probably the myth of Isis and Osiris, which spread out of Egypt into the whole ancient world, touching its life and religious beliefs thanks to Plutarch, the Greek historian. This myth can be roughly summarized in the following way.

The goddess of heaven Nut and the god of earth Geb begat Osiris, Isis, Nephthys, and Seth. Isis, goddess of love, loved Osiris since she was in the womb; the two became pharaohs and civilized the world. One day, Seth decided to kill his brother Osiris out of envy. He built, together with some accomplices, a sarcophagus made of wood and

---

9. Grouping of nine elements.
10. Grouping of eight elements.

precious stones; during a party, he proclaimed that he would give it to anyone who managed to fit in perfectly. When Osiris, encouraged by his brother, tried to enter, the latter locked him in and threw the sarcophagus in the Nile. The sarcophagus descended the river to the sea and eventually was stopped in Byblos[11] by the branches of an acacia tree. In later times, that acacia was cut, and from its trunk was obtained a pillar for the palace of the king of Byblos. In the desperate search for Osiris, Isis reached Byblos, where, under the guise of a mortal, she managed to join the royal court, gain the trust of Queen Nemano, and become nurse to the young prince of the city. One day Nemano discovered Isis while laying the prince child on burning embers. The queen, unaware that it was a ritual designed to guarantee immortality to the child, became alarmed, so that Isis was forced to take on her true appearance and reveal the reason she was in the city. Nemano then gave the goddess the sarcophagus, which was still contained in the acacia pillar. Isis magically brought Osiris back to life. They mated, getting her pregnant, but Osiris died a little later because the magic of Isis was not strong enough to keep him alive any longer. Isis therefore hid his body in Buto.[12] Some time later she gave birth to Horus and raised him in secret in the marshes of the Nile Delta. One day, Seth found Osiris's body. Furious, he dismembered it and scattered the pieces around Egypt, confident that Isis would finally give up and, for greater security, put Isis and Nephthys under lock and key. They were later set free by Selket and seven other goddesses and immediately sought out the parts of the body of Osiris. After reassembling it, they mummified him, so that the god could be born again in the Aaru fields, a sort of Egyptian paradise. Isis would eventually reunite with her loved one in the Underworld and live forever with him. It would be up to Horus, the son of Isis and Osiris conceived in Byblos, to defeat his uncle Seth in a series of battles, eventually becoming pharaoh to bring the glory of his father.

The themes of this story of love and resurrection are many, among them:

- the opposition between chaos (Seth) and universal balance (Osiris)

---

11. Byblos is a city in Lebanon. It is believed to have been first occupied between 8800 and 7000 BC and continuously inhabited since 5000 BC, making it one of the oldest continuously inhabited cities in the world. It is a UNESCO World Heritage Site.

12. Buto or Butosus was an ancient city located ninety-five km east of Alexandria in the Nile Delta of Egypt. It is today called Tell El Fara'in (Hill of the Pharaohs).

- the importance of the female figure as an element of protection and motherhood (Isis)
- the origin of mummification
- the birth of the first divine triad (Osiris, Isis, Horus)
- the definition of the kingdom of the underworld
- the flood cycle of the Nile, deeply connected to the rebirth of Osiris
- the legitimization of the figure of Pharaoh as guarantor of the cosmic order (Horus)

In later times, Pharaoh Amenhotep IV, who lived between 1375 and 1334 BC, attempted to impose a religion focused mainly on Aten (or solar disk). To stress its importance, he also changed his name to Akhenaten, which means "effective to Aten," as if there was a will to establish a monotheistic religion. Akhenaten's image as a religious revolutionary has produced many speculations, from hypotheses of specialists up to marginal or non-academic theories. Although the opinion that Akhenaten was one of the first monotheists of history is quite popular, it is more correct to say that Akhenaten practiced the enoteism (or monolatry), a term coined by the historian of religions Max Müller[13] to designate the religious attitude (observed by him particularly in the Vedas)[14] of the one who, in fervor of the adoration of a divinity, invokes and celebrates it as unique, without adopting a real monotheistic conception, as Akhenaten does not appear to have ever denied the existence of other gods besides Aten. The attempt, however, failed, and the cults and rites of the ancient Egyptian gods returned.

## Phoenician Civilization

Phoenicians is the name the Greeks gave to the people settled on the eastern coasts of the Mediterranean Sea and in its immediate hinterland, in correspondence with today's Lebanon, and of which there are accounts since the twenty-second century BC. Phoenicians were an ancient Semitic population; excellent sailors, they were masters of maritime and

13. Friedrich Max Müller (6 Dec. 1823–28 Oct. 1900) was a German-born philologist and Orientalist who lived and studied in Britain for most of his life.

14. The Vedas are a large body of religious texts originating in ancient India. Composed in Vedic Sanskrit, the texts constitute the oldest layer of Sanskrit literature and the oldest scriptures of Hinduism.

commercial shipments all over the Mediterranean basin and oceanic routes. They founded colonies on the northern coasts of Africa, in Spain, Sicily, and Sardinia, and they were the first to develop an alphabetic writing system, spreading it to Greece and Italy. The Greek historian Herodotus[15] wrote that they were the first to circumnavigate Africa.

The Phoenician religion varied from city to city with autonomous tendencies, each city-state having its own divinity protector. In Tyre,[16] next to *Astarte*, main goddess of the Phoenician religion who manifested herself in various figures (*Anath, Ishtar*), we find a divinity who appeared in the Iron Age and who would have greater power with time: *Melqart*, that is, "king of the city." He was the protector and inventor of the fundamental interests of society, from purple dye to navigation to the west. Dedications to Melqart, well-identified by the Greek Heracles, appear in Cyprus, Carthage, Sicily, Sardinia, Malta, and Spain, while his sanctuaries played a role as outposts in the context of expansion and Phoenician navigation.

The preeminent divine couple in Sidon[17] was made up of Astarte and a god designated as Ba'al of Sidon or "holy prince," probably to be identified with *Eshmun*. Like Melqart, Eshmun was a typical Iron Age god. He had the characteristics of a healing god and would be assimilated by the Greeks and Romans into Asclepius/Aesculapius, god of medicine.

In the western colonies, even with regard to religion, there were both aspects of continuity and innovation with respect to the mother country. For example, in Carthage[18] were revered Astarte, Melqart, Eshmun, and Resheph, but also, from the fifth century BC on, Tanit (or Tinnit) and Ba'al Hammon, already attested in the East, who were recipients of great

---

15. Herodotus (c. 484–c. 425 BC) was an ancient Greek historian, often referred to as the Father of History, a title first conferred on him by the first-century BC Roman orator Cicero.

16. Tyre is a city in Lebanon. It is one of the oldest continually inhabited cities in the world.

17. Sidon is the third largest city in Lebanon. It was one of the most important Phoenician cities, and it may have been the oldest.

18. Carthage was the center or capital city of the ancient Carthaginian civilization, on the eastern side of the Lake of Tunis in what is now the Tunis Governorate in Tunisia. Carthage was widely considered the most important trading hub of the Ancient Mediterranean. The city developed from a Phoenician colony into the capital of the Punic empire, which dominated large parts of the southwest Mediterranean during the first millennium BC. It was eventually destroyed by the Roman Republic in the Third Punic War in 146 BC.

veneration in the African metropolis. The goddess Tanit was sometimes called Mother, but more often Lady or Face of Ba'al to indicate her close relationship with divine companion Ba'al Hammon. The divine couple, venerated in all western Punic centers, was also the main recipient of the rituals that took place in the Punic sanctuary called *tofet*.

## Greek Civilization

The term *ancient Greece* indicates the civilization that developed in mainland Greece, in Albania, on the islands of Aegean Sea, on the coasts of the Black Sea and western Turkey, in Sicily, on the coastal areas of Southern Italy (collectively called, at the time, *Magna Graecia*), in North Africa, Corsica, and on the eastern coasts of Spain and the southern ones of France. Although Greece's geographic conformation favored the onset of multiple political units in their own right (*poleis*), Greek culture was a rather homogeneous phenomenon that incoporated all the Hellenic people, united by the same language. Greek culture attached much importance to knowledge and search of truth. For the Greeks, getting closer to the truth meant getting closer to divinity; therefore they attributed an almost religious value to knowledge and science. In this context, ancient Greeks understood the importance of mathematics in the research of a knowledge closer to the truth. This would explain how the Greek civilization succeeded, within a few centuries and with a numerically limited population, to achieve remarkable goals in philosophy, math, and science.

On Greek civilization, on its beauty, and on the importance its history has had in the evolution of humanity there is an immense historical literary production, to which anyone wishing to deepen his or her knowledge can turn. To underscore its importance and depth, we can just remember what the philosopher Emanuele Severino,[19] who recently passed away, said about Greece: "Philosophy was born already great."

Greek religion is the set of beliefs, myths, rituals, mystery cults, theologies, and theurgic and spiritual practices professed in ancient Greece, in the form of public, philosophical, or initiatory religion. The origins of this religion are to be found in the prehistory of the first peoples living in Europe, in the beliefs and traditions of different Indo-European peoples who, from the twenty-first century BC, migrated to those regions, in the

---

19. Emanuele Severino (26 Feb. 1929–17 Jan. 2020) was a contemporary Italian philosopher.

Minoan[20] and Mycenaean[21] civilizations, and in the influences of the civilizations from the ancient Near East which occurred over the centuries. The Greek religion ceased to be with the edicts promulgated by the Roman emperor of Christian faith Theodosius I,[22] who prohibited all non-Christian cults, including the Eleusinian mysteries,[23] and with the devastations inflicted by the Goths[24] in the fourth and fifth centuries AD.

Greek mythology is the collection of all myths and legends belonging to the culture of the ancient Greeks and Hellenes concerning their gods and heroes, their world view, their cults and religious practices. It consists of a vast repertoire of short stories (*logoi*) that explain the origin of the world and the life and events of a great number of deities, heroes and heroines, monsters, and other mythological creatures. These stories were initially composed and spread in oral poetic form, whereas they have come down to us mainly through written texts of the Greek literary tradition. Greek mythology has had a huge influence on culture, the arts and literature of Western civilization, and its legacy still remains in European languages and cultures.

The Mycenaean Cretan religion must be considered the natural origin of the religion of the Greeks, not only for the ethnic mix of the two bloodlines but also because the origin of the main myths and cults of classical Greece are to be found in the Minoan age. However, between the Mycenaean Minoan era (second and first millennium BC)

---

20. The Minoan civilization was a Bronze Age Aegean civilization on the island of Crete and other Aegean islands, flourishing from c. 3000 to c. 1450 BC until a late period of decline, finally ending around 1100 BC. The name Minoan derives from the mythical King Minos.

21. The Mycenaean civilization was the last phase of the Bronze Age in Ancient Greece, spanning the period from approximately 1600 to 1100 BC. The most prominent site was Mycenae, in the Argolid, after which the culture of this era is named.

22. Theodosius I (11 Jan. 347–17 Jan. 395), also known as Theodosius the Great, was a Roman emperor from AD 379 to 395. He issued decrees that effectively made Nicene Christianity the official state church of the Roman Empire. Theodosius is considered a saint by the Armenian Apostolic Church and the Eastern Orthodox Church, and his feast day is on January 17.

23. The Eleusinian Mysteries were initiations held every year for the cult of Demeter and Persephone based at the Panhellenic Sanctuary of Eleusis in ancient Greece. They are the among the most famous of the secret religious rites of ancient Greece. Their basis was an old agrarian cult, and there is some evidence that they were derived from the religious practices of the Mycenean period.

24. The Goths were a Germanic people who played a major role in the fall of the Western Roman Empire and the emergence of medieval Europe.

and the classical era there is a period of five centuries, called the Hellenic Middle Ages, in which also the religious conception underwent a series of progressive transformations: the gods as natural forces (sea) and the agricultural deities of the plebs (for example, Demeter and Dionysus) interpenetrate with Olympians gods narrated by Homer,[25] clearly anthropomorphic divinities who gradually acquire precise characterizations. It should be emphasized that, beyond the individualism typical of each Greek polis, religion always represented an element of strong cultural and social cohesion.

The Attic-Ionic canon[26] recognizes twelve Olympic gods: *Zeus, Hera, Apollo, Athena, Artemis, Poseidon, Demeter, Aphrodite, Ares, Hermes, Hephaestus,* and *Hestia*.

Zeus (Jupiter for the Romans), whose name means resplendent, was the main deity, initially god of heaven, the one who caused storms thunders and rains on earth. As supreme god, he gave power to kings, rules justice, and protected cities and the domestic hearth. As was noted by studying the progress of Greek religion, Zeus ended up absorbing many previous deities and their legends, thus explaining the many disparate myths and animal transformations related to his name. The main place of worship dedicated to him was the temple of Olympia[27] in Peloponnese,[28] where there was a colossal gold and ivory statue by Phidias.[29] Here took place the most important feast of all Greece, the Olympic Games.

Hera (Juno for the Romans), goddess of earth, was the jealous bride of Zeus and protector herself of marriages and motherhood.

Apollo was originally a foreign god, perhaps from Lycian[30] cults. Later he became son of Zeus and Leto, twin brother of Artemis, born

---

25. Homer is the presumed author of the *Iliad* and the *Odyssey*, two epic poems that are the central works of ancient Greek literature.

26. A group of official, authentic, or approved rules or laws, particularly ecclesiastical, or standards accepted as axiomatic and universally binding in a religion.

27. Olympia is a small town in Elis on the Peloponnesian peninsula in Greece, famous for the nearby archaeological site of the same name, which was a major Panhellenic religious sanctuary of ancient Greece, where the ancient Olympic Games were held.

28. The Peloponnese, or Peloponnesus, is a peninsula and geographic region in southern Greece.

29. Phidias or Pheidias (c. 480–430 BC) was a Greek sculptor, painter, and architect. His statue of Zeus at Olympia was one of the Seven Wonders of the Ancient World.

30. Lycians is the name of various peoples who lived, at different times, in Lycia, a geopolitical area in Anatolia (also known as Asia Minor).

on the island of Delos,[31] where his sanctuary was located. He was often represented as an archer with sunrays as his arrows, by which he stopped and healed epidemics and ailments. He is however a complex divinity, to which many epithets, and therefore many functions, were attributed: the god of legality and order, of peace and harmony, inventor of the lyre;[32] protector/keeper of the arts and the muse, he was also the preeminent god of oracles. In the temple of Delphi,[33] he gave his responses through the priestess Pythia. In this temple were written the sentences of seven wise men that became famous, like his statements "know yourself," "never too much," etc.

Athena (Minerva for the Romans), also called Pallas and *Glaukopis* ("with gleaming eyes"), was the goddess of war but also of wisdom, considered the favorite daughter of Zeus, born from his head, armed with helmet and armor. She was the protector of the city of Athens and there the inhabitants built a temple dedicated to her, the Parthenon[34] (*parthenos* means virgin). The most important celebrations and cults dedicated to her were also held in Athens, the Panathenaia.

Artemis (Diana for the Romans) was Apollo's sister, the virgin goddess of hunting and the woods, where she lived surrounded by nymphs. She was also the goddess of fertility, marriage, birth, and youth in general. The most important temple dedicated to her is located in Ephesus.[35] It

---

31. The island of Delos, near Mykonos, near the center of the Cyclades archipelago, is one of the most important mythological, historical, and archaeological sites in Greece. The excavations in the island are among the most extensive in the Mediterranean.

32. The lyre is a stringed instrument known for its use in Greek classical antiquity and later periods. The lyre is similar in appearance to a small harp but with distinct differences.

33. Delphi (formerly also called Pytho) is the ancient sanctuary that grew rich as the seat of Pythia, the oracle who was consulted about important decisions throughout the ancient classical world. The ancient Greeks considered the center of the world to be in Delphi. It is located in upper central Greece, on multiple plateaus along the slope of Mount Parnassus.

34. The Parthenon is a former temple on the Athenian Acropolis, Greece, dedicated to the goddess Athena, whom the people of Athens considered their patron. It is the most important surviving building of classical Greece and its decorative sculptures are considered some of the high points of Greek art.

35. Ephesus was an ancient Greek city on the coast of Ionia, three kilometres southwest of present-day Selçuk in Izmir Province, Turkey. Ephesus was one of the seven churches of Asia that are cited in the Book of Revelation. The Gospel of John may have been written here. The city was the site of several fifth-century Christian councils.

was the largest temple of antiquity, considered one of the Seven Wonders of the World.

Poseidon (Neptune for the Romans) was the god of the sea, the brother of Zeus and of Hades with whom he divided the dominion over the world (sky, sea, and the underworld). Earthquakes and storms, as well as the fate of castaways, depended on him. The symbol of his power was the trident, built by his sons the Cyclopes,[36] with which he would shake the earth and sea.

Ares (Mars for the Romans) was the god of war, always in contention with humans and gods.

Aphrodite (Venus for the Romans) was the goddess of beauty. According to Hesiod, she was born from the waters near Cyprus,[37] hence also the name of Cypris. Although married to Hephaestus, she had a baby from Ares: Eros the god of love, generally depicted as a boy, whose myth is masterfully narrated by Plato[38] in the Symposium[39] dialogue.

Hermes (Mercury for the Romans) was the messenger of the gods and therefore depicted with wings on his feet. Protector of shepherds, wayfarers, and thieves, son of Zeus and the nymph Maia, he was the one who accompanied the souls of the dead into the underworld. As messenger god, therefore skilled in rhetoric, he also gave his name to the art of text interpretation or hermeneutics. Again related to Hermes is the figure of Hermes Trismegistus[40] (thrice-greatest) and the related hermetic literature concerning magic.

Hephaestus (Vulcan for the Romans), son of Zeus and Hera, brother of Ares, Aphrodite's husband, was the god of fire and metals, which he

---

36. In Greek mythology and later Roman mythology, the Cyclopes are giant one-eyed creatures.

37. Cyprus is an island country in the eastern Mediterranean.

38. Plato (428/427 or 424/423–348/347 BC) was an Athenian philosopher during the classical period in ancient Greece, founder of the Platonist school of thought and the Academy, the first institution of higher learning in the Western world. He is widely considered the pivotal figure in the history of ancient Greek and Western philosophy, along with his teacher Socrates and his most famous student, Aristotle.

39. The *Symposium* is a philosophical text by Plato c. 385–70 BC. It depicts a friendly contest of extemporaneous speeches given by a group of notable men attending a banquet. The men include the philosopher Socrates, the general and political figure Alcibiades, and the comic playwright Aristophanes. The speeches are to be given in praise of Eros, the god of love and desire.

40. Hermes Trismegistus is the purported author of the Hermetic Corpus, a series of sacred texts that are the basis of Hermeticism.

forged in works admired by other gods. He built the weapons of Ares, the arrows of Eros, and especially the chariot and scepter of Zeus. The island of Lemnos[41] was the place where his cult was held.

Finally, among the Olympic gods, there is Hestia (Vesta for the Romans), sister of Zeus, goddess of the home and the city.

Furthermore, there are non-Olympic gods such as Asclepius, god of medicine; Dionysus, god of vegetation; and more ancient deities like Persephone, Gaia, and Chronos.

Also typical of Greek religion were the heroes, complex figures who in Homeric lyrics were very brave men who distinguished themselves in military prowess and prudence in councils, while in Hesiod's[42] works were already demigods coming from divine lineage, taking on therefore almost the function of mediator between humans and gods. The gallery of Greek heroes is very rich, and their adventures are narrated with great amount of fantastic details. Particularly significant are Heracles (Hercules), the only mortal, born from Alcmene and Zeus, and eventually risen among the gods, exemplary expression of strength, courage, and recklessness. Due to Hera's jealousy, he was forced to bear the twelve labors, according to some the symbol of the signs of the zodiac,[43] after which he was accepted by Zeus into Olympus, where he married Hebe. An important temple dedicated to him is in Agrigento; its remains can still be admired today.

We know Greek cosmogony (doctrine or complex of myths that explain the origin of the universe) and theogony (myth or complex of myths illustrating the birth or descent of the gods) both from Homeric poems and from the *Theogony* by Hesiod, who lived later than the Homeric age, in the second half of the eighth century BC. According to Hesiod, five ages succeeded one another in world history: gold, silver, bronze, heroes, and finally iron. At the beginning was Chaos,[44] from which pro-

---

41. Lemnos is a Greek island in the northern part of the Aegean Sea.

42. Hesiod was an ancient Greek poet generally thought to have been active between 750 and 650 BC, around the same time as Homer. Ancient authors credited Hesiod and Homer with establishing Greek religious customs. Modern scholars refer to him as a major source on Greek mythology, farming techniques, early economic thought, archaic Greek astronomy, and ancient time-keeping.

43. The zodiac is an area of the sky that extends approximately eight degrees north or south (as measured in celestial latitude) of the ecliptic, the apparent path of the sun across the celestial sphere over the course of the year. The paths of the moon and visible planets are also within the belt of the zodiac.

44. Chaos refers to the void state preceding the creation of the universe or cosmos

gressively the ordered cosmos was formed, after fratricidal struggles of the first deities, and the reign of Zeus began. The Earth was the center of this order, surrounded by the ocean. West of the Earth was Hades, the kingdom of the underworld, inhabited by the souls of the dead. It was surrounded by iron walls with iron doors, beyond which the dead passed the waters of the Styx river, which flowed into the lake Acheron. Here the boatman Charon would transport to the other bank, which was guarded by Cerberus the dog, the dead who had been buried. The importance of Hesiodic theogony also lies in the effort of uniting and interpenetrating various deities from different cults in order to provide Greece, which was in great territorial and commercial expansion at that time, with a common and harmonious pantheon which would reflect its homogeneity.

An important aspect of the religion of the Greeks is what we could today define as ethics, but which, in that context, was the relationship between humans and divinity. First of all, it is to be remembered that even though, as a general rule, the fate of humans was dependent on the will of Zeus, already in the Homeric era the idea of a higher law (*Moira* or Fate) developed. On the one hand, it counterbalanced the whim of the gods; and on the other hand, it represented the immutability of physical and moral laws that rule the cosmos. With Moira, even the very concept of divinity gained new dimension, as not even the gods could oppose that, and this spurred the moral conscience of the individual, who must realize within himself that same balance that Moira achieved in the cosmos. Hence also the concept of fault for the Greeks: it was what would break this balance, that is, *hybris*,[45] pride or arrogance, above all the pride to compare oneself to the gods. Another very serious fault was impiety (*asebeia*), the behavior contrary to the law, its disrespect, seen as sacrilege. The most famous case of impiety was against Socrates,[46] who was sentenced to death.

If the primitive places of worship were springs or caverns, which were however fenced to accentuate the separation of the sacred, over

---

in the Greek creation myths, or to the initial gap created by the original separation of heaven and earth.

45. In its ancient Greek context, it typically describes behavior that defies the norms of behavior or challenges the gods which, in turn, brings about the downfall of the perpetrator of hybris.

46. Socrates (c. 470–399 BC) was a Greek philosopher from Athens who is credited as one of the founders of Western philosophy and as being the first moral philosopher of the Western ethical tradition of thought.

time, real dwellings and temples gradually became increasingly large and architecturally relevant. Sacrifices and processions took place outside the temple, and ceremonies had two parts: prayer and actual sacrifice. The former (*eukai*) was directed to the divinity, both to obtain favor and to ward off evil. The Greeks brought their hand first to the mouth and then turned it to god. The sacrifices or gifts (*dora*) consisted of first fruits (to recognize the power of gods over the things of humanity) or immolation of animals. The victim was crowned, purified, and then sacrificed. The entrails were examined, then sometimes a part of the animal was destined for the gods; another part, roasted, was the object of the banquet.

Priests did not constitute a caste, nor were they custodians of theological knowledge, but they were to be immune from bodily defects, free from sexual impurities, and elected by the people. Sometimes they belonged to families, who passed on the position. Women were not excluded from priesthood and were generally intended for the service of female deities.

Different from priests, but always mediators between human beings and divinities, were the oracles,[47] who were consulted to get answers about the future of the nation as well as for individual matters. The importance assumed by some of those is manifest in the political history of Greece. The most celebrated oracles are Dodona,[48] which is the oldest, set among the mountains of Epirus, and Delphi. In later times, the Cumaean Sibyl[49] assumed importance in the *Magna Graecia* (Southern Italy).

The rites of classical Greece are many and can be divided into two groups: domestic and public. Domestic rites were centered on the hearth, the protector of the house and always burning, where also the spirit of ancestors lived. Such rites were celebrated on all events of family members:

---

47. An oracle is a person or agency considered to provide wise and insightful counsel or prophetic predictions or precognition of the future, inspired by the gods. As such, it is a form of divination. Oracles were thought to be portals through which the gods spoke directly to people. In this sense, they were different from seers, who interpreted signs sent by the gods through bird signs, animal entrails, and various various methods.

48. Dodona in Epirus in northwestern Greece was the oldest Hellenic oracle, possibly dating to the second millennium BC, according to Herodotus. The earliest accounts in Homer describe Dodona as an oracle of Zeus. Situated in a remote region away from the main Greek poleis, it was considered second only to the oracle of Delphi in prestige.

49. The Cumaean Sibyl was the priestess presiding over the Apollonian oracle at Cumae, a Greek colony located near Naples, Italy.

births, marriages, adoptions. Public rites (prayer and sacrifices) were related to the deities and marked in turn the Greek calendar. The names of the holidays are the same as the month, because initially those were related to life of nature and events of agricultural work. The most important to remember are *Buphonia*, in honor of Zeus, at the end of the harvest; *Panathenaia*, in honor of Athena, set in July-August, which eventually became a celebration of the union of the various states with Athens and also included gymnastic games; *Daphnephoria*, in honor of Apollo, celebrated every nine years, especially in Boeotia; *Hyacinthia, Carneia,* and *Thargelia*, in honor of Dionysus for the ripening of flowers and fruit; and the great and small *Dionysia* and *Anthesteria*.

Great value had the games, which affirmed the unity of the various polis and therefore were considered national holidays. There were four-most important games: 1) the Olympic Games, held every four years, which saw the participation of all Greek cities; in addition to the sports competitions happening in the large stadium, theatrical performances and poetry readings took place in the city; 2) the Pythian Games, in honor of Apollo, in Delphi, were also celebrated every four years; 3) the Isthmian games were held every two years at the Isthmus of Corinth in honor of Poseidon; and 4) the Nemean[50] Games were also celebrated every two years in Argos, in honor of Zeus.

## Etruscan Civilization

The Etruscans were a people of ancient Italy who lived between the ninth and the first centuries BC in an area called Etruria, corresponding roughly to Tuscany, western Umbria, and northern/central Lazio, with offshoots also to the north in the Po Valley, in current Emilia-Romagna, south-eastern Lombardy, and southern Veneto, and to the south, in some areas of Campania.

At the basis of the Etruscan religion was the fundamental idea that nature depended strictly on divinity. It followed then that every natural phenomenon was an expression of the divine will; or rather, a signal sent by the divinity itself to humans who, in turn, had to do everything to understand it, discover its meaning, and adapt to it—that is, to behave according to the divine will. Everything else was consistent with these principles, starting from the very conception of divinity. This was essentially

---

50. Nemea is an ancient site in the northeastern part of the Peloponnese, in Greece.

mysterious and coincided with forces that were above nature. In practice, these were supernatural beings, vague and uncertain in numbers, at least at their origins, since the influence of other religions, and especially the Greek one, overlapped at a certain point in this primitive conception. The process of assimilation of the Etruscan deities into the gods of the Greek Olympus began during the seventh century BC and came to an end in the following sixth century, when a series of precise correspondences is definitively documented. Thus,

- *Tin* or *Tinia* appears assimilated into Zeus (Jupiter)
- *Turan* to Aphrodite (Venus)
- *Turms* to Hermes (Mercury)
- *Fufluns* to Dionysus (Bacchus)
- *Sethlans* to Hephaestus (Vulcan)
- *Uni* to Hera (Juno)
- *Menerva* to Athena (Minerva)
- *Maris* to Ares (Mars)
- *Nethuns* to Poseidon (Neptune)

At the same time new gods were directly imported from the Greek world, almost keeping their names, for example, the goddess Northia, probably of fate, and that god Veltuna or Velta (in Latin Veltumnus or Voltumna) which, according to Varro,[51] should be considered as a sort of national god of Etruscans. However, numerous minor deities continued to exist, although unfortunately our knowledge is limited to a few quotations from Roman authors (Varro, Pliny,[52] and Seneca).[53] They mention twelve superior gods, who were "wrapped in darkness"; "*consentes* gods," councilors of Tinia, ruthless and nameless, also twelve in number;

---

51. Marcus Terentius Varro (116–27 BC) was one of ancient Rome's greatest scholars and a prolific author.

52. Gaius Plinius Secundus (AD 23/24–79), called Pliny the Elder, was a Roman author, naturalist, natural philosopher, naval and army commander of the early Roman Empire, and friend of Emperor Vespasian. He wrote the encyclopedic *Naturalis Historia (Natural History)*, which became an editorial model for encyclopedias. He spent most of his spare time studying, writing, and investigating natural and geographic phenomena in the field.

53. Lucius Annaeus Seneca (54 BC–c. AD 39), known as Seneca the Elder or (less correctly) the Rhetorician, was a Roman writer.

"shocker gods," nine in number; "hidden gods," divided into four classes of divinity, heaven, earth, and waters and human souls.

The conception of life was regulated according to the Etruscan discipline, which provided for ten eras of the world, but all eras and human events were dominated by Fortune, which the Etruscans tried to evoke and avert with the divinatory arts of the haruspices and augurs. The former interpreted the will of gods by observing the entrails of sacrificed animals; the latter predicted the future by observing the flight of birds. The Etruscans deeply felt the mystery of death and, believing in a happy or unhappy afterlife, had a particular cult for tombs. They built cities of the dead or *Necropolis*, which looked like real homes, rich in paintings and equipped with pottery, jewelry, mirrors, and objects of daily life. To honor the dead, they organized gladiator parties and games.

## Roman Civilization

The history of ancient Rome covers the historical events from the origins of Rome (in 753 BC) to the construction and fall of the Western Roman Empire (in 476 AD, the year in which the beginning of the Medieval Era is conventionally placed) and on which I will not linger, given its universal notoriety.

Roman religion is the set of religious beliefs in ancient Rome, considered in their evolution as a variety of cults, correlated to the political and social development of the city and its people. The origins of the Roman religion are to be found in the cults of pre-Indo-European peoples stationed in Italy, in the religious traditions of Indo-European peoples who migrated to the peninsula probably from fifteenth century BC, and in Etruscan and Greek civilizations, as well as in the influence of beliefs from the Ancient Near East over the centuries. In ancient Rome, the veneration of deities was based on a contractual relationship rather than adoration. Not very inclined to the theological character of the divine aspect, the interest of the Romans was mainly relative to achieve the intercession of the gods for the community of humans. In a continuous exchange of give and take, the Romans complied scrupulously to their duties towards divinity, expecting, in return, protection and luck in the various areas of private and public life. Every aspect of the life of the ancient Romans was linked to a specific divinity, so much so that every category of person had a god to whom to appeal in case of need. This aspect was strongly influenced also from the dominations over other populations, Greeks above all.

*Jupiter* was the head of the gods, a good and caring father, guarantor of moral order, law, and loyalty (*Optimus Maximus*), personified in sky, lightning, and rain (from which came his various attributes like *Lucetius, Fulgor, Pluvius*).

*Juno* represented the feminine principle of deity, patron of birth, marriages, and family.

*Minerva* was the divinity who presided over manual and intellectual works.

In the Roman pantheon we find other very important deities. Mars was a typically Italic god, to whose name are linked the legends of Roman tradition. He had two characteristics: a naturalistic one (the original one, although later overshadowed by the second), by which he protected the vegetation and gave his name to the first month of the Roman calendar, when spring begins; and the warrior one, by which he led the Romans into battle. With Rhea Silvia[54] he begot Romulus and Remus and was therefore the progenitor of the Roman people. The Suovetaurilia festivals, dedicated to him and celebrated by *salii*[55] priests, consisted in the consecration of war objects and dancing in arms. His emblem was the javelin, preserved in the temple of Vesta.

*Quirinus*, an original divinity of the Sabines, was the protector of farmers, but then he became an expression of the fullness of civil and political rights, the full Roman citizenship becoming known as *ius quiritium*.

Another ancient divinity of pre-Roman origin was *Janus*, spirit of the threshold, who therefore presided over all the *iani*, arches open in the public streets, and the private doors. As divinity of beginnings and returns, he was sometimes portrayed as two-faced.

In addition to divinities who merged with Greek ones (*Mercury, Neptune, Ceres, Saturn, Apollo, Aesculapius, Hercules*) we must remember *Vesta*, goddess of the domestic hearth, whose cult represented the very heart of the Roman house. Connected with this cult was that of the

---

54. Rhea Silvia (also written as Rea Silvia and also known as Ilia) was the mythical mother of the twins Romulus and Remus, who founded the city of Rome.

55. In ancient Roman religion, the Salii were the leaping priests (from the verb *salire:* to leap, jump) of Mars, supposedly introduced by King Numa Pompilius. They were twelve patrician youths dressed as archaic warriors: an embroidered tunic, a breastplate, a short red cloak, a sword, and a spiked headdress called an apex.

*Lares*, the *Penates*, and the *Manes*, divinities of the private sphere. Lares originally protected the fields, then the hearth and the home; Penates were gods of economics and dispensation; Manes, who entered the Roman cult only in the imperial age, were the protectors of the dead. Finally, there were abstract divinities who presided over some actions or conditions of individual and social life (*Salus, Febris,* but mainly *Pax, Concordia, Pietas*) or life in general (*Fortuna, Faunus, Silvanus, Flora*).

In 207 BC, all these numerous deities were grouped together in the number of twelve, almost to create in imitation of the Greeks and the Etruscans a pantheon of greater divinities. Two verses of Ennius[56] so enumerate them: "*Iuno, Vesta, Minerva, Ceres. Diana, Venus, Mars, Mercurius, Iovis, Neptunus, Vulcanus, Apollo.*"

In the Roman world the private and public spheres were clearly distinguished, and if the former was subordinate to the latter, both were rich in significant cultural moments.

The private cult, which maintained for a long time the characteristics of the ancient religion, was present in all circumstances of life: birth, marriage, death, and also in the ones relating to owning farms or fields. All cults took place under the authority of the *pater familias*, custodian of the ancient tradition. The ordinary ritual consisted of offering, during meals, libations to the hearth; there were also special consecration rites, for example of the newborn or the bride, as well as death rites, which were considered important and necessary, because the condition in the other life depended on the treatment given to mortal remains. Initially the Romans used the practice of burial; then they learned cremation from the Greeks and Etruscans. In any case, the deceased was accompanied by his dearest objects, considered useful for future existence. Purification rites followed; in the event of illustrious deaths, games were also held.

As far as public cults were concerned, most ancient ones took place in the woods, considered home to the gods. In later times, they took place in a more defined location, where an altar was built, for sacrifices that were held outdoors. Eventually, Romans started building sacred buildings, which were called both temples and *aedes*.

The priest was the expert of the rite, who performed the sacred action and sometimes led the state representative, who in turn represented the whole community, in the carrying out of the ceremony. The priests were gathered in a college, initially of six members, then of sixteen,

---

56. Quintus Ennius (c. 239–c. 169 BC) was a writer and poet who lived during the Roman Republic. He is often considered the father of Roman poetry.

headed by the *pontifex maximus*. Their task, as experts in sacred law, was to preserve the religious traditions of the city while adapting them to political and social development; in short, to keep the *pax deorum*, the good harmony between the city and its gods. Other priestly colleges were those of the flamens, the vestals, the augurs, the *quindecimviri sacris faciundis* ("fifteen men who carry out the rites"), and *septemviri*. Minor brotherhoods were the Arval Brethren, the *Salii,* and the *Luperci* ("brothers of the wolf").

Holidays of the Roman calendar, established by the pontiffs,[57] were divided into fixed or moveable (called annually by magistrates)[58] and extraordinary, ordered by pontiffs and magistrates for some particular event. The festivals followed the calendar and were also linked to the rhythms of the vegetative cycle, as well as dedicated to divinities; to be remembered are the Secular Games, held every hundred years to atone for previous sins and greet the new era; the *Feriae Marti* (holiday for Mars), which started the year; the *Liberalia*, in honor of the couple Liber and Libera; the *Cerealia,* in honor of Ceres; the *Parilia,* in honor of Pales protector of shepherds; the *Vestalia,* for the goddess Vesta; and the *Saturnalia,* in honor of Saturn, protector of the new sowing. Finally, many festivals were dedicated to Jupiter and culminated in the *Feriae Iovis* on the thirteenth and fifteenth day of each month.

As the Roman religion is not revealed, and therefore not dogmatic, the texts to which we can refer are the collections of rules held by the priests, such as *Libri sacerdotum populi romani*, which contained the formulas of prayers and the indications for the rite; the Commentaries of the Pontiffs, a collection of decrees and responses on sacred-juridical subjects; the *Fasti*, a list of the magistrates elected annually and the calendar; and the *Annales maximi*, a sort of chronicle of the main events of the year. Other news of high religious content we get from literature.

---

57. Members of the most illustrious of the colleges of priests of the Roman religion, the College of Pontiffs.

58. The Roman magistrates were elected officials in ancient Rome.

Cicero,[59] Virgil,[60] Ovid,[61] and Seneca, with their works, outline the progressive evolution of the Roman religion.

We have so far talked about the religions that were practiced in Fertile Crescent and in the Greco-Roman world, but at the same time there were other populations and other nations that had their own religious beliefs and rites.

## Viking and Germanic Civilizations

In Northern Europe there were Viking and Germanic[62] populations, who in most cases had in common the same gods. Here we will take a look at the religion of these Indo-European populations, who from 1400 BC settled in the area between southern Sweden and the Weser[63] and Oder[64] Rivers. Later they pushed towards east, west, and south. In the last period of the Roman Empire they were distinguished as Northern Germani (Normans and Vikings), Eastern Germani (Goths, Vandals, and Burgundians), and western Germani (Franks, Swabians, Saxons, and Lombards). Germanic religion had polytheistic traits in which peasant cults intertwined with war rites.

The major gods were divided into two large groups: Æsir and Vanir, where the distinction indicates a functional difference, the former being associated with sovereignty, law, and war, and the latter with fruitfulness

---

59. Marcus Tullius Cicero (3 Jan. 106–7 Dec. 43 BC), most commonly known as simply Cicero, was a Roman statesman, lawyer, and Academic Skeptic philosopher who played an important role in the politics of the late Republic.

60. Publius Vergilius Maro (15 Oct. 70–21 Sept. 19 BC), usually called Virgil, was an ancient Roman poet of the Augustan period. He wrote three of the most famous poems in Latin literature: the *Eclogues* (or *Bucolics*), the *Georgics*, and the epic *Aeneid*.

61. Publius Ovidius Naso (20 Mar. 43 BC–AD 17/18), known as Ovid in the English-speaking world, was a Roman poet who lived during the reign of Augustus.

62. The Germanic peoples (from Latin: Germani) are a category of Northern European ethnic groups, first mentioned by Greco-Roman authors. Broader modern definitions of the Germanic peoples include peoples who were not known as Germani or Germanic peoples in their own time, but who are treated as one group of cultures, mostly because of their use of Germanic languages.

63. The Weser is a river in northwestern Germany.

64. The Oder is a river in Central Europe and Poland's third longest river after the Vistula and Warta.

and peace. The Æsir were the sovereign gods. They dwelled in Asgard (enclosure of the Æsir), a heavenly fortress located in the center of the world accessed via the rainbow bridge called *Bifröst*, perpetually under the threat of the onslaught of giants, mortal enemies of the gods, representing the forces of evil, chaos, and darkness.

*Odin* was the most important god among the Æsir. His name is connected to the Indoeuropean root *\*Wat*, which expressed the concept of both inspiration and fury and which can be found in the Latin *vates*, in the ancient Irish *faith* (seer), in the Gothic *\*wots* (furious, possessed). Inspiration gave him a specific relationship to poetic art, inspired word and wisdom, whereas fury was related to war. He was at the same time the god of the living and the dead and could be either benign or malicious, positive or negative. In the myths of creation, it is said that Odin gave humans spirit and life; he was therefore the father of humans and gods. He, in particular, was the father of all who fell in battle. They were called *Einherjar* (chosen ones), welcomed into *Walhalla*, the hall of heroes, and were to have accompanied him during *Ragnarök*, the final cosmic battle which would end the world and allow a new cycle to start over.

*Tyr* also belongs to the lineage of the Æsir. He was a god of great importance, but very little is known about him. His attributes were courage and wisdom, which relate him respectively to war and peace, of which he was the guarantor. In fact, he was the divinity who presided over the assembly, the *Thing*.

*Heimdallr* was the guardian of the gods. He sat on the edge of heaven, near the *Bifröst* bridge. Heimdallr had the finest sight and hearing, in order to be able to see the attacks of the giants. He was the guarantor of the cosmic balance, so much so that his direct opponent was Loki, a figure who, conversely, embodied the constant threat to the order of the world. Heimdallr supervised the orderly unfolding of the cosmic cycle and knew exactly when the end of the world would come. At that dramatic juncture, he was to rise and blow in the *Giallarhorn*, the sound of which could be heard in all the nine worlds of Nordic cosmology, calling the gods to battle.

*Thor* was the god of thunder and as such very ancient. His presence was felt through thunder and lightning, the latter representing both sovereign and creating power, linked to fertility and destructive power. Thor performed a function of protection of gods and humans.

*Baldr* was the son of Odin and Frigg and was married to Nanna. Snorri Sturluson[65] describes him as the best of the gods, handsome and bright, wise and eloquent. His essence was as of a principle of light. Baldr was destined to die in tragic circumstances due to Loki's malice, but was to be reborn to preside over the new era that would follow *Ragnarök*.

*Loki* was a singular figure among the gods and rather ambivalent. In some myths he was Odin and Thor's companion and often got them out of trouble, thanks to his cunning and ability. In other ones, instead, Loki was the one threatening the cosmic order, a malicious and fearsome deceiver. Although he belonged to the Æsir, he begot monstrous creatures. From his union with the giantess Angrboda three sons were born: Hel, guardian of the kingdom of the dead; Fenrir, the great wolf; and Jörmungandr, the snake lying in the ocean, whose coils envelop the whole earth. He is present in the most ancient myths, to underscore how evil originates from the very principle of the world. His most heinous act was to engineer Baldr's death. For this fault he was captured by the gods and chained to three boulders while a poisonous snake was tied above him, so that poison dripped on his face. Loki would only free himself at the end of the world when he would head the forces of evil in Ragnarök.

*Njordr* was a god among the Vanir and was the father of Freyr and Freya. He ruled wind, sea, and fire, and was protector of sea travels and fishing.

*Freyr* was the god of fertility and had power over rain and sun. He also governed the riches of humans (his appellations are also "god of abundance" and "dispenser of wealth"). His name means lord. He lived in *Alfheimr*, the land of the elves, one of the nine worlds of Nordic geography. Freyr has been identified with Yngvi, the progenitor, according to Tacitus, of the tribe of the *Ingaevones* from which it derives; for Snorri Sturluson, the great lineage of the Norwegian kings, the *Ynglingar*.

*Freya* was the goddess of love, fertility, and lust. She was also in relationship with war and was entitled to half of those killed in battle (the other half was given to Odin). She was a teacher of magic, an art that is linked to sexual practices, and, for her beauty, was the object of the desire of the giants.

---

65. Snorri Sturluson (AD 1179–23 Sept. 1241) was an Icelandic historian, poet, and politician.

Important were the Valkyries, made famous by Richard Wagner,[66] young girls armed with spears who rode winged steeds, who chose the fallen in battle to be escorted to *Walhalla* where Odin lived.

Particular attention was paid to the cult of the *Matronae*, the embodiment of motherhood, adorned with spikes and fruits, which represented positive forces. These cults can be traced back to the Druids. They believed in the sacredness of the woods, and their astronomical knowledge is testified by the mysterious site of Stonehenge, considered to be an ancient celestial calendar that could predict the cycles of the seasons and the eclipses from the filtering of sun rays among the monoliths. In this rich pantheon we also find elves,[67] who are divided into good and bad. The former live in the sunlight, between heaven and earth, the latter in the darkness of the mountains or in the underworld.

In the Nordic-Germanic conception, time has a cyclical character. The present is based on the difficult balance between opposing forces (gods against the forces of chaos, i.e., the giants and monsters), destined to clash in a final fight (*Ragnarök*) that will also give rise to a new cycle of life. The end of the world also announces, inexorably, the fate of the gods. The myth says that first there will be a harsh and terrible winter. Three more long cold seasons will follow without interruption, during which there will be wars, assassinations, sacrileges. In the sky will occur unequivocal events: the wolf Sköll will swallow the sun, the wolf Hati the moon, the stars will disappear, and so on. Monsters will break free. Fenrir will come out from his den with his jaws wide open, puffing flames from his nostrils and eyes, and the snake Jörmungandr will rise from the ocean, causing floods and tidal waves. Heaven will split, and evil powers will assault the dwelling of the gods. Ahead of everyone will be Surtr, the demon of fire, then Loki, the ice giants, and the infernal demons. They will pass *Bifröst*, which will shatter as they pass. Heimdall will blow his horn and the gods will put on their armor, going to the battle, followed by the *Einherjar*. A fate of death awaits the gods; nevertheless, they will resolutely march towards it—active fatalism. Odin will be ahead of everyone. He will collide with the wolf Fenrir, who will swallow him,

---

66. Wilhelm Richard Wagner (22 May 1813–13 February 1883) was a German composer, theater director, polemicist, and conductor.

67. An elf is a type of humanlike supernatural being in Germanic mythology and folklore. In medieval Germanic-speaking cultures, elves seem generally to have been thought of as beings with magical powers and supernatural beauty, ambivalent towards everyday people and capable of either helping or hindering them.

before succumbing himself, killed by one of the children of Odin, Vidarr, who will push his sword down his throat to his heart. Thor will fight with the snake and eventually manage to kill him, but will die soon after because of its poison. Freyr will fight with Surtr and fall, too. The hell dog, Garmr, will face the god Tyr, and they both will die, like Loki and Heimdallr. Finally, Surtr will cover the earth with fire, destroying all of it, except some places where the dead will be gathered. After the fire, there will be a new beginning. The earth will emerge from the waters, green and flourishing again. A new sun will shine in the sky. The surviving gods—Vidarr (son of Odin), Vali (son of Thor), and Baldr, returned from the underworld—will begin a new divine lineage and, from a man and woman, a new human generation will begin. However, the dark dragon Nidhöggr will sail the skies as a sign that this regeneration of the world does not mean the breaking of the balance between opposing forces nor the definitive disappearance of evil.

All the information about the religion of the Germanic peoples comes from the poem *Edda*, consisting of two works written in ancient Icelandic: the *Poetic Edda* (800–1200 AD) and the modern or *Prose Edda* (1200 AD).

∽

These are some notes on the religions of ancient Europe and the Near East. At the same time, in other parts of the world, other peoples and nations worshiped their gods.

## Religion in Ancient Asia

In ancient Asia, the main religious forms were:

Religions of the Far East:

- Confucianism
- Taoism
- Shenism
- Shinto

Indian religions:

- Hinduism

- Jainism
- Buddhism

Iranian religions:

- Zoroastrianism

## Confucianism

The term Confucianism describes a Chinese school of thought that was formed around the work of Kong Fuzi, Latinized as Confucius. Although he cannot be considered a founder like the Buddha or Christ, he was however the organizer of the rearrangement of a vast material, the heritage of the ancient Chinese religion which, in a particular moment of the troubled Chinese life, assumed the value of a barrier to moral and spiritual decay. This religion's relationship with political-social life and therefore with the moral and intellectual substratum of the ancient civilization was very close. Therefore, if initially Confucianism can be defined (and so it has been defined) as an ethical humanism, since interest in the human being is one of its focal points, we must then focus on its indisputable religious dimension.

Confucius lived in the so-called Spring and Autumn Period (774–454 BC) and was born in 551 BC in today's town of Qufu;[68] even if his life is shrouded in legend, it seems that he wasn't particularly brilliant in assignments or commitments. Initially he was in the service of the feudal family of Qi as superintendent of barns and fields; at twenty-two, he became a teacher, surrounding himself with boys of all conditions. The decisive moment for a hitherto gray existence hitherto was the journey on which he embarked in Luoyi,[69] where he carried out research and where it seems he encountered the founder of Taoism, Lao-zi.[70] From that

---

68. Qufu is a city in East China's Shandong province, best known as the hometown of Confucius, who is traditionally believed to have been born at nearby Mount Ni. The three most famous cultural sites of the city are the temple of Confucius, the cemetery of Confucius, and the Kong family mansion. Together, these three sites have been listed as a UNESCO World Heritage Site since 1994.

69. Luoyang (formerly Luoyi) is a city located in the confluence area of Luo River and Yellow River in the west of Henan province. It was the capital of the Eastern Zhou Dynasty.

70. Lao Tzu, also rendered as Laozi and Lao-Tze, was an ancient Chinese philosopher and writer. He is the reputed author of the *Tao Te Ching*, the founder of

journey, Confucius returned with the reputation of a wise man, esteemed and respected, and he committed himself and his teaching to the reform of society both in the socio-political and religious senses, reinterpreting ancient rules and doctrines in order for them to be helpful for present times. Disgraced by Prince Ding of Lu, for whom he had meanwhile become a minister, Confucius spent the last years of his life wandering throughout China together with his disciples, dealing also with poetry and music. He also devoted himself to the collection of testimonies and memories of antiquity, contributing directly or indirectly to the creation of the Five Classics of Confucianism.

In the canon of Confucianism there are nine writings. There are five main books: the book of change, the book of history, the book of songs, the book of rites, and the spring and autumn annals. If at one time these texts were all attributed to Confucius, both as author and editor, contemporary scholars believe that only the nucleus of most of them dates back to him, and that each one later developed, and therefore variously increased, over time. Next to these are four more books: the Analects, in which the teachings of Confucius are present in the vivacity of the teaching and in the dialogue with his disciples; the Mencius, a collection of conversations; the Great Learning, a short philosophical political treatise; and the Doctrine of the Mean, indicated in the inner balance.

On ethics, Confucius devoted himself to the education of young people, because he was convinced that the reform of the community would take place only through the regeneration of the individual and the family. Above all, he believed virtue to be an inner wealth that everyone can acquire, as human nature in itself is neither good or bad; hence the importance of a proper education. The aim of Confucian ethics is to form wise people, that is, those noble of spirit. If this aim is not achieved, people will behave like fools. Its center is the concept of *Ren*, a concept introduced by Confucius who, however, re-elaborates the concepts of *Li* and *Tianming* already present in Chinese philosophy.

The term *Li* is a complex one, because it indicates both the harmonization of humans with nature and the observance of religious rules and rites, and finally the love for a peaceful social life. The *Li* is the ordering force that guides humans in their duties, both towards others (respect, courtesy, tact, decorum, and self-control) and towards higher spiritual beings, which, according to the ancient religion, were the *Tian* (heaven)

---

philosophical Taoism, and a deity in religious Taoism and traditional Chinese religions.

or supreme god from whom the sovereign receives the kingdom and the subjects over whom he governs through the mandate of heaven (*Ming* or *Tianming*). For Confucius, individual life and history of the nation were the subject of the particular providence of heaven, and each human was responsible to it. The *novum* of Confucian doctrine, though, is represented by the elaboration of the virtue called *Ren* or just organization of human relations.

*Ren* can indicate a complex of virtues: goodness, benevolence, and gentleness, which could be summarized as humanity. Whereas sometimes in China it was defined as a characteristic of the noble towards the lower human, for Confucius it was a universal virtue. It is the virtue that constitutes the wise one, the perfect human being, a stage that everyone can reach, even though Confucius divided humans into three categories: the wise or perfect ones, who constitute the model to follow, having reached the highest degree of perfection (for example the emperors of China); the noble superior ones; and finally the common ones, who make up the majority.

An important aspect of the Confucian religion is its outlet in the political order, or rather its presentation as a civil religion. The doctrine of *Ren* is, in fact, extended to the political sphere in the form of benevolent government, constituted of moral persuasion, whose chief is an example of moral integrity and selfless dedication. If the Confucian sage has been described as having the heart of the sage and the wisdom of the king, humans too are always conceived in harmony with themselves and with society and this, in turn, reflects spiritual and ethical perfection. As a civil religion, Confucianism also acquired, in addition to the role of state cult, a series of great rituals implemented by the emperor himself, to honor heaven (a very important cult in China until the twentieth century), earth, and ancestors. The worship of ancestors in particular is a very well-known aspect of the Chinese religion. Once the prerogative of only the nobility, it would later become part of state orthodoxy. Even today, in many Chinese houses in Hong Kong or Taiwan, one can find the altar of the ancestors, on which commemorative tablets are placed. Other rituals were dedicated to the sun, moon, and terrestrial spirits, or minor deities, as well as to those incorruptible wise men and magistrates revered as gods of the city. Later Confucius himself became a cult object.

Confucianism was further developed by the followers of Confucius, including Mengzi (Latinized as Mencius) and Xunzi. The former, who lived between 372 and 289 BC, perfected the thought of Confucius in a more optimistic sense, speaking of the innate goodness of humans and the universal love of God for all beings. In the book of Mencius there is a significant evolution of the term heaven. If it was sometimes considered as a personal divinity by Confucius, Mencius frequently stated: "Man carries heaven in his heart, so if one knows one's heart and nature, he also knows heaven," thus accentuating the value of heaven as an immanent force, source, and principle of laws and ethical values.

Xunzi (312–238 BC) had, on the contrary, a more pessimistic vision, but according to him, humans, although fundamentally bad, can nevertheless achieve perfection with a severe and just moral education. In his opinion, in fact, the evil present in human nature tends to its opposite and therefore educational work can be very important.

## Taoism

Taoism is the oldest Chinese religion. The term Taoism does not simply denote a school but a quantity of doctrines with philosophical and religious value. Their complexity makes it impossible to provide a single definition. First of all, the term *Tao* (the Way) appears in all currents of thought and in all Chinese religions. Moreover, Taoism has always been surrounded by an air of mystery and if as a philosophy, it prefers exposure through riddles and puzzles, as an esoteric religion, it reveals many secrets only to its initiates.

However, the philosophical (*Dàojia*) and religious (*Dàojiào*) developments are deeply intertwined and not always easily distinguishable, therefore both must be examined. The moment of origin is seen in the legendary figure of Laozi (Old Master, sixth or fifth century BC) to which the oldest Taoist text is attributed, the short and cryptic verse essay entitled with his own name, *Laozi*, also known as *Tao Te Ching*.

According to legend, Laozi's mother became pregnant with her son, conceived from a ray of sunshine, for eighty years and then gave birth to him from her left armpit, under a plum tree. After becoming an archivist in the city of Luoyang, Laozi supposedly met Confucius there, as he was worried about the serious political and moral crisis that China underwent, but unlike Confucius, this state of affairs drove Laozi to meditation and abandonment of the world. He gave up his job and headed on the back of a buffalo, always according to legend, towards the west, "towards the realm of soul rest," where he would obtain eternal life. According to other legends, Laozi might have gone west to spread his message to barbaric (i.e., non-Chinese) peoples, and from this arose the idea that Buddha was Lao-zi himself, who adapted his doctrine to Indian mentality. Be that as it may, before crossing the border he was asked by the Guard Yinxi to leave a testimony of his teaching, so he wrote the short work *Laozi* mentioned above. This text, also called *Tao Te Ching* (book of the principle and its virtue), focuses initially on the *Tao* as the first principle, absolutely indefinable.

In fact, it begins with these famous verses:

"The *Tao* that can be called *Tao* is not the eternal *Tao*. If its name can be pronounced, it is not its eternal name. What is nameless is the principle of heaven and earth."

A characteristic of Taoist thought stands out immediately, its dialecticity and its effort to identify, in the nameless Tao, the first immutable, indeterminate principle from which all things stem and then reach their own determination.

*Tao*, in fact, can be considered the mother of the world. Not only does it generate all beings, but it nourishes, shapes, and completes them. Furthermore, *Tao* is also conceived as a fundamental unity between beings, in which the particular differences and contradictions are resolved, hence the practical implication of this doctrine. Humans must regulate their lives according to the *Tao*, participate in it through *wu-wei* (literally, "not to act"), which does not mean an absence of action but rather a non-artificial action, a sort of support for the natural flow of things and the original cosmic order, without disturbing or modifying it. If we find in Taoism a certain form of asceticism and withdrawal from the world, its pleasures and the values promoted in it, the virtues of not acting are positively realized as modesty, humility, gentleness, tolerance, desire for tranquility, and altruism. Another fundamental work for the understanding of Taoist principles is the *Zhuangzi* (from the name of the author Zhuangzi, master of the fourth century BC), a collection of writings rich in parables, allegories, and fantastic descriptions. In addition to the concepts already described in the other text, here the focus is on the search for absolute bliss, which the author believes can be achieved by overcoming the distinctions between the ego and the universe, therefore in a sort of cancellation-transformation in the *Tao*. A higher knowledge is required that goes beyond distinctions, even that of life and death; knowledge is also defined as "fasting of the heart," in other words, an emptying of senses and mind. In this regard, we must remember the importance attributed by Taoist religion to meditation, which had the purpose of grasping a new self, to achieve harmony with the rhythm of the cosmos and to "dialogue with gods." Under the influence of Buddhism, Taoism developed meditation in a more spiritual sense, almost prefiguring an immortality that the spiritual self achieves after physical death. It is a mystical union with the *Tao*, as it has been said.

Linked to meditation is also the Taoist ritual, a very complex and complicated ritual, to which sacred value is attributed: initiation, purification, and renewal are its essential moments; important functions are performed by priests. The best known ceremonies are the Chinese New Year, with dragon dances and fireworks to drive out demons; the Cosmic Renewal Rite (at the time of the winter solstice, to remember the cosmic rebirth); and soteriological rituals that are affected by Buddhist influence. If as a philosophical doctrine, Taoism was of an individualistic type and represented a rationalization of previous conceptions, then as a true and proper religion, spreading over wider sections of the population, it would mix with elements of popular religions such as shamanism[71] and Buddhist doctrines. It would not totally identify with them and would also assimilate more general principles of Chinese thought, such as that of the *yin-yang* school, which conceives the natural order in the light of the two complementary and at the same time antithetical aspects: *yin*—moment of activity, *yang*—moment of passivity. The main purpose of the Taoist religion is the achievement of physical immortality, and the believer must strive for it through dietary, gymnastic, sexual, alchemical, and meditative practices. Regarding the death of the body, the Taoist religion believes that the body is only appearance and that in reality the immortals go to one of the paradises or to the islands of Happiness located beyond the borders of China. Next to the celestial immortals, there are also the terrestrial immortals, who wander in the sacred forests and on the mountains, and finally the human beings, who simply abandon their physical bodies.

In this perspective, popular religiosity, merging with Taoist principles, gives life to a pantheon very rich in divine figures, such as Huangdi, lord of heaven and father of nine daughters, who guides and governs the world together with the five divine sovereigns, who supervise the cardinal points (in China, in addition to the usual four, the center is added).

---

71. Shamanism is a religious practice that involves a practitioner, a shaman, who is believed to interact with a spirit world through altered states of consciousness, such as a trance. The goal of this is usually to direct spirits or spiritual energies into the physical world for healing or some other purpose.

This divinity, especially in official worship, will gradually lose its anthropomorphic characteristics, presenting himself more and more as a force and as an entity. It is interesting, however, to underscore, as Julia Ching[72] states, that if during the second century he was the supreme deity, immediately after the beginning of the Han[73] era people began to venerate a triad of gods who at different times would bear a different name: the Three Purities. They were the lords of three vital principles or respiratory movements. Their names were: Lord of Primordial Beginning, Lord of the Numinous Treasure, and Lord of the Way and its Virtue. From a metaphysical point of view, each of them represented some ineffable and transcendent aspect of the *Tao*, albeit able to incarnate, especially through the revelation of Laozi. Even the wise humans who reach immortality become part of this Olympus (*xianren*). To reach this goal, in some periods arose the figure of the "master of recipes," who made use of magical practices and invited the faithful to a retired life, according to the principle of Wu Wei mentioned above, which also led to the birth of monastic and priestly communities. Among the many Taoist sects should be remembered the Celestial Master, a title attributed for the first time (around the second century AD) to Zhang Ling, according to legend, by Laozi himself. He appeared to him, complaining about the absence of good in the world and entrusted him with the task of suppressing demonic practices and establishing true orthodoxy. In fact, bloody sacrifices were abolished, and confession of sins was introduced as a cure for diseases. Furthermore, Zhang organized his followers into communities led by priests and priestesses, in contrast to the numerous shamans or mediums of popular religion. This sect supports the existence of an invisible world beyond life and the need for earthly existence to be guided by a class of people in charge of spiritual mediation, that is, in charge of officially praying for the healing of certain diseases. As the sect grew stronger, the title of Celestial Master became hereditary and they moved to the Mount of the Dragon and the Tiger. After the communist conquest of power (1949), the base was transported to Taiwan, where the national Taoist Society, founded in 1965, is also located.

Another important, and still present, sect is the Supreme Clarity, which developed in northern China under the Yuan dynasty,[74] support-

---

72. Julia Ching (1934–2001) was professor of religion, philosophy, and East Asian studies at the University of Toronto.

73. The Han dynasty was the second imperial dynasty of China (202 BC–AD 220).

74. The Yuan dynasty (1279–1368) was the empire or ruling dynasty of China

ers of a life of celibacy and abstention. The monks of this sect followed the practices of meditation and mastered the techniques of alchemy. The Taoist writings, considered sacred, which constitute the canon that has been handed down to us from the fifth century, are divided into seven sections, distributed in turn into three parts called the Three Grottos. This term (*tung*) is probably used because the most important texts would have been revealed to hermits or discovered by them in caves.

The first cave includes the writings that surround the most important liturgical poem, *Shangqing*, with secret names of gods and spirits. The second cave is grouped around the *Lingbao* writings, composed like the previous ones in southern China, which reveal a Buddhist influence. The third cave was formed around the *Sanhuang* writings, of uncertain origin, perhaps the work of Taoist masters present at the court and in connection with the sect of the Celestial Master.

## Shenism

The term *Chinese popular religion* or Shenism is intended to bring together and describe the ethnic religious traditions that have represented the main belief system among the ethnic groups of China, especially the Han people, over the centuries up to now. Shenism includes Chinese mythology and involves the worship of the *shen* (divinity, spirits, awareness, conscience, archetypes), which can generally refer to the deities of the natural world, the clan deities (divinized ancestors), city and/or national deities, cultural heroes and demigods, dragons, and ancestors in general. The term Shenism was first used in 1955 by the scholar A. J. A. Elliot.

Sometimes this form of religion is associated with Taoism, since, over the centuries, when it found itself in an institutional position, Taoism tried to assimilate or at least administer local naturalistic/popular beliefs and faiths. More precisely, Taoism can be considered as a branch of Shenism, since it emerged from a mixture of popular religion and Chinese philosophy.

## Shinto

Shinto is the indigenous religion of Japan before the spread of Buddhism. The word shinto means "way of the gods," and this religion affirms the

---

established by Kublai Khan, leader of the Mongol Borjigin clan.

descent of the emperor, lord of heaven, from the *Kami* (or deity). Shinto must be considered as a set of very well-blended beliefs and rites that make up Japan's social, political, and cultural unity, which also allows for the coexistence with Buddhism, of which the Japanese declare themselves followers, together with the observance of Shinto.

The most important sacred texts and sources for the study are *Kojiki* (old written things) and *Nihongi* (chronicles of Japan). The first was supposedly written by a court dignitary, Yasumaru, and consists of three books with rich mythological narratives, information on the first rulers; the second constitutes the first official history of the country, made up of thirty books. Other important texts are the *Kogo-shui* (a text collected from ancient writings), which gathers the traditions not present in the previous texts and three collections of ceremonials.

The gods in Japanese are called Kami, a term that indicates both who is high or powerful and high things, as well as natural phenomena. Worshiped in particular places such as mountains and forests, ministers of worship were women called Miko, as they were more receptive and capable of being possessed. In mythology, there are numerous Kami, heroes or gods, considered ancestors of the imperial house.

The original mythology says that the islands of Japan were born from the divine couple Izanagi and Izanami, creators also of the divinities of nature. After this creation, Izanagi ascended to heaven and Izanami descended into hell. Izanagi in turn entrusted the dominion of the sky to the goddess of the sun, Amaterasu; that of the night to Tsukiyomi, god of the moon; and that of the sea to Susanoo, god of the storm. Amaterasu, a highly revered divinity, brought to earth the mirror, the sword, and jewels, still today symbols of imperial power. Through his grandson Ninigi, to whom he transmits them, there is the foundation of the empire; the Tenno[75] is in fact a descendant of Ninigi. Many other deities are revered (Inari, god of rice; Kane-no-Kami, god of metal; while local deities and abstract concepts to meet intellectual needs are also considered Kami).

In addition to a series of ethical precepts such as loyalty to duties, contempt for death (the survival of the soul is part of the beliefs), and love for the nation, worship includes purification, offering, and the recitation of prayers.

---

75. In Japanese, the emperor is called Tenno, literally heavenly sovereign or Emperor of God. The Japanese Shinto religion holds him to be the direct descendant of the sun goddess Amaterasu.

The places of worship are built on the model of ancient Japanese houses, so they are very simple: a group of wooden houses, some of which are inaccessible, and for the performance of the ceremony, a hall of worship, or *Haiden*, which is in the front. The shrine is preceded by a triple arch in the shape of a pi.

## Hinduism

The term Hinduism indicates the third and final phase in the history of the religions of India, after Vedism (c. 1500–900 BC) and Brahmanism (900–400 BC). It must be stressed, however, that this tripartition reflects a Western way of seeing and is not a self-denomination of an Indian religion. The followers of this religion, recognizing the common stock with the writings of Brahmanism, define their faith with the latter term. The Persian word Hindu was initially used by Muslims who entered India, to indicate the inhabitants of that region crossed by the great Indus river. In later times it designated with a more religious connotation those who did not convert to Islam, and only from the sixteenth century the Europeans would separate the concept of Indian, to which they attributed a profane meaning, from Hindu (and then Hinduism), which was given a religious meaning.

In general, to avoid misunderstandings, it must be added that Hinduism is a vast and complex composite of religious ideas, conceptions, and aspirations that are expressed in different movements. These movements, while clearly showing a common origin, show very precise doctrinal and liturgical differences. On the one hand, we are aware that a multiplicity of positions is necessary to find one's own path of access to the divinity; on the other, the multiplicity is such only on the surface, and below we find unity of purpose, as all religions work to help build the path to the absolute and salvation. As we read in one of the fundamental texts, the *Bhagavadgita*, Krishna[76] himself states: "Even the faithful of other gods who honor them with full faith, they also do nothing but venerate me although not quite in the right form."[77] The common background that allows this unity in differences is the Vedic[78] religion (with

---

76. Krishna is a major deity in Hinduism. He is worshipped as the eighth avatar of the god Vishnu and also as the supreme God in his own right. He is the god of compassion, tenderness, and love and is one of the most popular and widely revered among Indian divinities.

77. Bhagavadgita, 9:23.

78. The historical Vedic religion (also known as Vedism) and subsequent

the sacred language, Sanskrit), a patrimony of beliefs, liturgies proper to the Indo-Aryans, those people originating in Central Western Asia who settled in India in the first half of the second millennium BC. This population was also the progenitor of all Indo-European bloodlines, and it is significant that the Vedic religion shows remarkable similarities with the Greek, Roman, and Germanic beliefs. Following emigration, Hinduism spread also to the rest of Asia, Africa, and Latin America, giving rise to significant forms of syncretism in Bali, while in Europe it is known more for the presence of new religious movements such as the Hare-Krishna, Ananda Marga, Transcendental Meditation, Satya Sai, and Divine Light Mission. As the figure of a founder is missing, it is not easy to pinpoint with precision the birth of Hinduism. Scholars agree in placing its original elaborations around the first half of the first millennium BC. Referring in particular to the individual movements of Hinduism, we summarize here what are the common foundations accepted by all the faithful, even if not dogmatically recognized by any authority:

1. Faith in *brahman*, beginning and end of reality and operating force in it

2. Acceptance of a dynamic order in all levels of physical and moral reality (*dharma*), therefore linked to a cyclical conception of time without beginning and without end

3. Conception of *karma*,[79] *samsara*[80] and *moksha*,[81] already present in Brahmanism, with a reworking of the ways of liberation, which can

---

Brahmanism refer to the religious ideas and practices among some of the Indo-Aryan peoples of the western Ganges plain of ancient India during the Vedic period (1500 BC–500 BC). These ideas and practices are found in the Vedic texts.

79. Karma means action, work, or deed. It also refers to the spiritual principle of cause and effect where the intent and actions of an individual (cause) influence the future of that individual (effect). Good intent and good deeds contribute to good karma and happier rebirths, while bad intent and bad deeds contribute to bad karma and bad rebirths.

80. Saṃsara is a Sanskrit word that means wandering or world, with the connotation of cyclic, circuitous change. It is also the concept of rebirth and the cyclicality of all life, matter, and existence, a fundamental belief of most Indian religions. In short, it is the cycle of death and rebirth.

81. Moksha is a term in Hinduism, Buddhism, Jainism, and Sikhism for various forms of emancipation, enlightenment, liberation, and release. In its soteriological and eschatological senses, it refers to freedom from saṃsara, the cycle of death and rebirth. In its epistemological and psychological senses, moksha is freedom from ignorance: self-realization, self-actualization, and self-knowledge.

be many but not incompatible with each other: meditative way, way of ritual executions, and way of devotion

4. Faith in the Vedas, which implies the belief in the sacral state of the Brahmins and in the supremacy of the aristocracy of blood with the relative stiffening of the division into castes[82]

The main Hindu movements can be divided into theist currents and philosophical movements. The first are three, namely Vishnuism, Shaivism and Saktism; the second are six, namely Samkhya, Yoga, Nyaya, Vaisheshika, Mimamsa, and Vedanta.

We mentioned theist currents. In fact, the rich Indian pantheon (which includes a multiplicity of powers that operate, destroy, or conserve earthly affairs, such as celestial gods or *Devas* and underground gods or *Asuras*) acquired particular popularity and importance in the cults of Vishnu and Shiva, which, with Brahma, constitute the Trimurti or divine triad. The pantheon is meant to personify, even in various aspects or qualities, unity. Therefore, Brahma is the vital and creative force of the universe, Vishnu the conservative (the goodness of the world), and Shiva not only the force that destroys the world but the one which transforms it. In this sense, it is not accurate to speak of polytheism when referring to Hinduism; or at least this is possible only in relation to the celestial gods, who will later be considered on a lower level than the Trimurti. It can be added that while Brahma, due to his abstract and speculative character, was never the object of popular worship, the other two figures and Shakti originated real devotional currents:

- Vishnuism. Although many schools and various sects can be found within Vishnuism, here we recall only the more general characteristics. Vishnu, who was a minor divinity in Vedicism, arises as a main figure, however bringing together various peculiarities, such as that of being a beneficial force, supporter of the universe, merciful lord (*Ishvara*), defender of law and truth. His wife (*Shakti*)

82. The caste system in India is a hierarchical mechanism, at the level of social stratification, of a strictly hereditary nature. This millennial system, despite having been officially abolished in 1950, still partially influences the division of works, the balance of power, and the transfer of goods and is based on very ancient and deeply rooted religious foundations. The castes were divided as follows: the Brahmins (priestly people), the Kshatriyas (also called Rajanyas, who were rulers, administrators, and warriors), the Vaishyas (artisans, merchants, tradesmen, and farmers), and Shudras (labouring classes). This categorisation implicitly had a fifth element, being those people deemed to be entirely outside its scope, such as tribal people and the untouchables.

is Lakshmi. In his work of opposition to negative forces, Vishnu presents himself to humans in various incarnations or apparitions (*avatar*), which were a kind of perceivable revelation of his divinity. So far, nine have occurred in past ages, whereas the tenth (and last) will take place at the end of the current era; if the oldest ones are in the form of fish (*Matsya*) and wild boar (*Varaha*), in other times he became incarnate in *Rama*, the main protagonist of the epic poem *Ramayana*, and in *Krishna*, a divinity present in the other Indian poem *Mahabharata*. Finally, as proof of the assimilation capacity of Hinduism, it can be remembered that a further incarnation of Vishnu is in Buddha. This conception of incarnations also allows us to understand the idea of time, which is cosmic and cyclical, without beginning or end, in which are identified four ages. In times of danger, the god Vishnu intervenes, interrupting the cosmic cycle to restore order. Hence also the concept of power of god, that is, the ability to want, know, and act. For Vishnuites, these powers have not made themselves autonomous (as it will be for Shivaites) but are part of Vishnu, who through them manifests his omnipotence. In particular, Vishnu has the power to transform, simulate, and enchant, a power summed up in the term *maya* (illusion, fantasy or game), whereby Vishnu is considered divine player and *maya* his partner in this game. The diversity between Vishnu and Shiva (which we will discuss shortly) consists precisely in the active participation by Vishnu in this game: he is always present and attentive to the world, ready to intervene when the situation may seem dramatic, so he is a good god, sometimes cunning, always balanced. In content, some Vishnuite schools support a form of monism, in that they believe that all realities (individual souls, world of material things, and god—Vishnu), although distinct, are inextricably linked. Others, however, profess a clear dualism, in that Vishnu is autonomous, and the souls and the world depend on him who is the mover. Finally, some currents try to harmonize dualism and monism by comparing the relationship of the god with other substances to that of the ocean with the waves.

- Shaivism. The followers of the god Shiva believe him to be the personification of the Absolute, the destructive and regenerating principle of the world, the one who dispenses life and death. This dynamic sort of a game (*Lila*) will only end when a human, realizing his or her identity with Shiva, will flow into him. Shiva, therefore, is the god whose tensions set the world in motion; his generative and destructive capacity is unlimited. The fear of the wrath of god, also present in other religions such as Judaism, Christianity, and Islamism, in Hinduism can be explained according to the primitive history of certain areas and certain populations, in which religious conceptions had to struggle to have their autonomy recognized. Another difference, compared to Vishnu, consists in the individualistic spirit that circulates in Shaivism, since Shiva is, first of all, god of the ascetics and he is himself ascetic, immersed in yoga, already disinterested in the world. Secondly, when he is awakened and annihilates the demons, these are to be understood within humans as concupiscence, spiritual blindness, selfishness, and lack of love. In other words, Shiva works for individual liberation. Shiva too, as said of Vishnu, can assume different forms, characteristics, and names (one thousand and eight, according to tradition). We remember only the most important: creator and lord of the universe (*Mahashiva, Mahadeva, Maheshvara*), ascetic and yogin (*Mahayogi*), destroyer (*Mahakala, Ugra, Bhairava*), and finally fine cosmic dancer (*Nataraja*), to always symbolize the rhythm of births and of deaths. Later on, that is, in the pre-Christian era, he became the lord of knowledge and not only of supreme knowledge but also of arts, sciences, and dance. Also in Shaivism there are currents which are variously diversified according to whether they follow forms of absolute monism, qualified monism, or pluralism. In general, however, dialectic is among the individual souls, kept away from god and always eager to rejoin it by overcoming matter and through meditation and devotion (*Bhakti*).

- Shaktism. The faithful of this current practice the cult of the mother goddess Shakti or bride, a cult that in certain forms comes to support the prevalence of the female principle. The most venerated is Durga-Kali-Parvati, wife of Shiva, but also adored are the bride of Vishnu, Lakshmi, and that of Brahma, Saraswati. In this school, the creative energy of divinity, its strength and power, gets emphasized. The goddess becomes a central element, because she alone is the operative driving principle, to the point that, with a play on words, some say that without Shakti, Shiva would be only a corpse (*Shav*). In a more balanced way, it could be said that Shiva and Shakti are, from the beginning, in a mutual relationship which also allows overcoming of the distance between divine transcendence and earthly immanence; the male principle, in fact, acts through his bride. It is also believed that female energy itself constantly generates and nourishes material nature. Another typical characteristic of Shaktism lies in the almost emotional bond that unites the faithful to the great goddess. Whereas in other currents one never finds the definition of Vishnu or Shiva as father, Shakti is almost carnally revered as a life-giving mother, though sometimes, however, she becomes a disdained mother who chastises and punishes. It follows that in Shaktism, more than in other schools of Hinduism, women enjoy high esteem and consideration, as the perfect union of God with his bride is mirrored in the union between man and woman.

As we mentioned before, according to scholars, the classical philosophical systems present in Hinduism are six (in the Indian tradition they are ordered in pairs, since their development has been in a dialectical relationship): *Samhkya, Mimamsa, Vedanta, Yoga, Vaisheshika,* and *Nyaya,* each one being the result of a complex speculative doctrinal elaboration that can be drawn from the vast literature that derives from them. The common feature is that they are all born to provide an interpretation of the world, with the aim of indicating to humans the way to liberation, which can be achieved through knowledge:

1. *Samkhya* is one of the oldest and most characteristic schools of Indian spirituality. The term means enumeration, since it maintains the need to enumerate and investigate the categories of the phenomenal world. *Samkhya* conceives two fundamental realities: *prakriti* or unconscious active principle, the cause of the universe, a sort of *natura naturans*; and *purusha* or soul, an intelligent and conscious but passive principle, not subject to joy or pain. From the opposition of these two moments flows the whole life of the universe, according to the rhythm of samsara. In particular, then, the primordial matter consists of three elements or *gunas* (threads): *sattva* (intelligence), *rajas* (energy), *tamas* (resistance). As long as they are in balance in prarikti, there is a state of rest, but once the balance is broken with the prevalence of one over the other, the dynamic process of the universe begins, the birth of matter and the five elements. It should be stressed that this development scheme would be adopted by other Hindu schools. In turn, individual consciousnesses, purushas, are

inherently immaterial but linked (or precipitated) in matter, from which they must detach by recognizing their own extraneousness and returning to a state of calm.

2. *Mimamsa*, which means investigation, proposes the systematic exegesis of Vedic texts and rituals, thus insisting on the importance of these and of sacrifice, to interrupt the cycle of *samsara*.

3. *Vedanta*, also called the Shankara school, named after the founder, who was one of the most famous Indian philosophers. Supporter of a rigid monism, he believed that multiplicity and duality are only appearance, or rather they are the illusory veil (*maya*) that covers the pure unity and identity (*advaita*) of universal Brahman and individual Atman.[83] A scale of knowledge from the lower to upper allows the achievement of the absolute truth of this identity.

4. *Yoga* is one of the most famous Hindu schools. The term, which means union, generally indicates the method to obtain the dominion of all spiritual forces and the achievement of inner peace. While admitting two opposing and eternal substances, purusha and prakriti, yoga also affirms the existence of a god (Ishvara) as the supreme regulator of the motion of nature, the intelligent cause of its evolution. About the yoga path, as outlined by Patanjali,[84] it must be remembered that the term is ambivalent, as it means both harnessing, controlling the functions of the body, the senses, the thought itself, and the result of this, the union of individual and absolute ego, *atman* and *brahman*.

Yoga includes eight grades, divided into two phases. At first, control of the body is achieved through physical exercises, then comes the suspension of the multiplicity of inner representations, and finally the path ends with the mystical ecstasy, that is, the separation of the purusha from prakriti, a lightning-fast and

---

83. Atmanis is a Sanskrit word that means inner self, spirit, or soul. In Hindu philosophy, especially in the Vedanta school of Hinduism, Atman is the first principle, the true self of an individual beyond identification with phenomena, the essence of an individual.

84. Some traditions say that Patanjali lived around 500 BC and that he was a philosopher and a great yoga teacher. It is said that he was an evolved soul who decided to reincarnate as a human being, to help humanity. In his life, in fact, he decided to experience the joys and pains of life, and finally he found a method to overcome the sufferings of humanity, which he put in writing in the *Yoga Sutras*.

all-encompassing illumination of knowledge, a moment not easily accessible, and not by everyone.

5. *Vaisheshika*, a school founded by the wise Kanada, maintains the need to define the fundamental categories of the world, and therefore proposes an atomic theory, specifying the nature of atoms, their combination, etc. The Absolute controls atoms and their unions, thus controling *karma* as well.

6. *Nyaya*, founded by the Brahman Gautama, is very similar to the previous one and has developed over a period of twenty centuries with many differentiations. A typically philosophical school, it considers the dialectical speculative effort as the essential moment for the knowledge of reality, not proposing a new view of the world but striving to provide the means to give logical consistency to argument.

## Vedism

The term Vedism refers to the most ancient phase of the Indian religion, founded on the Vedas. They are the fundamental sacred texts of the Hindus. The name means knowledge, since it is believed that some very ancient seers and poets heard this knowledge; and at the same time it is believed that these are eternal revelations without principle, not produced at a certain moment by the gods. This knowledge is also necessary to maintain a proper relationship with the supernatural powers, from which the well-being of everyday life will derive. This characteristic of revealed religion remains in all Hindu currents, just as the connection with the Vedic tradition is very strong. Although the content of the revealed texts in force today has little to do with the content of the Vedas, they are an expression of the beliefs developed in India after the immigration of populations of Indo-Aryan[85] language and culture who, between 1800 and 1600 BC, moved from Southern Russia and Central Asia to the east. In India these warrior populations clashed with the autochthonous Dravidian[86] culture. The light-skinned invaders called themselves *Arya*

85. The Indo-Aryan peoples or Indic peoples are a diverse collection of ethnolinguistic groups speaking Indo-Aryan languages, a subgroup of the Indo-European language family. Indo-Aryan peoples are native to the North Indian subcontinent and are presently found all across South Asia, where they form the majority.

86. Dravidian people or Dravidians are the present and past speakers of any of the Dravidian languages. Dravidian speakers form the majority of the population of South

(lords of the earth); the others, dark-skinned, who were subdued, took the name of *dasyu* (slave).

The composition of the Vedas cannot be traced back to a single period but, according to scholars, the oldest part dates back to 1500 BC, while the remainder is dated around 600 BC. These texts consist of four collections of hymns:

1. *Rigveda* or Veda of praise, the oldest and the most memorable Indic work from a linguistic and cultural, as well as religious, point of view. It is made up of ten books (*mandalas* or circles) including 1028 hymns for about ten thousand verses.
2. *Samaveda* or Veda of the sacred songs, consisting largely of ritual hymns already present in the *Rigveda*, with an original part (seventy-five stanzas).
3. *Yajurveda* or Veda of the yajus, a sort of manual with the necessary instructions for sacrifice, which, together with knowledge, represents an essential moment of Hinduism itself. It consists of two collections, called white Yajurveda and black Yajurveda.
4. *Atharvaveda* or Veda of the knowledge of magic formulas, composed of twenty books, is the most popular text, dealing with spells, protective or magic formulas, and exorcisms.

The Vedas are written in Sanskrit, and another peculiarity is their oral transmission, until recent times, by master to disciple, from father to son in the families of the Brahmins, hence another characteristic of the Hindu religion, faith in the direct activity of the divine word: "It is good if you understand it, but it works even without understanding it." The *mantras*, sayings which help thought and meditation, sometimes simple syllables that do not present any recognizable sense, according to the faith of the Hindus, have a particular creative force because of their superhuman origin and the inherent possibility of spiritual development. Coming to the cosmogony, which is obtained not without difficulty from the Vedas, we find at the origin of the world the absolute, indivisible and eternal Entity, the One, which manifests itself thanks to the energy generated by ascetic practices, energy that also gives rise to the world as known by humans, to shapes and names.

---

India and are natively found in India, Pakistan, Afghanistan, Bangladesh, the Maldives, and Sri Lanka.

In the *Rigveda*, the One is described as an androgynous divinity, having in itself the male and the female principle. From this union the cosmic man, or Purusha, is born, who has the whole universe within him. From its sacrifice, in fact, from his dismembered body, as we shall see, the world flows, made up of three areas (sky, atmosphere, and earth) and the four main castes. Before clarifying the conception of the world and of humanity, we must still outline the pantheon of the Vedic religion, which is rich in powers and entities that are benevolent or adverse to humanity, but which nonetheless come to represent the totality of natural phenomena, as well as supernatural forces. In particular, the *Rigveda* speaks of thirty-three divinities, eleven in each of the areas of the universe, which in turn are divided into two groups: the *Devas* with Indra at the head and the *Asuras* with Varuna at the head. Of the first, we can remember Dyaus Pitar (Father Heaven) and his bride Prthvi Matar (Mother Earth); Ushas (goddess of dawn), present in many hymns as a dancing figure; Surya (the sun); Vayu, god of the wind; and Parjanya, the rain. And if these are natural divinities, there is no lack of anthropomorphized figures, such as Indra, considered, in fact, the chief tutelary deity of the Aryans, with his wife Indrani; Agni, god of fire; Soma, divinity linked to sacrifice; the two twin gods Ashvin, protectors of agriculture and breeders; and Rudra, god of storms and devastation. It is interesting to note that in the *Rigveda* we find, albeit still with little importance, a divinity that would become central in classical Hinduism, Vishnu.

In the group of Asuras, who would be considered demons only later, we find Varuna, guarantor of order, winner of chaos and protector, together with Mitra, of law and truth; Aryaman; Prajapati; and other minor deities. It has been said that Purusha is the primordial male and represents the totality of the universe, but it is significant to underline that whereas the multiplicity of things that surround us is born from the sacrifice of Purusha and from his dismemberment, the ultimate goal is the recomposition of the unity, the return to the original principle. However, all life in the world (including the orbit of the sun, moon, and stars) derives from this dismemberment, and every event is regulated by the *Rta* or impersonal law. Even the division into castes, which was to establish the difference between light-skinned Ariya conquerors and darker-skinned indigenous population, is mythologically founded, in a song in the *Rigveda*, by the sacrifice of the cosmic man, which sounds like this: "The *brahman* was his mouth, his arms became *ksahriya*, his thighs *vaisya*, and *sudra* was born from his feet." The four castes (*varna*), as we have seen, therefore are the priests or *brahmana*, the warriors or *kshatriya*, merchants and farmers or *vaishya*, and indigenous slaves or *shudra*. The last aspect to remember of Vedic religion is the importance of sacrifice as a moment of bond between humanity and divinity. Sacrifices can be divided into two fundamental groups, one aimed at obtaining the intercession of the gods, the other for the purpose of atonement.

The term Brahmanism refers instead to the second (from tenth to sixth century BC) of the three phases into which the Hindu religion is divided—after Vedism and before actual Hinduism. The term Brahmanism is derived from brahman, a formula that has both religious power and magical character. The Brahmins, the ones who have brahman, are members of the priestly caste who, in this period, increasingly acquired importance and power as custodians of the sacred word transmitted by the Vedas and as the only officiants of sacrificial rites. In addition, the Brahmins also played an important role in the slow merger of the various religious currents within Hinduism: the role of selection, systematization, imposition, and conservation of norms. At the same time, they became the custodians of culture, from philosophy to grammar, from mathematics to medicine, from economics to politics, in addition to sacred and profane law. This supremacy lasted until the sixth century BC when, following the renewal movements (Buddhism and Jainism), profound transformations took place. In addition to the Vedas, the literary texts of Brahmanism are made up of the *Brahamanas*, the *Aranyakas*, and the *Upanishads*. The *Brahamanas*, or priestly texts, are closely linked to the *Vedas*, constituting the official exegesis and commentary on those. They are believed to date back to 900–700 BC and are written in Sanskrit prose. They contain very specific and detailed precepts on sacrificial rites and the interpretation of ancient legends. The *Aranyakas*, or texts of the forest, are written by hermits and addressed to hermits, having therefore a strong mystical-ascetic accentuation and reference to precise sacred rites. Finally, the *Upanishads* or secret doctrine (literally "sitting down near," referring to the closeness of teacher and pupil), also collectively called *Vedanta* or source of the *Vedas*, represent one of the most precious and lasting heritage of Indian spirituality. Religious thought in these texts rises to metaphysical speculation, with psychological and meditative angles on the supreme being, the ego, and the world. Composed in different ages starting from 800 BC, they are mystical-philosophical treatises (one hundred and eight, according to tradition) of esoteric content (secret doctrines for pupils of the Brahmins). Although their content is not systematic and bears some contradictions, they show the most important conceptions of this religion and its attempt to answer questions about the meaning of existence, the principle of the world. The oldest are *Brihadaranyaka* and *Chandogya*, in prose and verse, followed by *Kaushitaki*, *Kena*, *Shvetashvatara* and others, which mark the detachment from the Brahmana.

The main characteristic and difference of Brahmanism compared to the Vedic period is the lesser importance attributed to the divinity in favor of the priestly caste. Consequently, the main divinity is Prajapati, the lord of creatures, to whom the personification of the priesthood was also attributed. Father of the gods and demons, he frees the feminine principle from himself, which by coupling with the masculine principle gives rise to the empirical world. In addition, Prajapati becomes the image and manifestation of the Absolute or One, which takes the name of brahman. Another fundamental notion of Brahmanism is defined, *Karma* (act, action, notion), which, already present in Vedism, takes on new connotations. Karma, in fact, is the action carried out by the individual and also the work and the fruit that derives from it. Life then does not end in one existence, but from one, it passes into another, and the form of this is determined by actions previously performed.

It should be emphasized that the cycle of existences, with their flow that takes the name of *Samsara*, is an endless and joyless current of births and deaths, hence a more pessimistic vision is present in the *Upanishads* than the substantially serene and naturalistic one of the *Vedas*. In fact, a desire emerges to escape from this wheel of existences and to depersonalize in the peace of *Nirvāna*, even if with the doctrine of karma, ethical behavior begins to be preferred over correctness and ritual formality.

## Buddhism

The term Buddhism indicates the doctrine preached by Prince Siddhartha Gautama (563–483 BC) called Buddha (the Enlightened), a doctrine that was born in India as an alternative to Brahmanism, but later became one of the great world religions. It can also be characterized as a philosophy, view of the world, or ethical teaching without exhausting its complexity within these definitions.

The doctrine of Buddhism came through a tradition that is inspired, basically, by canonical writings. These date back to an oral tradition formed shortly after the death of the Buddha in order to establish the essential features of his teaching and the disciplinary norms for the monastic community. They were then increased by numerous additions, including a section dedicated to philosophical reflection, called *abhidharma*. Of the numerous canonical writings, belonging to different groups or schools, we have in its entirety only the Pali canon or *Tipitaka* ("three baskets"), written in the Pali language and composed, according to the Sinhalese chronicles, on the island of Ceylon (Sri Lanka) during the first century BC. Fragments in Sanskrit remain of other canons and some translations into Tibetan and Chinese. In the fourth century BC, a large Buddhist council was held in the city of Pātaliputra, where schismatic tendencies began to loom, which led to the subsequent division of Buddhism into *mahāyāna* (the "great vehicle") and *hīnayāna* (the "small vehicle"). The latter, named thus, not without contempt, by the followers of the former, is commonly known as *theravāda*. Many doctrinal elements are common to both groups, summarized in the statement of the four noble truths:

1. Everything is pain.
2. Pain has a cause.
3. Pain has a termination: *nirvāna*.
4. There is a path that leads to *nirvāna*. It is articulated in the eightfold path: right understanding (of doctrine), right thinking (and deciding), right speaking, right acting, right way of sustaining oneself, right effort, right concentration, right meditation.

This is the intermediate way between the two extremes of the life of pleasure and the life of excessive asceticism, of which the Buddha himself set an example with his life. The three precepts of righteous speaking, righteous action, and righteous self-sustaining are further clarified by the five great commandments (do not lie, do not steal, do not commit adultery, do not kill any living thing, do not make use of intoxicating substances) which, for the monks, translate into five corresponding vows: perfect sincerity, poverty, chastity, non-violence, abstinence from fermented drinks. The life of the monk is of support and example to that of the laity, who, without leaving the chores of daily life, must seek refuge in the three jewels of Buddhism: Buddha, *dharma* (the law), and *sangha* (the community). They also must financially support the monastic community with their offerings, acquiring merit for future reincarnations. Monks have the task of preaching dharma towards lay people, which leads to salvation. Common to all schools of Buddhism is also the enunciation of the laws that determine the origin of pain. In its most ancient formulation, the cause of pain is identified with thirst, that is, with that craving which produces attachment to existence and gives rise to new birth, followed by aging and death. Fundamental to all Buddhism is also the law of karma, or the law of retribution of deeds, which, according to some Buddhist schools, is the cause of the origin of the world.

On the other hand, there are many differences between schools in relation to nirvāna, which, although recognized by all as the extinction of pain, is variously qualified in its essence. It is considered by some to be an absolute, unconditional entity with a liberating function (*Sarvastivada* school); according to others, it does not have metaphysical substance, but is a simple event (*Sautrantika* school). According to the schools of the Great Vehicle, nirvāna is conceived as the true essence of humanity and of the whole reality, and therefore is immanentized. Not even the school of *Madhyamaka* (intermediate path), so often accused of nihilism, asserted that nirvāna was nothing, even though it claimed that everything is empty, that is, that reality, whether contingent or absolute, is conceptually indefinable. The *Madhyamaka* remained faithful to the silence of the Buddha, who, when asked about the main metaphysical questions, did not want to answer. However, the doctrine he preached was a message not only of the highest moral value, but also of profound mystical value. The Great Vehicle made explicit the highest mystical instance of original Buddhism, presenting it as the authentic doctrine of the Master, esoterically transmitted to some of the disciples, and universalized by emphasizing the possibility and reality of salvation for all.

Regarding salvation and the means to achieve it, according to the Small Vehicle, one must save oneself through the practice of virtues and become an *arhat* ("he who is worthy" to enter the nirvāna). The adept of the Great Vehicle instead can become a Buddha and receive the help of the bodhisattvas, that is, of those who delay their entry into the nirvāna to help other creatures save themselves. The Great Vehicle has also considerably developed meditation techniques intended to purify thought. It was the school called *yogāchāra* that developed those methods of yogic concentration and contemplative practice which subsequently gave rise to a new type of idealistic gnoseology,[87] culminating in the theory of *ālayavijñāna* or storehouse-consciousness of all knowledge. The path of

---

87. The investigation and philosophical doctrine relating to the problem of knowledge, that is, the verification of the forms and limits of human cognitive activity.

spiritual purification ends in wisdom, *prajñā*, which consists in seeing things as they really are: transient, passing, devoid of substantiality. Even this doctrine, which was later reworked in the *Prajñāpāramitā-Sāstra* (treaties of perfect wisdom), was radicalized to the point of leading to the paradox of the insubstantiality of the sensible world as a whole. This led to conceive the essence of reality in a sphere located beyond experience, reachable only through mysticism.

The Buddhism of *vajrayāna* (diamond vehicle), also called *mantrayāna* (vehicle of ritual formulas) or *tantrayāna* (vehicle of the book), had its first center of diffusion in the mid-Gangetic[88] region and Bengal,[89] but it spread even further outside India, to China, Tibet, Sumatra, Burma, and Japan. Contrary to primitive Buddhism and the Great Vehicle, which were open to all, Buddhist Tantrism was esoteric, that is, restricted to a few circles of initiates, led by spiritual masters. They practiced the worship of the Buddha, metaphysically conceived as the One who manifests himself in the various Buddhas, bodhisattvas, divinities, and forces of the cosmos; but they also venerated female figures, such as Prajñāpāramitā (personification of perfect wisdom) and other similar deities, through which erotic mysticism was also introduced into Buddhism as a means of achieving perfection. Buddhist Tantrism had a remarkable literary and artistic flourishing, especially in the elaboration of mandalas[90] and the architectural monuments that recall their motifs. Linked to this is Buddhist cosmology, which is characterized by the sense of the enormous grandeur of spaces and times. It starts from a cyclical course of world history, which somehow reflects on a cosmic scale the cycle of individual births. There are certain repeated evolutions of the world and repeated cosmic catastrophes, followed by new cosmogonies—infinite worlds, therefore, or infinite universes, some already existed or perished, just like the current one is destined to disappear. Each world lasts for a period called *mahakalpa*,

---

88. The Ganges is a transboundary river of South Asia that flows through India and Bangladesh. The 2,704 km (1,680 mi) river originates from the Gangotri Glacier of western Himalayas in the Indian state of Uttarakhand, and flows south and east through the Gangetic Plain of India and Bangladesh, eventually emptying into the Bay of Bengal.

89. Bengal is a geopolitical, cultural, and historical region in South Asia, specifically in the eastern part of the Indian subcontinent at the apex of the Bay of Bengal.

90. A mandala is a geometric configuration of symbols. In various spiritual traditions, mandalas may be employed for focusing attention of practitioners and adepts, as a spiritual guidance tool, for establishing a sacred space, and as an aid to meditation and trance induction.

equivalent to twenty *kalpas* (periods). The infinite universes also float in space or primordial substance (*akasha*), and each consists of four parts: a surface, a center, and a lower and upper zone. In the lower area are the beings who suffer temporary penalties as a result of their actions; above is the terrestrial disk with Mount Meru in the center, from which the four continents originate, surrounded by the sea and inhabited by animals, humans, spirits, and demons. Whereas the sun, moon, and stars revolve around Mount Meru, in the upper area, also called the region of pure form, live the gods.

As we can see, there is no theoretical systematization in Buddhism that lingers on the concepts of creation of the world or around the divinity. The monks who asked for explanations of complex metaphysical questions were answered by the Buddha with "a noble silence," indicating the way of an intense ethical practice combined with an anti-dogmatic attitude. He himself affirms in a canonical text: "There is much more that I have directly known but have not explained to you. What I have explained is a tiny amount. And why haven't I explained it? Because it's not beneficial or relevant to the fundamentals of the spiritual life. It doesn't lead to disillusionment, dispassion, cessation, peace, insight, awakening, and extinguishment."[91]

The Buddha frequently makes fun of the metaphysical philosopher who gets lost in words and opinions, and compares him to the man, injured by an arrow, who wants to know who shot him, what material the arrow is made of, and where it comes from, before having it taken out. The core of Buddhism is therefore a theoretically simple doctrine and a profound ethical sense. Hence the characteristic of this religion of being a non-doctrine doctrine, a teaching of non-teaching. Theories and doctrines, therefore, are useless for the purposes of enlightenment, and the Buddha is free from opinions. In the moment of enlightenment, he supposedly sensed a precise ethical imperative to free himself from opinions (*ditthi*). It is interesting, however, to point out how the eightfold path which represents, as we mentioned, the way of liberation, is a strong ethical discipline that leads to meditative practice.

---

91. Samyutta Nikaya, "In a Rosewood Forest."

# Jainism

Jainism is a religious current stemming from Hinduism as a reform of that. It eventually developed as a distinct religion, and today it has more than three million followers, mainly in the northwestern part of India.

The supposed founder is Vardhamana (aka Mahavira), who lived, according to tradition, between 539 and 467 BC. Around the age of thirty, he left his family and turned to ascetic practices and meditation, reaching complete dominion of samsara and the way of salvation. He was therefore given the title of *Jina* (the winner), hence the term Jainism. The first disciples gathered around him, and gradually the new religion spread considerably, even because it included, among his followers, a sovereign as well, the king Chandragupta (322–298 BC). The Jain religion suffered a split due to some divergences on monastic life. Some more radical and conservative followers called *Digambara* (air clothes) believed that the monks should live naked, being in need of nothing and not having anything to obstruct the path towards liberation; others, called *Svetambara* (dressed in white) accepted the use of monastic robe. The canon recognized by Svetambaras is called *Siddhanta* (didactic book), consisting of forty-five texts divided into two sections, whose oldest parts date back to the third or second century BC. Digambaras instead do not recognize the canonical value of this text and consider as such only the writings of some teachers of their schools, in particular the works in verses by Kundakunda.[92]

In terms of content, Jain doctrine has many similarities with Hinduism. The universe is eternal, and only through rigid ascetic practices one can overcome the law or karma that regulates the rhythm of the various lives or samsara. The souls saved in this way possess infinite knowledge, joy, and strength and dwell in a place above the heavens. In particular, ethical life is guided by five principles:

1. Absolute respect for any form of life (*ahimsa*). Therefore, absolute non-violence towards even the smallest and most insignificant animal creatures as well as towards plants and all the basic elements (earth, air, water). This explains why the followers of Jainism are

---

92. Kundakunda was a Digambara Jain monk and philosopher, who likely lived in the second century AD or later. He authored many Jain texts, such as *Samayasara, Niyamasara, Pancastikayasara, Pravachanasara, Astapahuda,* and *Barasanuvekkha.* He occupies the highest place in the tradition of the Digambara Jain leaders.

barred from many work activities and have dedicated themselves particularly to academic and commercial activities.

2. Sincerity
3. Respect for the property of others unless received as a gift
4. Chastity
5. Non-attachment to material goods. For monks, all five of these principles are mandatory; for laity, only the first three, but it should be emphasized that between the monastic communities governed by the *acaryas* (teachers) and the laity, there are deep bonds and very close relationships.

## Zoroastrianism

Zoroastrianism is the doctrine preached by Zarathustra (also known as Zoroaster, 630–550 BC) in Persia and followed there until the Arab conquest. Although the Zoroastrian conceptions always had an aristocratic character and did not really penetrate into the lower classes, many of their elements remain nevertheless alive, for example in the religion of the Parsis, who emigrated to India following the Islamic conquest of Persia and still reside in a region close to Mumbai. Zarathustra's life is full of legendary and mythological elements. Determined to become a priest, he opposed the cult of Mithra,[93] hitherto accepted in Persia, because it was too bloody. He went through a period of meditation, after which he received the enlightenment of the supreme god, *Ahura Mazda*, and began his work as a prophet and reformer. He encountered many oppositions and therefore moved to western Persia, where he had the protection of various sovereigns until the assumption of Zoroastrianism as state religion under Cyrus the Great (600–528 BC). After a period of eclipse, because of both the conquest of the Persian empire by Alexander the Great and the loss of the sacred text *Avesta*,[94] Zorostrianism returned

---

93. Mithra is the Zoroastrian angelic divinity (*yazata*) of covenant, light, and oath. In addition to being the divinity of contracts, Mithra is also a judicial figure, an all-seeing protector of truth, and the guardian of cattle, the harvest, and the waters. The Romans attributed their Mithraic mysteries (the mystery religion known as Mithraism) to Persian sources relating to Mithra.

94. The Avesta is the primary collection of religious texts of Zoroastrianism, composed in the Avestan language.

into vogue with the Sassanid empire (226–651 AD) and was eventually replaced by Islam following the Arab conquest. The general characteristic of Zoroastrianism is being more than a religion, a theological, philosophical, and moral doctrine, as Zarathustra, in addition to fighting polytheism, set out to spread a moral code made up of pure and high ethical norms, which would have brought also an orderly social coexistence. Hence his reference not so much to an exact material execution of prescriptions, but to a pure inner disposition, summarized in the motto "think well, speak well, act well."

Regarding the more strictly religious contents, Zarathustra speaks of the supreme divinity Ahura Mazda, creator of heaven and earth and all that is in them, guardian of the moral order and judge of merits and guilt at the end of time. Unlike the gods of polytheism, Ahura Mazda is not tied to physical phenomena; he is the Wise Lord, omniscient and good. He created the six *Ameshas Spentas* (immortal saints), similar to angels, who surround him and help him in the government of the world, actively supervising various moments of existence. An antagonist of Ahura Mazda is *Angra Mainyu* or destroying spirit, also surrounded by evil spirits, which help him tempt humans. If initially (for 120,000 years) there was only the principle of good, after three thousand years Angra Mainyu chose evil. From that moment on, the world was divided into two areas, among which humans, endowed with freedom, must choose. The whole history of the universe becomes the history of the struggle between the two principles and will eventually end with the victory of good. Great importance is attributed to the choice of humans, therefore to the ethical norms to be followed, as said: righteousness, equity, docility to divine command, integrity. Hence the lack of worship and the absence of a priestly class, always despised and fought by Zarathustra.

We mentioned the sacred text Avesta. The one known today, a sacred text for Parsis, reproduces only in part the Zoroastrian original, which was made up of seventeen hymns, sometimes in contrast with the conceptions of the rest of the Avesta.

## Religion in Ancient America

### Native American Civilizations

At the same time, in pre-Columbian America, the indigenous peoples had their own and differentiated forms of religion. Complex civilizations developed and settled in Mesoamerica (the region of Central and Latin America comprising the southern half of Mexico; the territories of Guatemala, El Salvador, and Belize; the western part of Honduras; Nicaragua; and Costa Rica) and in South America, whereas in North America, inhabited by nomadic tribes, there were simpler civilizations, which, however, had a common religious sense. These tribes believed in a cosmic power, the Great Spirit, generator of life, called by several names, mostly frequent *Manitou*. For the Sioux it is *Wakaonda*; for the Huroni, *Oki*; for the Iroquois, *Orenda*. This supreme being guides earthly events through the *Totem*.[95] This term indicates precisely the protective spirit and, at the same time, the bond that unites the members of a tribe. Other important elements of Native American religion are *kalumet* and dance. With the first, a sacred pipe, Native Americans of the Mississippi area sealed peace agreements and established religious sanctions; the second, of a ritual nature, was performed with a mask that represented the animal with whom to identify through rhythm, while the main purpose was always to propitiate the prosperity of the tribe. Important civilizations developed in Mesoamerica and South America, of which the best known are the Aztec, the Mayan, and the Inca civilizations, which had complex and different religious rites.

## Aztec Civilization

The Aztec religion is the religion of the indigenous peoples who settled in the Mexican plateau before the Spanish conquest of AD 1519–21. These populations reached a higher degree of civilization than other peoples of the same continent, so their religion cannot be associated with primitive ones. The maximum expansion of the kingdom of the Aztecs occurred first with King Izcoatl, who founded a league of three cities, and then with Montezuma, who further enlarged the conquered territory. In 1519, the landing of the Spanish conquistadors under the guidance of Hernan Cortès, seen by the Aztecs as a divine figure (Quetzacoatl), put an end to this kingdom.

---

95. A totem (Ojibwe: *doodem*) is a spirit being, sacred object, or symbol that serves as an emblem of a group of people, such as a family, clan, lineage, or tribe. While the term totem is derived from the North American Ojibwe language, belief in tutelary spirits and deities is not limited to indigenous peoples of the Americas but is common to a number of cultures worldwide.

The Aztec pantheon is very rich and complex. The highest deities were the couple *Tota* (our father) and *Totan* (our mother), also called by other names (respectively Tonacatecuhtl and Tōnacācihuātl, Ometecuhtli and Omecihuatl). Mother of all the gods was *Teteoh Innan*, also known as Coatlicue (the Christian Shrine of Our Lady of Guadalupe was built on the site of the temple dedicated to her—*Tepeyacac*). Other astral deities were *Huitzilopochtli*, God of the sun, who protected the population in wars, and *Tezcatlipoca*, God of the Ursa Major, lord of cold and death. The presence of divinities of the stars of the southern sky, such as the *Centzon Uitznahua* (the four hundred of the south), is also interesting. Numerous also were the divinities of the earth linked to fertility (*Tlazolteotl* and *Xipe Totec*): *Chihucoatl* was goddess of earth and births; the god of corn, the main food of the population, was *Centeotl*; the god of flowers and love was *Xochiqueztal*; while *Xochipilli* was the deity who presided over parties, music, and joy. *Tlaloc* was the god of the rain. Finally there were the divinities of the underworld, *Miclantecuhtli* and his wife *Mictlantcihuatl*.

The Aztecs' world view was composite. Heaven and the underworld were two very high and specular pyramids joined together at the base, represented by the earth's surface. The sky was divided into thirteen parts, each with a divinity, whereas the underworld was in nine parts. The kingdom of the dead was divided into three parts: the first (house of the sun in the sky) hosted those who were killed in the sacrifices, or those who fell in battle and the women who died in childbirth; the second (kingdom of the god of the rain) hosted the drowned, lepers, and paralytics; in the third (place of the dead), the underground kingdom, rested all the others. Closely related to the Aztec religious vision was the practice of sacrifice, including human sacrifice, which was part of their rituals, together with baptism of children in water and confession. During the sacrifices, which were supposed to contribute to maintaining life on earth and therefore carried out to ensure the tour of the sun in its orbit, prisoners of war were immolated. The forms of these sacrifices were many (offerings of the heart, gladiator sacrifices, bonfires, skinning). Alongside these practices, we also find bloodless sacrifices such as offerings of flowers, incense, and fruits. The places designated for worship (called *teocalli* or divine houses) included the pyramidal terraced temple, the house of priests, the homes of young nobles, and the places of the sacred ballgame (*ollama*), which symbolized the movement of the sun. At the top of the temple, reached by exceedingly steep stairs, were two shrines, with the facades facing west and the sacrificial stone.

At the top of social hierarchy were the king and priests, in particular the two who presided over the two main temples, dedicated to Huitzilopochtli and Tlaloc. Then followed the nobles, the free, the serfs, and the slaves. The rite of baptism, mentioned above, as well as the symbol of the cross and sacred banquets, persuaded the Spanish conquerors to believe that the Aztecs professed a sort of deformed or diabolical Christianity.

## Mayan Civilization

The Mayan religion is the religion of the peoples who inhabited the territories of Central America corresponding to today's Yucatan, Mexico; Guatemala; El Salvador; and Honduras. These peoples gave birth to a civilization considered one of the most advanced of the pre-Columbian age and a flourishing empire until the conquest of the Spanish. If at the origin of the Mayan religiosity there seems to be a monotheistic idea, as the upper classes believed in a supreme being not represented by any image, in later times this conception got modified and the pantheon was enriched with other divinities: *Itzamna*, god of the sun and the sky, protector of science and culture; *Ixchel*, his consort, goddess of the moon and fertility; *Bacab*, their son; *Kukulcan*, or green feathered serpent, protector of priests; *Chaac*, god of thunder; *Huracan*, still god of thunder and storm. At the head of the kingdom of the dead we find *Hun Hau*, depicted as a skeleton.

All such deities lived in the heavens, imagined in number of thirteen according to some scholars, while for others there were nine spheres in the upper world and nine in the lower one. According to tradition, the earth was shaped and formed by the gods before the creation of humans, generated from a corn cob after two failed attempts, one with clay, the other with wood. Very important was the official cult, with vast rituals of ceremonies, sacrifices, and processions, preceded by the priests' class, which had a precise hierarchy. These cults took place in the characteristic truncated pyramid temples with a large staircase, similar to those that can still be admired in *Uaxactun*[96] and *Chichen Itza.*[97] To prepare for

---

96. Uaxactun is an ancient sacred place of the Maya civilization, located in the Petén Basin region of the Maya lowlands, in the present-day department of Petén, Guatemala.

97. Chichen Itza was a large pre-Columbian city built by the Maya people of the Terminal Classic period. The archaeological site is located in Tinúm Municipality, Yucatán State, Mexico.

these ceremonies, the Mayans had to observe fasting, refrain from sexual relations, and confess sins. The rituals involved collective prayers and sacrifices, generally of firstfruits or game, more rarely of human beings.

## Inca Civilization

The Inca religion is the religion of the peoples who occupied a large area of Latin America (today's Peru, Bolivia, Ecuador, Venezuela, Chile, and part of Brazil). The Inca empire was called for this *Tawantinsuyu*, or of the four cantons or regions of the world. The Incas were the Quechua-speaking[98] population which prevailed over other indigenous peoples, founding a great empire, whose capital was Cuzco (navel), considered the center of the earth.

The official religion consisted of a solar cult, as the founder of the dynasty, *Manco Capac*, had received divine illumination near Lake Titicaca from the sun god, *Inti*, who had entrusted him with the task of spreading this knowledge to all the inhabitants. He had also given him a golden rod that would indicate the place where to found the capital. From that moment on, the king was also the religious leader, considered the representative of the sun on earth, where he resided only temporarily, as he would return to the celestial world after his death. Other deities were *Viracocha* and *Packakarmac*, previous to the sun god. The first was the god of the waters; the second for some was the supreme being of whom nothing could be said, creator of the world and father of Inti, while according to others, he was identified with the moon. Bride and sister of the sun is the goddess *Mama Quilla*, and their children (in addition to *Manco Capac* and her sister *Mama Ocllo*, considered the initiators of the dynasty) are *Pitua*, who represented the planet Jupiter, residence of the blessed, and *Chasca*, who represented the planet Venus. There was also the god of thunder and lightning called *Catequil*, represented as a snake with or without feathers.

From what we have seen, it can be understood that the Inca religion was animistic, in that all natural elements were considered forces

---

98. Quechua is an indigenous language family spoken by the Quechua peoples, living primarily in the Peruvian Andes. Derived from a common ancestral language, it is the most widely spoken pre-Columbian language family of the Americas, with a total of probably some eight to ten million speakers. Approximately 25 percent (7.7 million) of Peruvians speak a Quechuan language. It is perhaps most widely known for being the main language family of the Inca Empire.

(*huaca*), to which enormous stones were consecrated, which can still be admired today in the mysterious complex of Machu Picchu in Peru.

The belief in life after death was very strong. It was thought that souls would use their mortal remains, so the bodies were mummified, and useful objects in future life, often of great value, were placed in the tombs. This caused desecrations and stealings by the Europeans when, in 1532, the Spaniard Francisco Pizarro captured with a stratagem and then killed the last ruler, Atahualpa, putting an end to this empire.

The main festivals were in honor of the sun and were celebrated at solstices and equinoxes. The most important, *Intip Raymi* (sun dance), lasted nine days, preceded by three days of fasting; a sacred fire would be lit and would be kept by the virgins of the Sun until the following year. Other festivals were that of purification and harvest.

## Religion in Ancient Africa

Each African population has developed its own specific religion, which has become an integral part of its cultural heritage. It can therefore be said that there are as many traditional religions as there are African populations. Proselytism, that is, the attempt to convert others to one's own religion, is not widespread among African populations, precisely because each religion is directly linked to the identity of a particular population. It is, then, not possible to trace a common historical origin in the various traditional African religions, nor a single geographical spread that allows us to follow its expansion in the continent. The term traditional is generally used to distinguish those that have an African origin from the major imported religions, such as Islam or Christianity, which have attracted over the years a very large portion of the population. Talking about religion in Africa means talking about social organization, and therefore talking about the relationship between the young and the old, the relationship with nature, the relationship between genders, the perception of disease, the acceptance of death, and so on. Everything about social life in Africa is regulated by religion. As there is no written text, such as the Bible or the Koran, religious tradition is generally kept by the elderly and entrusted to oral transmission, often through tales and proverbs. In this regard, it is good to remember that the terminology used by Western scholars to classify the African religious dimension is sometimes very imprecise and impoverishes its extraordinary complexity and variety.

Despite the transformations that constantly take place in the African religious world, it is still possible to recognize some elements that unite its various religious traditions. First, at the center of all religions is the belief in a single god, mostly defined as the Supreme Being. The figure of this Creator God is similar in all African religions: after creating the world, he deals little with it and rarely interferes with human affairs. Although he is the guarantor of the established order of things, he no longer participates in it and therefore remains outside the relationship with humanity. The Supreme Being is rarely the object of veneration and worship. For example, the god of the Kikuyu[99] people of Kenya, called *Ngai*, has retired to the top of Mount Kenya and no longer participates in the vicissitudes of his creatures. However, the Kikuyu always pray by turning their faces towards the mountain, as a sign of respect. The Creator God is both good and bad; he inspires fear because his rare interventions can be violent, but people are also grateful to him for his generosity. The figure of the Supreme Being is the most important entity of a large series of spiritual beings. They act as mediators between the Supreme Being and humans. In African religions, various spirits have become more important than the Supreme Being, which is felt as too distant. It is to them that humans turn to see their requests fulfilled. Spirits are divided into spirits of non-human origin and spirits which, after having been human beings, have become ancestral spirits. Spirits of non-human origin are sometimes connected with certain natural places, such as the spirit of the forest or the spirit of the sea. Among the most active and present spirits for the Luo[100] of Kenya, for example, is the spirit of the lake. This is explained by the proximity of Lake Victoria, on whose banks the Luo have lived for a long time. Among the Dogon[101] of Mali, the spirit of water, called *Nommo*, is considered the progenitor of humanity, the one who taught humans the art of fire and the use of tools.

---

99. The Kikuyu are a Bantu ethnic group inhabiting Central Kenya.

100. The Luo are several ethnically and linguistically related Nilotic ethnic groups that inhabit an area ranging from South Sudan and Ethiopia, through northern Uganda and eastern Congo (DRC), into western Kenya, and the Mara region of Tanzania. Their Luo languages belong to the western branch of the Nilotic language family.

101. The Dogon are an ethnic group living in the central plateau region of Mali, in West Africa, south of the Niger bend, near the city of Bandiagara, and in Burkina Faso. They are one of the African peoples who have most intrigued the western world. Legend says they have come from the star Sirius and have had contact with a highly evolved extraterrestrial civilization.

The spirits of nature often do not have a well-defined personality. They are the guardians of the territory where a certain population lives and with whom they establish complex social relationships. Other spirits, instead, are identified with natural phenomena, such as the spirit of thunder, wind, storm, rain, and so on. All these spiritual entities, which some scholars also call secondary deities, can be beneficial or evil, or even possess an ambivalent nature. Sometimes they are friendly and well disposed towards humanity, other times they can be hostile. Some rarely intervene, others are always present in everyday life; some move easily, others are sedentary. All these spiritual entities are arranged in a hierarchical scale in order of importance, and their position codifies the relationships between them and between them and humanity. Some of these spirits enter into relationship with humans through trance or possession. Sometimes there are whole families of spirits who periodically own a person and indicate how to act for the good of the clan or the whole community. These are, for example, the *Bori* spirits among the Hausa[102] of Niger or the *Bisimba* among the Zela[103] of the Democratic Republic of the Congo. The ancestors belong to the category of ancestral spirits. Death does not automatically transform a relative into an ancestor. Specific rituals are needed in order to accompany the deceased into the afterlife and allow them to acquire the new spiritual essence. Among these rituals is the double funeral. After the first one, there is a period of time in which the spirit of the deceased becomes ill-disposed towards the living, and only the second funeral, which includes a series of offers and collective prayers, reconciles him with his relatives.

In all African societies, the link between the living and the dead is very strong. The deceased must always be taken into consideration and satisfied with offers of various kinds. They firmly hold their positions within the family structure, and nothing is more fearful than arousing their anger. The ancestors are the closest relationship with the spiritual world, and they are able to guarantee prosperity, health, and fruitfulness to their descendants. The social structure of the Kikuyu of Kenya is reflected and divided into the organization of the world of ancestors,

---

102. The Hausa are the largest ethnic group in Sub-Saharan Africa. The Hausa are a diverse but culturally homogeneous people based primarily in the Sahelian and the sparse savanna areas of southern Niger and northern Nigeria.

103. The Zela are a Bantu people from Central Africa, established mainly in the southeast of the Democratic Republic of the Congo, at the foot of the Mitumba Mountains.

called *Ngoma*, among which the immediate ancestors or *Ngoma cia aciari* stand out. They mainly communicate with the head of the family, who must regularly offer them food and drinks. Some African peoples are hunters (Pygmies, San, Khoekhoe), others are mainly dedicated to agriculture and breeding. Therefore religious beliefs reflect these characteristics: in general, there is a presence of cosmic forces, that are at the same time forces of nature and spirit of the ancestors, with great creative value of productive fertility. For the Pygmies, the supreme being is called *Epilipilia*, god of the hunt who manifests himself through his bow, that is, the rainbow; likewise the San people believe in a hunter god, *Kaggen*, also called father. The Bantu, who are breeders and farmers, have other divinities, also different from each other according to the various populations: *Ndjambi-Karunga*, lord of time and ruler of the underworld; *Mululunga*, the one who is in heaven, whose voice is thunder and whose anger is lightning; *Nzambi*, light propagator, revered with silence. For the inhabitants of northern Guinea and Ghana the Supreme Being is *Nyame*, the resplendent, or great friend. For the populations of East Africa, such as the Masai[104] of Tanzania and Kenya, the supreme divinity, as for the Kikuyu, is *Ngai*. There is also *Mawu*, adored in Togo and Nigeria with his two descendants who represent good and evil, elements always linked to life and death. The whole cultural ritual, despite some differences, is therefore guided by these forces and aimed at increasing them in order to obtain health, children, and abundant harvests. Important is the mediation of priests, warriors, and heroes, considered messengers of the will of ancestors. The main forms of worship are sacrificial prayer and dance, in particular masked dance. This is an expression of both subtraction and concealment in the face of the divine and of playful religiosity, of a sacred game of sinking into magical delirium. In the tribe, the high priest is generally the king, supported by the priest-magician, healer. The places of worship are always clearly separated. Often they are sacred woods or specific huts.

---

104. The Maasai are a Nilotic ethnic group inhabiting northern, central and southern Kenya and northern Tanzania. They are among the best known local populations internationally due to their residence near the many game parks of the African Great Lakes, and their distinctive customs and dress.

## Religion in Ancient Oceania

### Aboriginal Civilization

In Australia, we find Aboriginal tribal religions. Their characteristic is the cosmogonic conception (birth of the world), from which all other beliefs derive. At first the earth was an empty plain, in which mountains, rivers, etc. were later formed, thanks to the awakening of the ancestors, who spiritually joined these elements and the animals, giving rise to the totemic symbols. Human beings also derived from these. Each group has its totemic symbol (for example, the kangaroo totem), and each member is linked to it by a peculiar and essential bond, almost a family relationship. A particularly sacred object is the tiurunga wood (belonging to the spirit), a very thin disc-shaped wood that, when thrown into the air, produces a slight noise. This is the stones of the soul or words of the ancestors themselves. The rites and cults are also closely connected with the totemic ancestors. In the Bora[105] ceremonies, for example, young people are initiated into the traditional rituals and customs of the tribe after being subjected to various fasts, trials of fire, and circumcision. Through this initiation the young man becomes a *mirano* (wise man), and only from that moment can he participate in the cult. Even today the Aborigines live in close relationship, even in symbiosis, with the Earth. They religiously worship the myth of Dreamtime. It is a kind of system in which humans, the universe, and time come together in a single system made up of different beliefs. At the heart of this, the Aborigines practice totemism. If a human being is tied through it to an animal or a plant, he will have to respect a whole series of duties and prohibitions in his relationship with that species. This is the reason the Aborigines have immense respect for nature in its broadest sense, which includes all living species, down to the smallest pebble.

---

105. Bora is an initiation ceremony of the Aboriginal people of Eastern Australia. The word bora also refers to the site on which the initiation is performed. At such a site, boys, having reached puberty, achieve the status of men. The initiation ceremony differs from Aboriginal culture to culture, but often, at a physical level, involved scarification, circumcision, subincision, and, in some regions, also the removal of a tooth. During the rites, the youths who were to be initiated were taught traditional sacred songs, secrets of the tribe's religious visions, dances, and traditional lore. Many different clans would assemble to participate in an initiation ceremony.

For Aboriginal people, the world was created when *Warramurrungundji*[106] came out of the sea and created humans. Then came other spirits. Thanks to *Ginga* the crocodile, *Gandajitj* the kangaroo, and *Almudj* the snake, the forms of earth, which was flat until then, were created. Once the work was completed, they appeared in a dream to humans in order to guide them from one sacred place to another. In Australian Aboriginal mythology, the Dreamtime (or the Dreaming, the Law) is the era prior to creation (or formation) of the world. It is at the same time a common and unifying element of the numerous and diverse Aboriginal cultural traditions that developed in the different regions of the continent and a mythical justification of the differences between them. In the various Aboriginal languages, the Dreamtime is named in different ways. A few examples are:

- *jukurrpa* in the Ngarrkic[107] language group
- *tjukurpa* in the group of dialects of the western deserts
- *altyerre* in the Arandic[108] family

The myths of the Dreamtime aim to explain the origin of the culture of the Aboriginal peoples and the origin of the world, or more precisely its geographical and topographical characteristics. Although in fact the Dreamtime is often mentioned as an era of creation, some authors and scholars emphasize that they are more precisely myths of formation (of taking shape); in Dreamtime the world already existed, but it was undifferentiated. It was inhabited by metaphysical, totemic beings, generally represented as gigantic creatures in the shape of animals. By walking, hunting, dancing, or simply sitting on the ground, they left traces of their actions and signs of their passage in the physical world—mountains, rocks, pools of water, and any other object found in nature. Certain places, created by events of particular importance (for example, fightings,

---

106. One of the main Creation Ancestors is Warramurrungundji (Mother of the Earth), who travelled to Kakadu with her husband from the islands in the northeast. She sent out spirit children, telling them which languages to speak and teaching them how to hunt and gather food from their land. She created river systems, billabongs, and much of the wildlife in the region. Her journey completed, she sat down and rested, changing into a large rock, which marks her Dreaming site.

107. The Ngarrkic (Ngarga) or Yapa languages are a small language family of Central Australia, consisting of the two closely related languages Warlmanpa and the more populous Warlpiri.

108. Arandic is a family of Australian Aboriginal languages of Central-Northern Australia, consisting of several languages or dialect clusters, including the Arrernte group, Lower Arrernte, Pertame, and Kaytetye.

deaths, or other dramatic events) maintain a special power, called by the aborigines the dream of the place. Furthermore, at the end of Dreamtime, the gods themselves settled in certain places, becoming mountains, rocks, rivers, and so on. In Perth, for example, the Noongar[109] people believe that Darling Scarp[110] is the body of the *Waugal*, a snake-shaped being who crossed the area in Dreamtime, creating rivers, streams, and lakes. Depending on traditions and regions, a particular metaphysical being can be referred to as supreme or creator of the world; it is often called *Altjira*, *Alchera* (Arrernte language), *Alcheringa*, *Mura-mura* (Dieri[111] language), or *Tjukurrpa* (Pitjantjatjara[112] language). The Aboriginal vision assigns a sacredness to every place on earth, and establishes a network of original relationships between every living being and every place.

Dreamtime is not confined to the historical past of the world. In the Aboriginal world view, it is both a time and what Westerners would call a dimension. It remains accessible to Aboriginal people precisely through dreams, a fundamental tool for communicating with spirits, deciphering the meaning of omens, or understanding the causes of illness and bad luck. Each Aboriginal group or nation keeps a number of Dreamtime tales, for which it is responsible. The elders of each group play this role of custodians of the stories and must pass them on to new generations in the ways and times required by tradition. This millennial tradition (perhaps tens of thousands of years) was interrupted in many regions (especially in Southeast Australia) during colonization. In reaction to the destructive action of the settlers towards their culture, today the Aborigines try to preserve the surviving tales by spreading their knowledge as much as possible. The Aboriginal tradition also requires that some particularly important stories are secrets that can be revealed only to particular groups or individuals. There are, for example, stories from the Dreamtime that only women know or only men. Given the strong link between the stories of the Dreamtime and the geographical reality of the country, it is not

109. The Noongar are Aboriginal Australian peoples who live in the southwest corner of Western Australia, from Geraldton on the West Coast to Esperance on the South Coast.

110. The Darling Scarp, also referred to as the Darling Range or Darling Ranges, is a low escarpment running north–south to the east of the Swan Coastal Plain and Perth, Western Australia.

111. Diyari or Dieri is an Australian Aboriginal language spoken by the Diyari people in the far north of South Australia, to the east of Lake Eyre.

112. Pitjantjatjara is a dialect of the Western Desert language traditionally spoken by the Pitjantjatjara people of Central Australia.

surprising that there are correspondences between the stories that each group can know and tell and the sacred places to which that the same group is authorized to go. Thus, many stories that Aboriginal people refuse to tell white people are related to places prohibited to tourists. Due to the effect of colonization on the one hand and the secrecy of myths on the other, only a small fraction of Aboriginal mythology is actually known to anthropologists. As reported by Bruce Chatwin[113] in *The Songlines*, the tales of Dreamtime are handed down in the form of songs. Each of these songs describes the path followed by an ancestral creature on its original journey and has a musical structure that corresponds, like a sort of map, to the morphology of the territory crossed by this path.

## Maori Civilization

The Maori religion is the beliefs of the peoples of New Zealand who follow tribal religions. In general, Maori religion presents a monotheistic creed grafted on primitive polytheistic beliefs. In fact, they believe in the Supreme Being or *Io* or *Kio*, head of all divinities and master of the universe. Heaven and earth, which came from nowhere, are inhabited by twelve spirits of nature called *Atua*. These include *Tangaroa*, lord of the seas; *Tane*, ruler of the woods; and *Tu* and *Rongo*, respectively lords of war and peace. Lower deities, like *Hina*, goddess of the moon, and *Atea*, goddess of space, are called *Aitu*. A characteristic of the Maori religion is the animist conception, whereby almost all natural elements are in contact with the divine; hence their respect for what is considered taboo, that is, endowed with mysterious strength. "The person who owns the taboo can exercise his power, or mana, over human affairs, and the priests are the mana guardians of the tribal groups." At the origin of the Maori religion is the god *Tane*, who gave humanity three baskets of wisdom, which contain the history of creation and many other useful teachings. They believe that all living things are descended from gods; and rivers, lakes, mountains, and trees are permeated with the gods: everything has a soul (*wairua*). Some geographical elements of the North Island are fundamental points of reference and considered sacred for the Maori, the Wanganui River and the Ngaruahoe and Ruapehu Mountains. These beliefs represent a reason for their strong bond with the earth. The funeral

---

113. Charles Bruce Chatwin (13 May 1940–18 Jan. 1989) was an English travel writer, novelist, and journalist.

is an important moment in religious life. After death, there is a vigil over the body of the deceased until the moment of burial. Then the spirit of the deceased flies to the top of the sacred mountains to descend into the sea and re-emerge in the Three Kings Islands (a small archipelago near the northwest tip of the North Island) for the final farewell, before reaching the ancestors.

∽

We took a bird's-eye view of the religious sentiment of humanity, and we found that, in all times and places, whether in primitive or advanced civilizations, we have always felt the need to find something metaphysical to face and accompany life. Thus, as we have seen, thousands of gods have arisen and disappeared all over the world, different from each other and with different characteristics, but with a single purpose: to explain the inexplicable.

# 2

## Jewish and Christian Religions

### Jewish Religion

I LEFT LAST THE Jewish religion, which is one of the oldest and still alive religions of the world. It has accompanied (guided) and accompanies (guides) the history and life of the Jewish people so as to make it an inseparable whole; but above all, the Christian religion was born from it, the religion which has become the most widespread religion in the world, which still permeates our life, and for which I write this book.

The Jewish religion is divided into two phases: the Hebrew religion and Judaism. The first refers to the worship and faith of the twelve tribes[1] of the sons of Jacob (also called Israel), Abraham's grandson, and ends with the fall of the kingdom of Judah.[2] The second designates that period in the history of the Jewish people which includes, after the end of the kingdom of Judah, the Babylonian exile, but is basically the continuation of the traditions of the ancient tribes. Both belong to the Semitic religions of Asia Minor and are counted among the universal religions. Already from what has been said above, a characteristic of this religion emerges, its close connection and dependence on the historical events

---

1. In the Hebrew Bible, the twelve tribes of Israel descended from the twelve sons of the patriarch Jacob (who was later named Israel) and his two wives, Leah and Rachel, and two concubines, Zilpah and Bilhah.

2. According to the Hebrew Bible, the kingdom of Judah resulted from the breakup of the united kingdom of Israel (1020 to about 930 BC) after the northern tribes refused to accept Rehoboam, the son of Solomon, as their king. The two kingdoms, Judah in the south and Israel in the north, coexisted uneasily after the split until the destruction of the kingdom of Israel by Assyria c. 722/721.

through which this people were formed. To understand that dependence, it would be necessary to follow the sacred history of the Jews, a process that is millennia long, which is not possible here. We therefore stick to brief historical notes, to eventually focus on Judaism itself as faith, life, doctrine, and ethical and cultural law. Scholars today generally agree in considering the ancient Jews as a group of Habiru[3] mentioned in various documents of the second millennium BC as *apatrides*, stateless people who served as military and workforce. The name Habiru probably is derived from Eber, descendant of Shem, son of Noah (Gen 10:21) or from *ahar* (to pass), which would indicate a people who came across the river. The Jews narrated that their progenitor Abraham had abandoned by order of God the Mesopotamian area in the second millennium BC and moved with his people to the south of Syria, and the community made up of the twelve tribes of the sons of Jacob was called Israel (another name of Jacob himself).

Moses is considered the initiator of Hebrew religion (which is in fact also called Mosaic) and is the first historically delineated figure, albeit with many features still blurred in legend. He was born in the house of Levi during the period of Pharaoh Ramesses II (1290–1224 BC), who had subjugated the Jewish nomads as slaves, but his name of Egyptian origin (meaning son) informs us about the events of his childhood. The Pharaoh had ordered the Jews to kill all the newborns, but Moses's mother placed him in an ark and concealed the ark in the bulrushes by the riverbank, where the baby was discovered and adopted by the Pharaoh's daughter, and raised as an Egyptian. As an adult, however, he had sensed his status as a Jew, had fled following a murder committed to defend a Jew, and had settled with the shepherds of Midian.[4] There, on Mount Horeb,[5] considered sacred by the nomadic tribes of the desert, he

---

3. In ancient Eastern texts, a particular social class, probably similar to refugees, from foreign lands. These are people particularly experienced in the art of warfare, which in the firmly governed states were controlled and subject to service, while in the weaker ones they constituted a constant element of disturbance.

4. Coastal district of Saudi Arabia. It overlooks the Red Sea in the Gulf of Aqaba, on the border with Jordan. A mountainous and impervious region, with a thin, flat coastal fringe, it forms the northwestern edge of the Arabian plateau, with elevations approaching 3000 m.

5. Mount Horeb is the mountain at which the book of Deuteronomy in the Hebrew Bible states that the Ten Commandments were given to Moses by Yahweh. In other biblical passages, these events are described as having transpired at Mount Sinai, so most scholars consider Sinai and Horeb to have been different names for the same place.

had a vision of a burning bush which would not be consumed by flames, that is, the theophany or manifestation of Yahweh. Yahweh ordered him to free his people from slavery. Moses returned to Egypt, and after various vicissitudes and clashes with the pharaoh, the Jews managed to abandon that country under his leadership. In the Sinai desert, Yahweh made a covenant pact with them: he would be their only God and would give them prosperity and victory over their enemies. With this act, the Hebrew religion was formally founded (Exod 19:24), which would have visible expression in the tables of the law, preserved since then in the ark of the covenant, the sacred point of the community.

After forty years of wandering, the Jews began the conquest of the promised land (Canaan), the land Yahweh had promised to Abraham, forming a monarchy with Saul first, then David and Solomon, and making Jerusalem capital of the state (around 1000 BC). Solomon's reign is remembered for the enlargement and embellishment of Jerusalem, as well as for the extraordinary culture of Solomon himself, believed to be the author of numerous books of the Bible (Proverbs, Canticle of Canticles, Ecclesiastes, and the book of Wisdom).

However, national unity did not last, and in 993 BC, after the death of Solomon, two kingdoms were formed. The kingdom of the north (Israel) ended in 721 BC after being conquered by the Assyrians, and many inhabitants of this area went into exile in Media and Mesopotamia. In the southern kingdom (the kingdom of Judah), at some point, foreign cults were introduced, so it was necessary, around the middle of 700 BC, thanks to the preaching of prophet Isaiah,[6] to initiate a religious reform, the deuteronomist[7] reform, to restore the authentic cult of Yahweh.

Later, no reform happened in response to the preaching of Jeremiah,[8] who announced the end of Judah by the hands of Babylonians; in 598 BC, there was the first siege of Jerusalem and the first exiles. Another siege, that lasted a year and a half, followed, and in 587 BC, Jerusalem and the temple of Solomon were destroyed. The kingdom of Judah ceased to exist

---

6. Isaiah was the eighth-century BC Israelite prophet after whom the book of Isaiah is named.

7. In 622 BC, Josiah launched his reform program, based on an early form of Deut 5–26, framed as a covenant (treaty) between Judah and Yahweh, in which Yahweh replaced the Assyrian king.

8. Jeremiah (probably after 650–c. 570 BC), also called the weeping prophet, was one of the major prophets of the Hebrew Bible (Old Testament of Christian Bible). According to Jewish tradition, Jeremiah authored the book of Jeremiah, the books of Kings, and the book of Lamentations.

in 586 BC with mass deportation to Babylon. During this forty-year exile, the Jews maintained and strengthened their religious traditions. After the fall of the Babylonian kingdom to the Persians (539 BC), there was a return to the homeland, and Palestine was recognized as a Persian province. The Jews were able to rebuild the temple and, under the leadership of high priests, developed a theocratic system.

More than remembering the subsequent historical events (revolt of the Maccabees,[9] rebuilding of the temple by Herod the Great,[10] domination of Rome, and consequent rebellions), it is interesting to underscore the relationship between Judaism and surrounding cultural areas, especially the Hellenistic world. In fact, in the last years before Christian era, Judaism came into contact with Hellenistic civilization and the Latin world in two different ways, on the one hand, through the communities of the diaspora,[11] on the other, with the entrance of the Near East (and therefore Palestine) in the Greek and Roman orbit after the conquests of Alexander the Great.[12] If this second relationship ended generally in clash due to the intention of the various sovereigns (from Antiochus Epiphanes[13] to

---

9. The Maccabees were a group of Jewish rebel warriors who took control of Judea, which at the time was part of the Seleucid Empire. They founded the Hasmonean dynasty, which ruled from 167 to 37 BC, being a fully independent kingdom from about 110 to 63 BC.

10. Herod I (c. 74–73 BC), also known as Herod the Great, was a Roman client king of Judea, known for his colossal building projects throughout Judea.

11. A diaspora is a scattered population whose origin lies in a separate geographic locale. Historically, the word diaspora was used to refer to the involuntary mass dispersion of a population from its indigenous territories, in particular the dispersion of Jews. This has since changed, and today there is no set definition of the term, because its modern meaning has evolved over time.

12. Alexander III of Macedon (20/21 July 356–10/11 June 323 BC), commonly known as Alexander the Great, was a king (*basileus*) of the ancient Greek kingdom of Macedon and a member of the Argead dynasty. He spent most of his ruling years on an unprecedented military campaign through Western Asia and Northeast Africa, and by the age of thirty, he had created one of the largest empires of the ancient world, stretching from Greece to Northwest India. He was undefeated in battle and is widely considered one of history's most successful military commanders.

13. Antiochus IV Epiphanes (c. 215–Nov./Dec. 164 BC) was a Hellenistic king of the Seleucid Empire from 175 BC until his death in 164 BC. Notable events during the reign of Antiochus IV include his near-conquest of Egypt, his persecution of the Jews of Judea and Samaria, and the rebellion of the Jewish Maccabees.

Vespasian[14] and Hadrian[15]) to Grecianize Palestine, not only from a political but also religious point of view, things went differently in the countries of the diaspora.

In fact, the communities of exiled or dispersed Jews, born in the great Hellenistic cities (Antioch, Ephesus, Athens, Corinth, Alexandria) and in Rome, which were cosmopolitan centers where tolerance of ideas and religions reigned, worked for a sort of interpenetration between the two cultures (Jewish and Hellenistic). They started a reflection on the religion of the fathers in light of the speculative categories of Hellenism, since the educated Greeks themselves considered Jews as philosophers. First, since the Jews spoke Greek like their fellow citizens, they not only introduced this language into worship, but also translated the Bible into Greek (the so-called Septuagint, or Bible of the Seventy),[16] a task performed by the Jewish communities of Egypt. This was met with appreciation by the Greek world, which found Greek philosophy in biblical writings, but also an awareness on the part of Hellenistic Jews of the superiority of biblical monotheistic thought over the Greek polytheistic one. Furthermore, these diaspora communities would be the starting point of the missionary activity of the new-born Christianity, even if later on the relations between the two religions would increasingly wear out, and unfortunately the religious struggle would be reflected in social life in a very painful way for the Jews.

As for doctrinal contents, the central nucleus of the Jewish religion, its strength and its contribution to the history of culture, is monotheism (as opposed to the polytheism of neighboring peoples who deified the forces of nature) and at the same time faith in the intervention of God in the history of his people. In the account of the burning bush (Exod 3:14), that is, in the manifestation to Moses, the God Yahweh defines himself as "I will be present as the one who will be present" (to intervene) or "I am who I am," according to the translation of the Septuagint. Another name

14. Vespasian (17 Nov 9–24 June 79) was Roman emperor from AD 69 to 79. The fourth and last in the Year of the Four Emperors, he founded the Flavian dynasty, which ruled the empire for twenty-seven years.

15. Hadrian (24 Jan. 76–10 July 138) was Roman emperor from AD 117 to 138.

16. The Greek Old Testament, or Septuagint, is the earliest extant Koine Greek translation of books from the Hebrew Bible, various biblical apocrypha, and deuterocanonical books. The full title, "The Translation of the Seventy," derives from the story recorded in the Letter of Aristeas that the Hebrew Torah was translated into Greek at the request of Ptolemy II Philadelphus (285–47 BC) by seventy Jewish scholars or, according to later tradition, seventy-two.

for God is Elohim, plural form of El, the deity for the Semites; the name of El is sometimes used in conjunction with Shaddaj (Almighty). Yahweh is in fact the only God of the universe, almighty Creator of heaven and earth, just, independent, but also fearful to those who manifest themselves as his adversaries or disobey his will. The profession of Judaic faith on the eternity and uniqueness of God, which must be recited morning and evening by each adult, repeats the biblical words (Deut 6:4): "Listen, Israel (*Shema Israel*), Yahweh is our God, Yahweh is one." If we remember that another appellative connected to the name of God is Sebaot (armies) we can also understand how the religious experience represented for those nomadic tribes a moment of self-awareness on the path of unification. Initially the individual tribes manifested beliefs different one from another. Therefore the covenant with God on Mount Sinai and the revelation of the law became a common experience and a constitutive element of the union. The core of the Sinaitic law is represented by the Decalogue (or Ten Commandments):[17] they have, anyway, to be followed with the right attitude by the faithful, who understands how the way to God's help passes through the recognition of the royalty and uniqueness of God. He also grasps that sin is not only a rebellion against sacred laws but is showing oneself as sinner before God; it is a failing, a deficiency in opposition to integrity, a transgression of the covenant whereby God is the protector of the nation on condition that it is faithful to him.

This particular bond to the one God finds its support in the action and teachings of the spiritual leaders of Israel in the various eras of its history, from Moses to the Judges.[18] Later, when monarchy was established, David[19] became the prototype of the just and pious king and, since then, messianism (that is, the expectation of a descendant of David, faithful to God like him, and defender of his people) became a constant of Judaism. Other essential figures of this religion are the prophets,[20] who began to

---

17. The Ten Commandments, also known in Christianity as the Decalogue, are a set of biblical principles relating to ethics and worship. These are fundamental to both Judaism and Christianity.

18. The biblical judges are described in the Hebrew Bible, mostly in the book of Judges, as people who served roles as military leaders in times of crisis, in the period before an Israelite monarchy was established.

19. David is described in the Hebrew Bible as the third king of the united monarchy of Israel and Judah, mentioned mainly in the books of Samuel, Chronicles, and Psalms. He is honored in the prophetic literature as an ideal king and the forefather of a future messiah, and many psalms are ascribed to him.

20. In religion, a prophet is an individual who is regarded as being in contact with

act around the ninth century until the third century BC, very particular figures of custodians of the original and authentic religious message, and therefore many times floggers of the masses or violent critics of the kings when these yielded to the fascination of polytheistic and orgiastic cults. The prophets, for example Amos[21] and Isaiah, also tried to spiritualize the cult itself without forgetting the defense of the humblest classes. Gradually, however, prophetism lost its power and gave way to the precepts of the rabbinic schools, in which were privileged formality and quantity, and in this period the arrangement of the sacred texts of Judaism was completed.

This vast Jewish heritage is divided into three parts that reflect different times and genres:

1.  Biblical literature (eleventh century BC to first century AD), which includes the Hebrew Bible and the Apocrypha.[22] The Bible (from the Greek *Biblia*, books) is divided into three parts: Torah, Nevi'im, and Ketuvim.

    The *Torah*, which in Hebrew means teaching (while in Greek is used the word *Pentateuch*, five scrolls) includes the five books attributed to Moses: Genesis, Exodus, Leviticus, Numbers and Deuteronomy.

    *Nevi'im* includes the first prophets (Joshua,[23] Judges, Samuel [two books],[24] Kings [two books]) and the last prophets (Isaiah, Jeremiah, Ezekiel),[25] plus the twelve minor prophets.

---

a divine being and is said to speak on that entity's behalf, serving as an intermediary with humanity by delivering messages or teachings from the supernatural source to other people. The message that the prophet conveys is called a prophecy.

21. In the Hebrew Bible and Christian Old Testament, Amos was one of the twelve Minor Prophets.

22. Apocrypha are works, usually written, of unknown authorship or of doubtful origin.

23. Joshua or Jehoshua is the central figure in the Hebrew Bible's book of Joshua. According to the books of Exodus, Numbers, and Joshua, he was Moses's assistant and became the leader of the Israelite tribes after the death of Moses.

24. Samuel is a figure who, in the narratives of the Hebrew Bible, plays a key role in the transition from the period of the biblical judges to the institution of a kingdom under Saul and again in the transition from Saul to David.

25. Ezekiel is a Hebrew prophet and the central protagonist of the book of Ezekiel in the Hebrew Bible.

*Ketuvim* (writings) includes the Psalms (an admirable poetic text), Proverbs,[26] Job,[27] Canticle of Canticles,[28] Ruth,[29] Lamentations,[30] Ecclesiastes,[31] Esther,[32] Daniel,[33] Ezra-Nehemiah,[34] and Chronicles[35] (two books).

Esther's book, together with the Torah, was first transcribed in parchment scrolls. The scrolls are still read on the occasions of the

26. The book of Proverbs, "Proverbs (of Solomon)," is a book in the third section (called *Ketuvim*) of the Hebrew Bible and the Christian Old Testament. Proverbs is not merely an anthology but a "collection of collections" relating to a pattern of life that lasted for more than a millennium. It is an example of biblical wisdom literature and raises questions of values, moral behavior, the meaning of human life, and right conduct. Its theological foundation is that "the fear of God" (meaning submission to the will of God) is the beginning of wisdom.

27. Job is the central figure of the book of Job in the Bible. In rabbinical literature, Job is called one of the prophets of the gentiles. Job is presented as a good and prosperous family man who, with God's permission, is beset by Satan with horrendous disasters that take away all he holds dear, including his offspring, health, and property. He struggles to understand his situation and begins a search for the answers to his difficulties.

28. The Song of Songs, also Song of Solomon or Canticles, is one of the *megillot* (scrolls) found in the last section of the Tanakh, known as the Ketuvim, and a book of the Old Testament. The Song of Songs is unique within the Hebrew Bible: it shows no interest in law or covenant or the God of Israel, nor does it teach or explore wisdom; instead, it celebrates sexual love.

29. Ruth is the person after whom the book of Ruth is named. In the narrative, she is not an Israelite but rather is from Moab; she marries an Israelite. Both her husband and her father-in-law die, and she helps her mother-in-law, Naomi, find protection. The two of them travel to Bethlehem together, where Ruth wins the love of Boaz through her kindness. She is the great-grandmother of King David, therefore mentioned in the genealogy of Jesus found in the Gospel of Matthew.

30. The book of Lamentations is a collection of poetic laments for the destruction of Jerusalem in 586 BC.

31. Ecclesiastes is presented as the biography of Kohelet.

32. The book of Esther relates the story of a Hebrew woman in Persia, born as Hadassah but known as Esther, who becomes queen of Persia and thwarts the genocide of her people.

33. The book of Daniel is a second-century BC biblical apocalypse combining a prophecy of history with an eschatology.

34. The book of Ezra-Nehemiah covers the period from the fall of Babylon in 539 BC to the second half of the fifth century BC and tells of the successive missions to Jerusalem of Zerubbabel, Ezra, and Nehemiah, and their efforts to restore the worship of the God of Israel and to create a purified Jewish community.

35. Chronicles contains a genealogy from Adam, the first man, and a narrative of the history of ancient Judah and Israel until the proclamation of King Cyrus the Great.

five main feasts of the Jewish calendar: Passover,[36] Feast of Weeks,[37] Mourning for Jerusalem,[38] Feast of Booths,[39] and Purim.[40]

The Hebrew Bible was translated into Aramaic and used in synagogal worship, whereas the Septuagint is the one translated into Greek in the second century AD, accepted by Christianity with the name of the Old Testament and, together with the books of the New Testament, constitutes the Christian Bible. It should be emphasized that this text has also influenced populations extraneous to Judaism and represents one of the most widespread literary works in the world.

The Apocrypha and Pseudo-Apocrypha are texts of lesser importance because, unlike the previous ones, they are not considered having been inspired by God, and therefore not binding from a doctrinal point of view.

2. Talmudic-midrashic literature (up to the ninth century AD), represented by the so-called oral teaching, that is, post-biblical teaching of the law, reported in the Mishnah and in the Talmud.[41] The latter work is, after the Bible, one of the cornerstones of Jewish literature and collects a vast material of the tradition from the first century BC to the fifth century AD. Strictly speaking, it includes only the Gemarah; in a broader sense, the Mishnah as well.

The *Mishnah* (what is learned several times) represents the oldest nucleus of oral teaching and focuses on both the legislative

---

36. Pèsach or Pesah, also called Passover, is a Jewish holiday that lasts eight days and reminds participants of the liberation of the Jewish people from Egypt and their exodus to the promised land.

37. This Jewish holiday corresponds to our Pentecost but with a different meaning. In fact, it celebrates the harvest of the crops with a particular offering of first fruits to the Lord and also completes the memory of the liberation from salvery in Egypt. This feast falls seven weeks after Pèsach (the Jewish Passover that Jesus also celebrated).

38. In memory of the destruction of the first temple in 586 BC by Nebuchadnezzar and of the second temple by Roman emperor Titus in AD 70.

39. Sukkot is a seven-day festival, also known as the Feast of Booths, the Feast of Tabernacles, or just Tabernacles. It commemorates the years that the Jews spent in the desert on their way to the promised land and celebrates the way in which God protected them under difficult desert conditions.

40. Purim is a Jewish holiday which commemorates the saving of the Jewish people from Haman, an Achaemenid Persian Empire official who was planning to kill all the Jews.

41. The Talmud is the central text of rabbinic Judaism and the primary source of Jewish religious law and Jewish theology.

doctrine as handed down and the interpretation of the law. It is made up of six *sedarim* (orders), each with other treaties for a total of sixty-three. the content is indicated by the short titles: seeds, festival, women, damages, holy things, purities.

The *Gemarah* (completion) represents a commentary on the Mishnah written by Amoraim.[42] Two parts can be distinguished, according to the content: the Halakah, more legislative, and the Haggadah, more narrative. To understand the great importance of the Talmud and its influence on the Jewish people, one must consider its inspiring principles: the belief that there is an oral law alongside the written one and that holiness, the ideal of life for everyone, is achieved precisely by observance of divine precepts.

Finally, midrashic literature indicates that literature of commentary on the Bible (*midrash*, interpretation) written with consoling intents to help meditation, whose characteristic is the narrative tone.

3. Rabbinic literature (until 1800 AD). Rabbinism is the complex of exegetical, moral, juridical and ritual doctrines of the rabbis, that is, the official teachers of religion, and therefore includes the Mishnah and the Talmud in a more specific sense. By rabbinic literature we define post-talmudic and post-misdrashic productions up to the nineteenth century, during which the talmudic academies were transformed into institutes with a broader and more varied research purpose. This literature includes commentaries on the Bible and the Talmud and codification of talmudic law. Kabbalistic and Hasidic writings also fall within this sphere. The first are mystical texts, the result of various currents, which combine the interpretation of midrash with a more in-depth biblical exegesis, through the interpretation of characters and numbers. Hasidism is a most recent religious mystical movement, founded in the mid-1700s by the Ukrainian rabbi Israel ben Eliezer, which spread to Eastern Europe and has its roots in the Kabbalah.[43] It deepens the value of devotion, felt as a moment of joy and leading to the ecstasy of union with God.

---

42. Jewish scholars of the period from about AD 200 to 500, who "said" or "told over" the teachings of the Oral Torah. They were located primarily in Babylonia and the land of Israel.

43. A complex of Jewish mystical and esoteric doctrines about God and the universe, which were allegedly revealed to a small number of people and passed down from generation to generation.

There are 613 divine precepts, of which some are positive imperatives (248), others prohibitions (365). In the positive commandments, in addition to the actual ethical laws, of great importance are the rules of purity, the alimentary rules, and the norms concerning marriage. In fact, the distinction between pure and impure prescribes cultic ablutions, hand washing before morning prayer and before and after meals. Even food rules are precisely coded, based on the existence of perfect foods and separation of meat and dairy products, as well as on the ban on eating the meat of particular animals. Other fundamental commandments of the Jewish religion are prayer, the Sabbath holiday (*sabbath*, rest) and the obligation of circumcision. Saturday is the seventh day of the week, dedicated to sanctification and rest, in memory of Yahweh's rest at the end of creation. If on the one hand it has the typical characteristics of a *via negationis* (abstention from work, refusal of any trouble or occupation), on the other hand, it takes on a much greater significance as the holiness of time, as remembrance of the covenant and anticipation of eternity. Prayer can be said at home or in the synagogue (*Bet ha-Keneset*, meeting place or house of prayer), at fixed times or on specific occasions. The most used form is the one already mentioned, Shema Israel, expression of faith in the one God; another prayer is the *Berakhah* (blessing or praise) which begins "blessed are You, Lord our God, King of the Universe." Community prayer is the *Amidah* (nineteen blessings), which includes requests of various types, spiritual, material, and patriotic.

The other fundamental commandment, circumcision, represents the symbol and the rite of initiation, the sign by which one becomes part of the covenant that Abraham entered into with God (Gen 17:10); it is performed eight days after birth. At thirteen, then, the young man (and in the Reform Jewish communities, also girls) becomes *Bar-mitzvah* (son of the commandment), that is, obliged to follow the commandments, and becomes part of the religious community in all respects. Even marriage has the value of a divine commandment and takes place under the *chuppa* (wedding sky), a tent supported by four poles.

An important moment in Jewish religious life is the holidays, which are divided into joyful holidays, solemn holidays, happy commemorations, and sad commemorations. The first include *Pesach* (Passover), *Shavuot*, and *Sukkot*, which are the pilgrimage celebrations, recalling three fundamental moments in the history of the people of Israel: the liberation from Egyptian slavery, the giving of the *Torah* on Mount Sinai, and the peregrinations in the desert. Solemn celebrations include New

Year's Eve (*Rosh Hashanah*) and the Day of Atonement (*Yom Kippur*). Happy commemorative days are *Hanukkah* (rededication of the temple) and *Purim* (in memory of the danger they escaped, according to the story of the book of Esther). There are five sad holidays, and the most significant of these are the Mournings for Jerusalem, in memory of the first (587 BC) and second (AD 70) destruction of the temple, during which fasting is observed.

There were many currents or religious movements within Judaism: Samaritans, Sadducees, Pharisees, Zealots, Essenes, and Damascus community, in addition to the already mentioned Rabbinism and Hasidism.

The Samaritans were a population made up of the union of Jews who remained at home after deportation and Assyrian settlers, who took their name from the city of Samaria, capital of the Northern Kingdom. Later, when the Jewish community in Jerusalem was restored, its leaders (Ezra and Nehemiah) forbade relations with "the mixed population," and the Samaritans have since formed an autonomous current of Judaism.

The Sadducees were the representatives of the high clergy, mostly aristocrats and conservatives, who opposed the Pharisees. In fact, they recognized as imperative only the written law (Torah) and rejected the oral law, as supported by Pharisees; moreover, they denied any development in the eschatological[44] sense of the Jewish religion. They were very authoritative within the *Sanhedrin* or high council, being able to designate the high priests.

The Pharisees were not only a religious but also a political current, as they awaited redemption from Roman rule but did not believe they had to resort to force like the Zealots, who in fact detached from them. From a religious point of view, they supported a strict observance of the law, also favoring its formalistic aspects, with an attitude of uncompromising closure towards sinners.

The current of the Zealots, or fanatics, began around the year AD 67 on the initiative of Judah the Jew, who claimed the need to rebel against foreign rulers. They lived by raids in the desert, and for this reason the historian Josephus calls them brigands. Due to their pressure, a war against Rome broke out in AD 66, ending in AD 70 with the fall of Jerusalem, where their leader John of Giscala had barricaded himself. They eventually

---

44. Doctrine concerning the ultimate destinies of humanity and individuals. It is part of the beliefs coessential to the very idea of religion, which explains why eschatological beliefs are found in both the so-called primitive populations and more complex religions.

took refuge in Masada,[45] where after a long siege and a long resistance, they all killed themselves, in order not to be captured by Romans.

The Essenes (the pure ones) were an ascetic community, organized as a monastic order, born in controversy with what they considered an excessive Hellenization of Judaism. They developed mainly in Palestine, and the head of the community was a priest, called master of justice, as opposed to the priest of the temple of Jerusalem, called false priest. An important center of the Essenes was the monastery of Qumran, on the shores of the Dead Sea, reserved for famous members of the community, on which essential information was found after the discovery in 1947 of remarkable manuscripts. The faithful led a life in common, governed by obedience and silence with a particular care for bodily purity, culminating in frequent ablutions that also assumed the value of spiritual purification. Other characteristics of this community were respect for the Mosaic law; detachment from bodily pleasures; the belief that the human soul comes from heaven and, if deserving so, returns there after the death of the body; openness to one's neighbor; and refusal to any use of violence.

The Damascus community stemmed from Hasideans (pious or devout), who date back to the second century AD and who founded the community of the New Alliance under the guidance of a master of justice. Persecuted, they moved to Damascus waiting for a messiah, then returned to Palestine. Their organization was similar to that of the Essenes, and there were theological similarities with the Judeo-Christian group of the Ebionites.

## Jesus of Nazareth and the Early Stages of Christian Religion

In this historically, socially, and religiously complex context of the history of Jewish people, at the time when Octavian Augustus was the emperor in Rome, Jesus of Nazareth was born in Roman-occupied Palestine. He began a preaching that revolutionized the world and is still part of our life. The human events and the preaching of Jesus are known to all. What is less known and then more interesting to follow is how and why they came to us in the way we know them. After the death of Jesus, the first Christian nucleus, the first church, was formed, naturally, in Jerusalem,

---

45. Masada is an ancient fortification in the Southern District of Israel, situated on top of an isolated rock plateau. It is located on the eastern edge of the Judaean Desert, overlooking the Dead Sea, about 100 km southwest of Jerusalem.

and from there, it spread to all Asia Minor and up to Rome, through the travels of the apostles[46] and with the spread of news (keep in mind that it was the heyday of Roman Empire, and communication was relatively easy). Thus many churches arose, autonomous from each other, of which the most famous were those of Jerusalem, Antioch, Alexandria, Caesarea of Palestine, the Seven Churches of Asia, Anatolia, Rome, Carthage, and many others scattered from India to Britain.

Jerusalem, as said, was the first center of the church; the apostles lived and taught there in the times after Pentecost.[47] Paul and Barnabas arrived there, about AD 50, to meet Peter, John, and James, giving body to what later would be called Council of Jerusalem. Among other decisions, the council confirmed the validity of the mission of Paul and Barnabas to the gentiles, namely non-Christian pagans, and freedom for gentile converts from the majority of the Mosaic laws, especially from circumcision, which repelled Hellenic mentality.

In AD 66, the Jews rose up against Rome, and Rome besieged Jerusalem for four years, eventually bringing it down in AD 70. The city was destroyed, including the temple, and the population was exterminated or deported. Still, according to Epiphanius of Salamis,[48] the Cenacle of the Last Supper survived at least until the visit of Hadrian in AD 130. However, only a minimal part of the population survived the devastation. Eusebius of Caesarea[49] (in his work *Ecclesiastical History*) and Josephus Flavius[50] (in *Jewish Wars*) report that the Christians of Jerusalem took refuge in Pella, in the Decapolis (a territory made up of ten cities between

---

46. The apostles of Jesus Christ, as described in the New Testament, are the disciples commissioned by Jesus to give continuity to the message of salvation proclaimed by him. He chose twelve, like the number of the tribes of Israel.

47. Pentecost, which is celebrated on the forty-ninth day (the seventh Sunday) after Easter Sunday, commemorates the descent of the Holy Spirit upon the apostles and other followers of Jesus Christ while they were in Jerusalem celebrating the Feast of Weeks, as described in the Acts of the Apostles.

48. Epiphanius of Salamis (c. 310/320–403) was the bishop of Salamis, Cyprus, at the end of the fourth century. He is considered a saint and a Church Father by both the Orthodox and Roman Catholic Churches.

49. Eusebius of Caesarea (260/265–339/340) was a historian of Christianity, an exegete, and a Christian polemicist. He became the bishop of Caesarea Maritima about 314.

50. Titus Flavius Josephus (37–c. 100), born Yosef ben Matityahu, was a first-century Romano-Jewish historian who was born in Jerusalem—then part of Roman Judea—to a father of priestly descent and a mother who claimed royal ancestry.

present-day Syria, Jordan, and Israel), and there they waited for the Jewish wars to end.

In the second century, Hadrian rebuilt Jerusalem as a pagan city, calling it Aelia Capitolina, and placing statues of Jupiter and himself on the site of the destroyed temple, the Temple Mount. Bar Kokhba,[51] the Jewish leader who started the third Jewish war against Rome, also presented himself as messiah, but Christians refused to accept him as such. When Bar Kokhba was defeated, Hadrian excluded the Jews from the city, except on the day of *Tisha b'Av* (day of mourning for the Jewish people, which is celebrated on the ninth day of the Jewish month of Av, which falls between our July and August). Consequently, the successive bishops of Jerusalem were gentiles (uncircumcised) for the first time.

The general significance of Jerusalem for Christians experienced a period of decline, especially during persecutions by the Roman Empire. It gained new importance after the pilgrimage which Elena, mother of Emperor Constantine, made in the Holy Land around 326/328, when she allegedly found the cross of Christ under a temple dedicated to Venus, which she had had removed. The relics of the cross are kept in the Basilica of Santa Croce di Gerusalemme in Rome, which she specially built.

## Early Centers of Christianity

Jerusalem later became part of the Pentarchy, which was the name given to the five most important episcopal seats in the Roman world, namely Rome, Constantinople,[52] Alexandria, Antioch, and Jerusalem, to which the whole Christian government was jointly entrusted.

Antioch, now in ruins, one of the major centers of Hellenistic Greece and the third most important city of the Roman Empire, was located near the city of Antakya, in modern Turkey. It is there where Christians got their name: "in Antioch for the first time the disciples were called Christians" (Acts 11:26). It was also famous for a church, whose remains are still preserved, commissioned by Peter, where the apostle preached the

---

51. Simon ben Kosevah, known to posterity as Bar Kokhba (died AD 135), was a Jewish military leader who led the Bar Kokhba revolt against the Roman Empire in 132. Bar Kokhba fell in the fortified town of Betar after a prolonged siege of three and a half years.

52. City founded by Emperor Constantine on the site of ancient Byzantium in AD 330; capital of the empire.

good news for the first time. Antioch was also a bishopric and one of the major religious teaching centers.

Alexandria, located on the Nile Delta, was founded by Alexander the Great and took its name from him. Still known as the second city of modern Egypt, at the time of Jesus, it was a large, very lively city of the Roman Empire, with a particularly animated cultural life. Its legendary library was an extraordinary center of studies and conservation of the cultures of the time. In this favorable environment, texts of great qualitative depth were written, and people of historical importance were formed, such as Origen[53] and the Fathers of the Church Clement[54] and Athanasius,[55] as well as the gnostic Valentinus.[56] The library suffered various destructive events that undermined its integrity, until the Arabs completely destroyed it in 642; the Alexandrina Library was inaugurated in 2002 in its memory.

Caesarea of Palestine, located on the coast northwest of Jerusalem, in the stretch between the current cities of Tel Aviv and Haifa, was founded by Herod the Great around 25–13 BC. It was an important port and a center of large commercial exchanges, as well as the political and military seat of Roman Judea. It was served by a double aqueduct and had a vast amphitheater, whose ruins can still be admired today. Peter stayed and baptized the first Christian convert there, the centurion Cornelius. Paul stopped there many times and was imprisoned there for two years, before being taken to Rome. Origen wrote some of his works there and organized a theological school and an important library, later destroyed by Saracens.

---

53. Origen (Alexandria, Egypt, 185–Tyre, 254), also called Adamantius ("resistant as the diamond"), was an ancient Greek theologian and philosopher. He is considered one of the leading Christian writers and theologians of the first three centuries.

54. Titus Flavius Clemens, also known as Clement of Alexandria (c. 150–c. 215) was a Christian theologian and philosopher who taught at the Catechetical School of Alexandria.

55. Athanasius of Alexandria (c. 296/98–2 May 373), also called Athanasius the Great, was the twentieth bishop of Alexandria (as Athanasius I). His intermittent episcopacy spanned forty-five years (c. 8 June 328–2 May 373), of which over seventeen of them encompassed five exiles, when he was replaced at the order of four different Roman emperors. Athanasius was a Christian theologian, a Church Father, and the chief defender of Trinitarianism against Arianism.

56. Valentinus (c. 100–c. 160) was the best known and, for a time, most successful early Christian gnostic theologian. He founded his school in Rome. According to Tertullian, Valentinus was a candidate for bishop but started his own group when another was chosen. See below.

Eusebius of Caesarea, the first historian of the church and friend of Emperor Constantine, was bishop there from about 314 to 339.

Damascus is the capital of Syria, unfortunately known in our days for the terrible events happening in that area, and is considered the oldest city in the world among those continuously inhabited, tracing its foundation back to the time of the Mesopotamian civilizations, about eleven thousand years ago. On the road to Damascus was the famous conversion of Paul, who from being a persecutor of Christians became one of the most authoritative apostles.

The Seven Churches of Asia were small communities, all set in today's Turkey, and owe their fame to the fact that the only words that Jesus ever spoke directly to his church on earth are precisely addressed to them, according to Revelation: "I, John, your brother and companion in the suffering and kingdom and patient endurance that are ours in Jesus, was on the island of Patmos[57] because of the word of God and the testimony of Jesus. On the Lord's Day I was in the Spirit, and I heard behind me a loud voice like a trumpet, which said: 'Write on a scroll what you see and send it to the seven churches: to Ephesus, Smyrna, Pergamum,[58] Thyatira,[59] Sardis,[60] Philadelphia[61] and Laodicea.[62]'" Each one had a cathedral and was an episcopal seat; famous bishops were Melito of Sardis[63] and Polycrates of Ephesus.[64] The councils of Ephesus and Laodicea also took place in two of them. In addition to the seven churches, there were

---

57. Patmos is a small Greek island in the Aegean Sea. It is the location where the disciple John received the visions found in the book of Revelation of the New Testament and where the book was written.

58. Pergamon or Pergamum was a rich and powerful ancient Greek city in Mysia. It is located twenty-six km from the modern coastline of the Aegean Sea on a promontory northwest of the modern city of Bergama, Turkey.

59. Thyateira (also Thyatira) was the name of an ancient Greek city in Asia Minor, famous for its dyeing facilities and for being a center of the purple cloth trade.

60. Sardis was the capital of the ancient kingdom of Lydia, in Asia Minor—West Anatolia.

61. City in Asia Minor, was a highly important center in the early Christian and Byzantine periods, also called the little Athens because of its festivals and temples.

62. Laodicea on the Lycus was an ancient city built on the river Lycus in Asia Minor.

63. Melito of Sardis (died c. 180) was the bishop of Sardis near Smyrna in West Anatolia and a great authority in early Christianity.

64. Polycrates of Ephesus (c. 130–196) was an early Christian bishop who resided in Ephesus, best known for his letter addressed to Pope Victor I, bishop of Rome, about Quartodecimanism. See below.

other Christian settlements in Anatolia, thanks to the preaching of Paul, who was originally from those areas, namely from Tarsus, a city located in the central and southern part of Anatolia, and Ignatius of Antioch.[65] The place where major communities developed was Pontus, an area on the Black Sea where there was an ancient Greek colony and where most conversions took place.

Rome, at the height of its power and beauty, capital of the empire and future center of Christianity, is believed to have seen the first Christian settlements around AD 40, with the arrival of some Judeo-Christians from Asia Minor, among which were the spouses Aquila and Priscilla. The Christian community of Rome was certainly already substantial and well established in 57, the year in which Paul wrote the letter to the Romans from Corinth. It was made up of people of all social backgrounds, from the most humble (servants, artisans, shopkeepers) to intermediate ones (merchants, apothecaries) to the highest ones (state officials, notables, high military positions), as can be seen from the epigraphs found in the catacombs.[66] Peter and Paul also came to Rome and founded the Holy See[67] of Rome as an organized Christian community, which grew in importance over time until it was recognized as the leader of the church. Peter and Paul were martyred in Rome, and later various and violent persecutions (particularly bloody were those of Valerian and Diocletian)[68] decimated the church of Rome, which however survived, increasingly fortified in its Christian faith.

Carthage was the most important Christian settlement in Africa. It became a bishopric, and the bishop of Carthage was the primate and

---

65. Ignatius of Antioch was an early Christian writer and bishop of Antioch. He is considered a saint and a Church Father by both the Orthodox and Roman Catholic Churches.

66. Catacombs are human-made subterranean passageways for religious practice. Any chamber used as a burial place is a catacomb, although the word is most commonly associated with the Roman Empire.

67. The term Holy/Apostolic See was used to refer to any see founded by one of the twelve apostles, but with time, it became specific, in the Catholic Church, to the see of the bishop of Rome, whom that Church sees as successor of Saint Peter.

68. Valerian (193/195/200–260 or 264), also known as Valerian the Elder, was Roman emperor from AD 22 Oct. 253 to Spring 260. Emperor Diocletian, who lived between the third and fourth centuries, had a very high sense of the state and fought his whole life to defend traditional institutions and social structures, which were in crisis. Precisely the strenuous defense of that world and the obstinate refusal of new values produced the strongly negative image that most historical sources transmitted to us.

metropolitan of proconsular Africa, Numidia,[69] Tripolitania,[70] and Mauretania.[71] Tertullian[72] and Cyprian,[73] the father of the church, were born there. However, it was also traversed by several currents which then resulted in heresy.

Malta[74] had a Christian community dating back to the apostle Paul, who on a journey to Rome was shipwrecked and remained there for about three months, during which he met the Roman governor Publius, who converted to Christianity and became the first bishop of Malta. The beautiful catacombs of Rabat[75] remain as evidence of that period and of the fact that Malta was among the first Christian communities.

Salona was the Roman capital of Dalmatia,[76] and ruins found there testify how Christianity had arrived from the early years, so much so that Titus, Paul's disciple, preached there, and there were several martyrs. The Roman emperor Diocletian, author of a fierce persecution of Christians, was born in Salona. The city was destroyed by the Avari barbarian tribe in 639, and the surviving population took refuge in a fort, which later became the city of Split.

The church on the island of Cyprus was founded by the apostles Paul and Barnabas, who was a native of that land. They left Antioch in 46 and came to Salamis, an ancient Greek and then Roman city, located in the northeastern part near Famagusta, in the territory now under the control

---

69. Numidia was a Roman province on the North African coast, comprising roughly the territory of northeast Algeria.

70. Tripolitania is a historic region and former province of Libya.

71. Mauretania is the Latin name for a region in the ancient Maghreb. It stretched from central present-day Algeria westwards to the Atlantic, covering northern Morocco, and southward to the Atlas Mountains.

72 Tertullian (c. 155–c. 240) was a prolific early Christian author from Carthage in the Roman province of Africa. Of Berber origin, he was the first Christian author to produce an extensive corpus of Latin Christian literature. He was an early Christian apologist and a polemicist against heresy, including contemporary Christian Gnosticism. Tertullian has been called the father of Latin Christianity and the founder of Western theology.

73. Cyprian (c. 200–Sept. 14, 258) was bishop of Carthage and a notable early Christian writer of Berber descent, many of whose Latin works are extant. He is also recognized as a saint in the Christian churches.

74. Malta is a Southern European island country consisting of an archipelago in the Mediterranean Sea.

75. Rabat is a town in the Northern Region of Malta.

76. Dalmatia is a historical region, a narrow belt of the east shore of the Adriatic Sea.

of Northern Cyprus. From Salamis, the two apostles crossed the whole island from east to west towards Paphos, which was the Roman capital of Cyprus and where there was a large Greek community devoted to the cult of Aphrodite (born, according to Greek mythology, precisely from crystal clear waters close to Paphos and to whom was dedicated one of the most beautiful temple in ancient Greece). Here the two apostles began their preaching, and Paul made his first conversion, turning to Christianity the Roman proconsul Sergius Paulus, but also experiencing the first persecution on his skin, because he was sentenced to be whipped, for having created disorders. He suffered this penalty by being tied to a column, which is now referred to as the Pillar of Saint Paul in the archaeological area of Paphos. Barnabas returned to Cyprus few years later, accompanied by the Evangelist Mark, and became bishop of the island, continuing his mission of preaching Christianity until he was martyred. On his grave, discovered a few centuries later in Salamis, was built a monastery that still exists but has now been transformed by the Turkish authority into a museum of icons.[77]

In Greece, there were Christian communities from the very beginning of the spread of Christianity. Thessaloniki, the largest city in northern Greece, was a very important Christian center, from which Christianity radiated towards Macedonia, Bulgaria, Thrace[78] (especially in the city of Philippi, made famous by the battle between the armies of Anthony and Octavian[79] against those of Brutus and Cassius).[80] Corinth was a large city in southern Greece and had from the beginning a large Christian community, where Paul stayed several times, too. Paul sent to the Christians of these cities some of his famous letters, which remain not only a testimony

---

77. An icon is a sacred representation painted on wood, produced in the context of Byzantine and Slavic Christian culture.

78. Thrace is a geographical and historical region in Southeast Europe, now split among Bulgaria, Greece, and Turkey,

79. Marcus Antonius (14 Jan. 83–1 Aug. 30 BC), commonly known in English as Mark Antony or Anthony, was a Roman politician and general who played a critical role in the transformation of the Roman Republic from an oligarchy into the autocratic Roman Empire. Octavian was a Roman statesman and military leader who became the first emperor of the Roman Empire as Augustus, reigning from 27 BC until his death in AD 14.

80. Marcus Junius Brutus (85–23 Oct. 42 BC), often referred to simply as Brutus, was a Roman senator and the most famous of the assassins of Julius Caesar. Gaius Cassius Longinus (3 Oct. c. 86–3 Oct. 42 BC), often referred to as simply Cassius, was a Roman senator and general best known as a leading instigator of the plot to assassinate Julius Caesar on 15 Mar. 44 BC.

of his faith, but also confirmation of the rapid spread of Christianity in those lands. Paul also went to Athens, the capital of Greece, which was and still is its largest city, where he found a small but rapidly developing community. In fact, a few years later, Athens was the birthplace of Hyginus, who became bishop of Rome and the ninth pope of the Catholic Church. It is believed that the first bishop of Athens was Dionysius the Areopagite,[81] who met Paul and was convinced by him to embrace Christianity.

In that part of Gaul of Narbonne[82] and the land called Occitania,[83] which is now French Provence, there were important early Christian settlements, particularly in the cities of Lyon,[84] Avignon,[85] Arles,[86] Vienne[87] and Marseille,[88] where persecutions also took place. The most violent one was of Marcus Aurelius,[89] during which the bishop of Lyon, Pothinus, lost his life and was succeeded by Irenaeus.

---

81. Dionysius the Areopagite was a judge at the Areopagus Court in Athens, who lived in the first century. A convert to Christianity, he is venerated as a saint by multiple denominations.

82. Gallia Narbonensis (Latin for Gaul of Narbonne) was a Roman province located in what is now Languedoc and Provence, in Southern France.

83. Occitania is the historical region in Southern Europe, with no political borders, where Occitan was historically the main language spoken. This cultural area roughly encompasses the southern third of France, as well as part of Spain, Monaco, and smaller parts of Italy.

84. Lyon is the third largest city and second largest urban area of France.

85. Avignon is a city in Southern France, known as an ancient papal city, following the choice of Pope John XXII in 1316 to make it his home. This period is better known by the name of the Babylonian Captivity. In total, eight popes ruled over the city seat, of which two schismatics, residing in the castle called Popes' Palace, which was gradually enlarged by the various popes.

86. Arles is a Southern French city, an ancient Roman city. Its prestigious Roman monuments (the amphitheater, the ancient theater, the baths of Constantine, the necropolis of the Alyscamps), together with the Romanesque cathedral of Saint Trophime and other famous ancient and medieval buildings, were listed as UNESCO World Heritage Sites in 1981.

87. Vienne is a city in Southeastern France, which was a major center of the Roman Empire and also an important early bishopric in Christian Gaul.

88. Marseille is the second largest city in France, known to the ancient Greeks as Massalia and to the Romans as Massilia. Marseille is now France's largest city on the Mediterranean coast and the largest port for commerce, freight, and cruise ships.

89. Marcus Aurelius (Marcus Aurelius Antoninus, 26 Apr. 121–17 Mar. 180) was Roman emperor from AD 161 to 180 and a Stoic philosopher.

In Spain, the first Christian settlements (dating back to apostolic times) are found in what is modern Seville,[90] which at the time was the capital of the Roman province of Southern Spain. In those years Gerontius, bishop of Italica[91] (whose ruins can be admired near Seville), preached in the apostolic age in Betica, which is the Roman name of that region. From there Christianity, crossing the Strait of Gibraltar, spread to Roman Mauretania. Similarly, in its initial period, Christianity did not stop within the borders of the Roman Empire, but spread to other nations such as Armenia,[92] where Bartholomew the Apostle and Judas Thaddeus[93] arrived during the first century, and the kingdom of Edessa.

Edessa was an important Christian city since the apostolic period. Located in the south of modern Turkey, on the border with Syria, in what was at the time northwest Mesopotamia, it was the capital of the eponymous kingdom and the fulcrum of Syrian Christianity. The Christians expelled from Antioch found a refuge there, after they had started their mission towards gentiles and had thus been persecuted. These dramatic events confirm that the church of Edessa saw its beginning in the apostolic period, which gave it a great development, so that Christianity became a state religion for a certain period, and the members of the royal house converted to Christianity. This conversion seems to be due to a request that King Abgar V of Edessa made to Jesus, to come and visit him and heal him, and that he received an answer. In fact, the apostle Thomas sent the missionary Addai to the king after the resurrection, who converted the whole city. Addai (or Thaddeus) was accompanied in this mission by a disciple called Mari, with whom he is considered the founder of the church, according to the liturgy of Addai and Mari, which is still the liturgy of the Assyrian Church. The *anaphora* (Eucharistic prayer) of Addai and Mari is famous. Addai evangelized Mesopotamia, roughly present-day Iraq, and became the first bishop of Edessa. Many Christian priests moved from there to evangelize eastern Mesopotamia and ancient

---

90. Seville is a city of Spain, of Iberian-Punic origin, located in the southwestern part of the Iberian Peninsula.

91. Italica was an Italic settlement founded by the Roman general Scipio in the province of Hispania Baetica, which become an elaborate urban centre, obtaining the highest status of Roman city.

92. Armenia is a landlocked country in the South Caucasus region of Eurasia.

93. Jude, also known as Judas Thaddaeus, was one of the twelve apostles of Jesus, according to the New Testament. The Armenian Apostolic Church honors Thaddeus along with Saint Bartholomew as its patron saints. In the Roman Catholic Church, he is the patron saint of desperate cases and lost causes.

Persia, now Iran. A council was held in Edessa in 197, and in 325, its bishop Atillâtiâ participated in the Council of Nicea.

## The Spread of Christianity in the Ancient World

The spread of Christianity to the East happened in vast territories up to India and the island of Ceylon, now Sri Lanka, thanks to the work of itinerant bishops and missionaries who, following Paul's example, moved from one place to another, procuring themselves a living by practicing various crafts.

The progressive advance of this penetration meant that the city of Arbela, on the banks of the Tigris River, assumed the role previously held by Edessa as a center for spreading Christianity. The most important cities for Christianity in that period, however, were those of Seleucia and Ctesiphon, twin cities, born on the opposite banks of the Tigris, where was established a patriarchate with jurisdiction over the entire church of the eastern territories, including also India and Ceylon. As many as nine metropolises were subordinated to this patriarchate of Seleucia.

Bardaisan, a Syrian writer and philosopher, narrates in his writings of 196 that in Media, the current Iran; in Parthia, a region southeast of the Caspian Sea; and in Bactria, now Afghanistan, there were already substantial Christian settlements. It was the same in the Arabian Peninsula, where Paul stayed for three years, and where they developed especially in the southwestern part of the peninsula, where is currently Yemen, called at that time Sheba and famous for the events of its queen and King Solomon.

The evangelization of India is due to Thomas and Bartholomew, but mainly to Thomas, who arrived by ship in the southwestern part of India, on Malabar Coast in the state of Kerala, near Kochi.[94] There he preached to all classes and had a great number of conversions, even among the major castes, and ordered teachers and elders, who became the first priests of the church of Malabar. He then traveled to the southeastern coast of India, that of Coromandel, and carried out his apostolate in what is currently the Madras region, where he converted many other people and a local king. He also went through Malacca to China, where he stayed for some time and from where he returned to Madras. The king of Mylapore

---

94. Kochi is a major port city on the southwest coast of India, bordering the Laccadive Sea.

imprisoned him and, after questioning him, sentenced him to death. He also ordered the sentence, for fear of popular unrest, to be carried out on a nearby mountain, where Thomas was led and, after being allowed to pray, was stoned and then finished with a spear.

There is also news of Thomas's presence in northern India, and a tradition, considered a legend until recent archaeological finds, is grafted onto this presence. It is said that Thomas had a night vision, in which Jesus invited him to leave for India and to proclaim the word, so that, having overcome a certain reluctance and reassured by the presence of the grace of Jesus, Thomas accompanied an Indian merchant who led him in the northwestern part of India, where he lived. Here Thomas placed himself at the service of King Gondophares,[95] who converted to Christianity, together with his brother and many other people. This tale was considered a legend, and the historical truth of King Gondophares was also denied, until his existence and his importance, indicating him as one of the most prominent personalities of northern India in the second half of the first century, was confirmed by modern archaeological finds of coins of his kingdom and remains of his palaces. There is little information on the development of the church in those places, although it is learned from Bardesain that in Upper India existed Christian communities, who claimed to have been converted by Thomas and also preserved some relics. The remains of Thomas, however, were brought to Edessa and later transported to the Greek island of Chios, from where in 1258, the naval commander Leone Acciaiuoli[96] of Ortona, a city on the Abruzzo coast, took them to his city, where they still rest in the basilica dedicated to him.

The great diffusion of the churches demonstrated the extraordinary vitality of Christianity but also saw the inevitable multiplication of the discussions about the figure of Jesus, due not only to the large number of Christian communities, but also to the diversity between them, in culture and traditions.

Early Christianity, in fact, developed from Roman Judea through existing Jewish faith centers, and the first followers were known as Judeo-Christians. Later, it spread throughout the Roman Empire, coming into contact with all the other populations and cultures that formed it.

---

95. Gondophares I was the founder of the Indo-Parthian Kingdom and its most prominent king, ruling from AD 19 to 46.

96. Leone Acciaiuoli (Ortona, c. 1220–Florence, 1300) was an Italian politician who lived in the thirteenth century, a member of the Florentine Acciaiuoli family.

# Jewish and Christian Religions

## The Many Gospels and the Controversies about Them

### Before the Canon: A Variety of Writings, Some Long Lost and Recently Found

The first Christians met in private houses, called domestic churches, to remember Jesus and his teachings. The information on the life, acts, and teachings of Jesus were passed down orally at first, but soon were drafted several written accounts, called Gospels. The oral tradition of the life and acts of Jesus took place in the years immediately following his death, and the various passages could also have led to modifications of the original narrative. For this reason, the oral tradition started to be transformed in written form, in order to create a version that could be shared and spread among the different communities. Thus, in the first period immediately following the death of Jesus, a rich literature flourished, aimed at telling the story of his life and his teachings. Due to the differences in culture, origin, and language (they were written in Greek, Aramaic, Armenian, Coptic, and later Latin), a vast quantity of writings was created, the majority of which is now lost and of which we know only a small part, mainly through citations and other writings that refute their contents.

Some relatively recent discoveries have brought to light a series of documents relating to the writings that circulated in the period immediately following the death of Jesus, which help us understand how large and how different the narratives were about his life and acts. Research by the nineteenth-century Greek Orthodox bishop of Nicomedia Philoteos Bryennios led to the discovery of some papyri containing the *Didache*, or doctrine of the twelve apostles, a Christian text by an unknown author, with moral and behavioral indications for the communities. Its main value lies in the fact that it offers extra-biblical data on the institutions and life of the first Christian communities. The *Didache* wanted to codify moral, liturgical, juridical, and other rules and dispositions, considered convenient and necessary at the time it was written. It presents an exclusively practical orientation and, with the exception of chapter 16, leaves out any dogmatic element.

In Oxyrhyncus, Egypt, were found writings, known as the papyri of Oxyrhyncus. These are a large collection of handwritten fragments, many on papyrus, found between the late nineteenth and early twentieth centuries in an ancient landfill, thanks to the work of various archaeologists, including in particular Bernard Grenfell[97] and Arthur Surridge Hunt.[98] Most of the manuscripts found in Oxyrhyncus consist of public and private documents, such as codes, edicts, registers, inventories, deeds of sale, and letters, but also fragments of a religious nature referring to apocryphal texts of both the Old and New Testaments. Among these, in particular, are the Gospels of Thomas, Mary, Peter, James, the Shepherd of Hermas (texts we will find in full form in the papyri of Nag Hammadi), and the *Didache* just mentioned. In addition, there are also some manuscripts of unknown gospels. The papyri of Oxyrhyncus are kept in various institutions around the world; a significant number are in the Ashmolean Museum at the University of Oxford.

The greatest discovery, however, occurred in 1945. In a town in Upper Egypt, Nag Hammadi, a terracotta jar was found in a cave, at a cenobite monastery[99] founded by Saint Pacomius in the fourth century. It contained thirteen papyri with writings that referred to the first and second centuries, that is, the years immediately following the death of Jesus. Given their importance, let us analyze in a synthetically descriptive way these documents, which have instigated a copious literature, to which I would like to refer those who wish to deepen their knowledge. The texts are almost all gnostic, so I will briefly recall what gnosis is.

Gnosis, a Greek word meaning knowledge, is a form of philosophy and religion, present in the ancient world with its philosophical and religious concepts long before the birth of Jesus (some scholars trace it back to the conquest of Babylon by Cyrus the Great[100] in 539 BC). It was only after Jesus's death, though, that it insinuated itself into the Christian world and thought, giving form to what is called Gnosticism. Gnosticism had Alexandria and Rome as centers of major importance, but it also spread to monastic circles with ascetic currents, especially in Syria and

---

97. Bernard Pyne Grenfell (Birmingham, 16 December 1869–18 May 1926) was an English Egyptologist and papyrologist and a member of The Queen's College in Oxford.

98. Arthur Surridge Hunt (Romford, 1 Mar. 1871–Oxford, 18 June 1934) was an English papyrologist and Egyptologist.

99. Cenobitic (or coenobitic) monasticism is a monastic tradition that stresses community life. Often in the West, the community belongs to a religious order, and the life of the cenobitic monk is regulated by a religious rule, a collection of precepts.

100. Cyrus II the Great was an extraordinary personage, celebrated by the ancients for his great endeavors. He lived in the sixth century BC and conquered Media, Lydia, and the Babylonian Empire, giving birth to the Persian Empire. During his reign, the Jews, deported to Babylon from Nebuchadnezzar, were able to return to Palestine.

Egypt. Gnostic thought was attractive in the past, as it still is now, but it was severely fought, as we will see later, as heresy.

Returning to the Nag Hammadi Codes, the texts are written in ancient Coptic, although most of them have been translated from Greek. The most important work among them is the Gospel of Thomas, the only manuscript of the collection to be complete. Thanks to this discovery, scholars found the presence of fragments of these texts in the papyri of Oxyrhyncus, as we have already seen, and also traces of them in the citations present in the writings of the Church Fathers. The dating of the manuscripts goes back to the third and fourth centuries, while for the original Greek texts, although still controversial, dating to the first and second centuries is generally accepted. Here is a list of the most important texts:

- The Gospel According to Thomas is an apocryphal Gospel that collects one hundred fourteen sayings of Jesus. The vision that emerges from the Gospel of Thomas is that the kingdom of God is already present on Earth and that divine light, present inside all humans, can allow them to see the kingdom and enter it.

- The Secret Book of James, also known as the Apocryphon of James, is a gnostic gospel, written in Coptic in the first half of the second century. It describes secret teachings given by Jesus to Peter and James in the period between the resurrection and the ascension. The pseudepigraphic[101] author is James, the first-person narrator.

- The Treatise on the Resurrection or To Rheginos is a gnostic-Christian work dating back to the last thirty years of the second century, preserved in a single copy in Coptic language. The author states that salvation occurs through the resurrection, which however should not be understood as a rebirth of the flesh but as the ascent of the spirit to its heavenly home.

- The Epistle of Eugnostos (or Eugnostos the Blessed) is a gnostic treatise in the form of an epistle addressed to Eugnostos (right thought). The text contains an exposition of gnostic cosmology. Its content is very similar to that of the Christian gnostic work Wisdom of Jesus Christ, so much so that some scholars believe that Wisdom

---

101. Pseudepigrapha are falsely attributed works, texts whose claimed author is not the true author, or a work whose real author attributed it to a figure of the past.

is a version of the epistle to which, according to this thesis, were added Christian themes.

- The Wisdom of Jesus Christ or Sophia of Jesus Christ (Latin: *Sophia Jesu Christi*) is a gnostic gospel, written in Coptic language between the first and third centuries. Jesus, already risen, before ascending to heaven instructs the apostles on heavenly truths. There is no hint of the biographical life of Jesus.

- The Dialogue of the Savior, written in Coptic language in the second century. The remaining text contains a dialogue between the Savior (Jesus) and some disciples—somehow similar, or possibly based, on the Gospel of Thomas—in which he expresses gnostic cosmology.

- The Apocalypse of Paul or Coptic Apocalypse is a gnostic text, originally in Greek language but preserved only in Coptic language. For the composition, various dates have been proposed by scholars, ranging from the middle of the second century to the beginning of the fourth, with a preference for the second half of the second century. The pseudepigraphic attribution is to the apostle Paul of Tarsus.

- The First Apocalypse of James is a gnostic New Testament apocryphal, attributed to James the Just,[102] probably composed in Greek language but preserved in Coptic language. The title of the work is Apocalypse of James, but it is called first to distinguish it from the apocalypse of the same name present immediately after in the fifth code, called Second Apocalypse of James. It was composed between the last two decades of the second and the first half of the third century. It is a dialogue concerning a revelation (apocalypse) between Jesus and James the Just, Jesus's "brother," regarding salvation, understood in the gnostic sense as liberation of the soul from earthly suffering and its return to the primordial state.

- The Second Apocalypse of James is a text of primitive Christian literature, believed lost for centuries and eventually found among the Codes of Nag Hammadi in a Coptic language version. It was probably composed in the middle of second century, in the Greek language, in a gnostic environment; the pseudepigraphic attribution is to James the Just, "brother of the Lord."

---

102. James the Just was the head of the church of Jerusalem after Jesus's death. He is believed to be the author of the New Testament letter of James.

- The Apocalypse of Adam is an apocryphal of the Old Testament, from the first or second century AD, written in Coptic, of Judeo-gnostic or Christian-gnostic origin. It belongs to the apocalyptic genre. The Apocalypse of Adam is particularly notable for its radical rewriting of the main episodes of biblical history, and in particular Genesis, the Gospels, and the last judgment. They are revisited in a gnostic sense, in light of the conflict between the false god of matter, identified with the divinity of the Old Testament, and the true God of the spiritual world, identified with the divine Father of the Messiah.

- The Hypostasis[103] of the Archons[104] is a Coptic gnostic treatise; it is an exegesis of Gen 1–6, which exposes Gnostic mythology on the creation of the cosmos and humanity.

- The "Thunder, Perfect Mind" is a gnostic poem in Coptic language (but originally composed in Greek) which takes the form of an extended monologue, in which an immanent savior exposes a series of paradoxical statements about the feminine nature of the divine. These paradoxical statements recall the Greek enigmas on identity, a poetic form common in the Mediterranean area, particularly in the Egyptian and Jewish areas, in which similar female deities (Isis and Sophia respectively) list their virtues to an attentive audience and exhort them to strive to achieve them. The riddles of the poem could presuppose a classical gnostic myth, such as the one found in the Archontium Hypostasis or in the Apocryphon of John.

- The Exegesis of the Soul exposes the primordial elements of the gnostic dualistic conception and the theology of the Sacred Feminine. The mythology and theology contained in it, which are the basis of all Christian gnostic thought, were fully elaborated already in the first century, and consequently the Christian gnosis was born in the first century and not later.

- The Coptic Apocalypse of Peter, also known as the Gnostic Apocalypse of Peter, is an apocryphal of the New Testament, of pseudepigraphic attribution to the apostle Peter. It should not be confused with another Apocalypse of Peter, in Greek, also apocryphal.

---

103. Hypostasis is the underlying state or substance, the fundamental reality that supports all else.

104. Archons, in gnostic cosmogony, are the judges and rulers of the material world.

These works, coexisting with the Gospels of Matthew, Luke, Mark, and John and certainly with other works that never arrived to us, make us understand how important the debate on the figure of Jesus and his teaching must have been. This huge number of writings, which spread among Christian communities, representing different understandings on the interpretation of the life and acts of Jesus, caused not only a vast debate, but the birth of fractures and antagonisms within Christianity, which even turned into communities fighting each other to affirm the value of their interpretations. Among the best known communities are the Ebionites, the Nazarenes, the Montanists, the Marcionites, the Quartodecimans, and that of Melito of Sardis.

## Ebionites and Elchasaites

Ebionites is the name by which the representatives of Judaizing Christianity were generically designated or, in particular, some specific current of them. The name derives from the Hebrew 'ebhyonim—poor, and this is likely to be understood in an economic and social meaning, although, based on the use of the word poor in Jewish literature, the title is also thought to have a political-religious meaning, especially assumed in the times of the Maccabean wars (second century BC). Another almost insoluble question, connected to that of the etymology to be attributed to the word Nazarenes, is that of the relations between Ebionites and Nazarenes, clearly distinct from each other by Epiphanius.[105] It is plausible to think that Ebionites were the members of the extreme Judeo-Christian currents in the Jerusalem community that, starting from 70, spread in the regions of Judea and Samaria, eastwards in Jordan and Syria and southwards in Egypt. St Jerome[106] attests to their existence still at the end of fourth century. A characteristic of them was the extreme attachment to the practices of the law, considered indispensable to achieving salvation.

---

105. Epiphanius of Salamis (c. 310/320–403) was the bishop of Salamis, Cyprus, at the end of the fourth century. He is considered a saint and a Church Father by both the Orthodox and Roman Catholic Churches. He gained a reputation as a strong defender of orthodoxy for composing the Panarion, a compendium (with several quotes) of all heresies known at the time.

106. Jerome (c. 347–30 Sept. 420), also known as Jerome of Stridon, was a Latin priest, confessor, theologian, and historian. He is commonly known as Saint Jerome. He is recognized as a saint and Doctor of the Church by the Catholic Church, the Eastern Orthodox Church, the Lutheran Church, and the Anglican Communion.

For them, the world wass the creation of God, and Christ was the son of Joseph and Mary. The Ebionites, like other Judeo-Christians, did not believe in the virgin birth of Jesus and considered him as only a man or rather a thaumaturge prophet but not of divine nature.

For this reason, the Gospel of the Ebionites probably did not contain the story of the virginal birth of Jesus (Origen testifies to us that some of them believed in the miraculous birth of Jesus). They rejected the letters of Saint Paul (whom they considered apostate) and used a Gospel similar to the canonical Matthew, identified by some with the Gospel of the Nazarenes, by others with one of the Jews (written at the beginning of the second century in an Egyptian environment), of which many fragments remain. Critical analysis generally leads us to keep these fragments separate from those of a Gospel used by the Ebionites and referred to by Epiphanius, which must almost certainly be the Gospel remembered by Origen and was probably written in the second century in the Judeo-Christian communities east of the Jordan or of eastern Syria.

A particular expression of the Ebionites were the Elchasaites (also known as Elcasaites or Elcesaites). They were a group of gnostic Ebionites, originating in Sassanid Mesopotamia, who flourished in the third century and followed the teachings contained in the book of Elchasai, written at the beginning of the second century by Elchasai himself. The group spread to Rome under the pontificate of Pope Callixtus I, around 220, when Alcibiades of Apamea went there to preach the book of Elchasai. The group survived until the end of the fourth century. Hippolytus of Rome[107] says that under Pope Callixtus I (217–22), Alcibiades, an Elchasaite missionary, arrived in Rome from the city of Apamea in Celesira (region of present-day Lebanon), bringing with him a book allegedly given to him in Parthia by a righteous man named Elchasai. The contents of the book had been revealed to Elchasai by a gigantic angel, who was the Son of God, accompanied by his sister, the Holy Spirit (in Semitic languages, the word spirit is feminine). Alcibiades announced a new remission of sins, proclaimed in the third year of Trajan's reign (100), and described a baptism capable of granting forgiveness of sins to even

---

107. Hippolytus of Rome (Asia, c. 170–Sardinia, 235) was a Roman theologian and writer, the first antipope in the history of the church; before his death, he reconciled with the legitimate pope, Pontian, with whom he suffered martyrdom. He is revered as a saint by the Catholic and Orthodox Churches; therefore, he is the first of only two antipopes in history who received canonization, the other being Felix II (antipope from 356 to death).

the most hardened sinners. Origen, who appears to have met Alcibiades, says that this current was recent. A century and a half later, Epiphanius of Salamis affirmed that the book was in use by the Sampseans, descendants of the first Elkasaites, as well as by the Essenes and other Ebionite communities.

## Nazarenes

With the name of Nazarenes or Nazoreans, Epiphanius designates the members of a pre-Christian Jewish sect, established in the regions beyond the Jordan, who, while accepting numerous Jewish institutions (circumcision, Sabbath observance), denied that the law registered by the Pentateuch was the one promulgated by Moses; they made no sacrifices and did not eat animals. The same name is used by several writers to generally designate the Judeo-Christians, that is, those Christians coming from Judaism, who, on the question of observance of the law and acceptance of the gentiles in the Christian ranks, assumed a strictly conservative attitude, although being less rigid than Ebionites. It is also known that Christians themselves, without distinction of tendency, were called Nazarenes or Nazoreans (see testimony already in Acts 24:5) and that the name has remained, in this sense, in rabbinic literature and in the Eastern countries.

The Gospel of the Nazarenes is an apocryphal gospel that has been lost, of which traces have come down to us only through occasional testimonies provided by some Fathers of the Church. It was in use among the Judeo-Christians present in Palestine in the second century. It should probably be identified with two other equally Judeo-Christian texts, the Gospel of the Ebionites and the Gospel of the Hebrews. The Nazarenes, like other Judeo-Christians, did not believe in the virgin birth of Jesus and considered him as only a man, or rather a thaumaturge prophet but not of divine nature. Furthermore, his personal resurrection was not seen with the same importance that it has gained in the subsequent Christian tradition, that is, the means by which all humans reach salvation. For these reasons, the Gospel of the Nazarenes probably did not contain the episode of the virginal birth of Jesus and his resurrection (the passage quoted by Epiphanius testifies to the integrity of the text, but also admits that he has never seen it in person).

## Montanists

The Montanists were followers of Montanus, a convert to Christianity in the Phrygian area in central Anatolia, who claimed to be in contact with the Holy Spirit, with whom he communicated through his ecstasies and those of two of his priestesses. Montanism initially spread to Phrygia and nearby areas and then expanded rapidly throughout the Roman Empire, at a time when Christianity was generally tolerated or legal. Despite the prevalence of the orthodox current of Christianity, which had branded Montanism as a heresy even though it had initially accepted it, this movement survived in isolated areas until the eighth century. Some have found similarities between Montanism and Pentecostalism,[108] hence the denomination of Neo-Montanism sometimes used for the latter.

The best known Montanist was Tertullian who, before his conversion, was the main Catholic apologist and the first to use the term Trinity. Montanism did not have a true doctrinal apparatus. It was based instead on Christian doctrine modified by a series of behaviors and precepts. The contrasts with the orthodox Catholic Church arose because the Montanists affirmed the superiority of their prophets over the institutional clergy and allowed, in open contrast to the official Church, the participation of women in the rites, making them especially central in revelations and prophecies: Maximilla and Priscilla above all. They were also convinced that the prophecies of their founders completed and rediscovered the doctrine proclaimed by the apostles. Other contrasts arose because Montanists preferred prophecies in a state of ecstasy, in contrast to the more rigid and disciplined approach of the dominant theology in Christian orthodoxy. They were also convinced that Christians who left divine grace could not redeem themselves, in contrast to the Christian idea that repentance could lead to a remission of sins by the church. According to the Montanist view, the prophets were messengers of God, and spoke in his stead to believers: "I am the Father, the Son, and the Paraclete,"[109] said Montanus, in a way similar to the prophets of the Old Testament. This communication of the Spirit of God who spoke through the prophet is described thus by Montanus: "Behold, man is like a lyre and I fly over

---

108. Pentecostalism or classical Pentecostalism is a Protestant Christian movement that emphasises direct personal experience of God through baptism with the Holy Spirit.

109. Paraclete means advocate or helper. In Christianity, the term paraclete most commonly refers to the Holy Spirit.

it like a plectrum; man sleeps, and I watch; behold, it is the Lord who immerses the hearts of men in ecstasy and who gives a heart to men."[110] A strong emphasis was placed on the elimination of sin, carried out by practicing chastity, avoiding second marriages, and in rare cases, marriage itself. They also observed very severe periods of fasting, were inflexible with those who committed *peccata graviora* (serious sins—adultery, murder, apostasy), and came to condemn those who fled during the persecutions, praising, indeed, self-denunciation. However, the real focal point of the movement was the millenarian spirit, the expectation of the *parousia* (presence of the divine), suggested, perhaps, by the influence of the Apocalypse of John on the Christian world of that time. This belief resulted in the total absence of interest in the world and in history, considered things that would perish soon. The same belief made the followers of Montanist doctrine morally inflexible. Some Montanists were also Quartodecimans, that is, they celebrated Easter on the fourteenth day of the Jewish month of Nisan (the period between March and April, whose beginning was established by the March moon), regardless of the day of the week, and not on the following Sunday.

## Marcion

Marcion is one of the most interesting personalities of Christianity in the first century, associated with a movement that opposed the Roman Church, the largest and most widespread movement before the Arian controversies. Marcion was born in the last years of the first century in Sinope, on the southern shores of the Black Sea. His father was the bishop of the city; Epiphanius says that the father was forced to excommunicate the young son because he was guilty of seducing a girl. Whether this was true or not, it is certain that Marcion had to leave his hometown. As a merchant and shipmaster, he accumulated a huge fortune. It seems that the acceptance of traditional faith had always raised many doubts in him. In any case, Marcion had to go to Rome around 140. At first, he remained on good terms with the official congregation, which accepted a donation of two hundred thousand sesterces from him. It seems probable that the Roman relations between Marcion and Cerdo (Syrian gnostic theologian), reported in agreement by Irenaeus, Tertullian, Hippolytus, Eusebius, and Epiphanius, had little influence on the spiritual crisis of

---

110. Cited in Epiphanius, *Panarion*, vol. 2, ch. 48, v. 4.

Marcion (Adolf von Harnack's[111] radically negative opinion seems excessive). The definitive rupture between Marcion and the Roman community (a moment that Marcionites would later celebrate as that of the foundation of their church) happened in July 144. In that month, Marcion faced the priests of the community. He explained to them his belief that it was impossible to reconcile the faith revealed by Jesus and Paul with the religious heritage of Israel accepted by the church. He was shown how the passages of the Gospel mentioned by him (Luke 5:36; 6:43) were susceptible of a harmonious interpretation. He did not want to be convinced, so he was excommunicated and was returned the sum he had paid to the community. It is probable, in the opinion of Harnack, that on this occasion Marcion delivered a written declaration to the Roman congregation about the reasons for his dissent from them. Further information on Marcion's activity is missing; the date of his death should probably be placed around 160.

The loss of Marcion's original writings forces those who want to draw a picture of Marcionite doctrine to refer above all to the five books of Tertullian's *Adversus Marcionem* which—if only for the lively, often crude realism—is perhaps the least suitable for understanding Marcionite spirituality. Moreover, the heresological tradition—starting with Irenaeus—was all too focused in drawing up genealogical lists of heretics and establishing kinship relationships between them. The arbitrary inclusion of Marcion in the framework of the gnostic heresy has greatly contributed to the overestimation of Marcion's relation with the gnostic Cerdo, leading to misunderstanding of the true sense of Marcion's religious experience, rich like few others, with profound originality.

Today, however, the reconstruction of Marcion's work and thought, traced by Harnack, allows us to place his figure in the right framework. The tradition of the Roman church was in agreement, at that time, in linking the Christian message to the religious traditions of Israel with no interruption, through a typological-allegorical interpretation of the books of the Old Testament: the facts narrated therein were therefore interpreted as an announcement and prefiguration of the Christian plan of salvation, which had been inaugurated by Jesus, the promised and awaited Messiah. Marcion totally rejected this interpretation. His temperament was

---

111. Carl Gustav Adolf von Harnack (7 May 1851–10 June 1930) was a Baltic German Lutheran theologian and prominent church historian. He produced many religious publications from 1873 to 1912 (in which he is sometimes credited as Adolf Harnack).

far from any erudite subtlety, from any form of allegorism, as from any philosophical speculation. Guided by a linearity of thought, adamantine in its simplism, he did not doubt for a moment that the Old Testament should be interpreted only literally and accepted as the true and faithful history of humanity and the world. Reading the Old Testament with this spirit, Marcion, who reveals an instinctive, almost pathological repugnance towards all matter and the very laws of life, could not see anything in it but the story of a God who creates a man full of imperfections, a world full of evils, and who places a series of obscene and repulsive acts at the origin of life. A God himself imperfect as his work, victim of a thousand inconsistencies—a God who is not, as in Persian dualism, a principle or hypostasis of evil, but who, whatever his plans and wishes may have been, has not shown adequate means and powers for his intended work, to organize the world of matter. Because of his inability, in order to curb his imperfect work, he resorted to a severe and despotic law, in the observance of which he laid the foundation of all morals, the fulfillment of which is guaranteed by a series of penalties, all based on the idea of the law of retaliation, which he applies with unyielding cruelty also on the children of sinners and up to the fourth generation. But this attitude of Marcion towards Jewish religiosity and holy books would have remained only negative and sterile, if he had not read in Paul the statement that the Jewish law had been definitively removed and abolished by Christ. In fact, the message of Christ, who in the Sermon on the Mount had announced the new precept of love, forgiveness, mercy, appeared to Marcion as something absolutely, ineffably new, in perfect contrast with the whole Jewish religiosity and law, which was therefore to be banned forever.

Marcion's originality, the distinctive note and the keystone of all his thought, must be sought precisely in this affirmation of the absolute novelty of Jesus's preaching. From this opposition of two religious visions, Marcion was drawn to formulate a true dualism between the Creator God (the just God of the Old Testament) and the good God, the foreign God (according to Saint Paul),[112] hitherto unknown, who revealed himself in Christ. This dualism (which, anyway, never materializes in a metaphysical duel between two antithetical principles fighting each other)

---

112. Paul announces a foreign god: the Christian God is a foreign god not only with respect to the Greco-Roman pantheon but also with respect to the metaphysical principle of philosophy. He is a foreign god because he is the God who turns himself into a man in order to save men.

is anyway inessential to Marcion's thought; at most it is the inevitable consequence of some essential premises.

Christ, the revealer of the good God—the relationships between this and that, not clearly distinct from each other, reveal in Marcion singular affinities with modalistic positions (a term used by Harnack to indicate beliefs in the uniqueness of God, which excludes the Trinity)—suddenly appeared in the world during the fifteenth year of the reign of Tiberius, a man already made, not born of a woman,[113] to preach the new law of love, to abolish the law of the just God. But the apostles of Jesus betrayed the spirit of the Gospel and continued to accept the Old Testament tradition, identifying the God of the Hebrews with the good God and Jesus with the Messiah expected by them. Paul had had the merit—although his correspondence is not immune to legalistic infiltrations—to bring Christian society back to the truth of the Gospel. But how can those who opt for Christ and the Gospel come to salvation? Harnack asserted that, for Marcion, the achievement of salvation requires nothing more than an act of faith in the merits of Christ the Redeemer. This affirmation of Harnack, who, with a very strange anachronism, gives Marcion the mentality of a Lutheran, is denied by the fact that in Marcion there is the idea of the kingdom, conceived as already implemented in Christ and in the preaching of the Gospel (*"initiatio Evangelii, in quo est Dei regnum, Christus ipse"*).[114] This idea implies another, of the salvation achieved through participation in Christ's reign, which is possible only to those who, through a deep inner palingenesis,[115] renounce forever the rules of the Creator God.

Ultimately, for Marcion there are two Gods: the Creator of the world, revealed to humanity from the beginning, in the works of creation and in the Old Testament, and the foreign God, who manifests himself in his son Jesus Christ, to save humans from the overwhelming dominion of the Creator.

Behind this theological vision, at first sight very bizarre, hides a particular interpretation of the Bible. Over ten centuries before Luther,

113. This is the doctrine of docetism, that is the doctrine of those who, especially in the first centuries of Christianity, claimed that the body of Christ existed only as φάντασμα, ghost, apparent form, without the substance of the flesh. They therefore excluded his human conception and birth, as well as the full reality of his passion and death. Docetists never formed a group or a sect but spread among the most diverse groups and individuals.

114. Tertullian, "Tertulliani adversus Marcionem."

115. Renovation, rebirth, regeneration; used in the New Testament to define the inner renewal of one by effect of faith in God.

Marcion claimed the independence of the Gospel from the Mosaic law with extreme radicality, so much so that the Old and the New Testament are the work of two different deities. As Pope Benedict XVI himself recently recalled, referring specifically to a text by Harnack, Marcion represents at the same time the greatest threat but also the greatest challenge launched on Christian doctrine and still represents today an obligatory passage for Jewish-Christian dialogue.

Once he declared his clear dissent with the official church, Marcion had to turn all his activity to constitute a competing church, inspired by his ideas. What the means used by Marcion were and what particular nuances his propaganda had, it is difficult to say, for lack of direct data. It is anyway certain that, already in the second century, Catholic polemicists in Italy, Gaul, Africa, Greece, Crete, Asia Minor, and Egypt denounced loudly the Marcionite danger. In them, such is the harshness of the controversy, so clear is the feeling of the threat represented by the spread of Marcionism, that the assertion of Ammon[116] is not farfetched, when saying that probably, in almost all the cities of some importance a Marcionite church rose up against the Catholic community.

Between the middle of the third and fourth centuries, Marcionism followed the downward curve of its trajectory, at least in the West. In the East, after successfully passing the test of the persecutions of Valerian and Diocletian, Marcionism continued to live a prosperous life, especially in southern Syria and Palestine. In the face of the persecutions of the Roman Empire and the fight without quarter of the Catholic bishops, Marcionism—presumably allied with Manichaeism[117]—gradually abandoned cities for the countryside, the coastal areas for the interior. At the end of the fourth and fifth centuries, it still represented a danger to the Syrian-speaking Christian communities, and then it disappeared almost completely. Reliable traces of Marcionism can be found in the Khorāsān (region of present-day Iran) still in the tenth century.

Marcion codified his ideas in the Marcionian Code. Taking into account the numerous refutations of Marcion and in particular that of

---

116. Kaspar Ammon (Hasselt, 1450–1524) was a Belgian theologian.

117. Manichaeism is a religion that, starting from the third century AD, spread to Asia, Europe, and Africa. According to the Manicheans, reality is based on the incessant conflict between good and evil, light and darkness, and the task of religion is to free the light trapped in matter. This dualistic conception of reality inspired the current use of the adjective Manichean, which indicates he who considers things either white or black, without taking any nuances into account.

Epiphanius of Salamis, one can thus try to reconstruct it: the Gospel of Marcion (*Evangelikon*) is a part of Luke's, to which nothing is added. The main identified omissions are the following:

1. The entire chapter 1: the prologue; the narration of the birth of the Baptist; the annunciation, the Magnificat ("he helped Israel as he had promised to our fathers"), and the Benedictus.
2. The entire chapter 2: the birth and infancy of Jesus.
3. The Baptist's invitation to the uprising and the genealogy of Jesus from chapter 3.
4. Various sentences in the intermediate chapters, all with references to Israel and the Old Testament.
5. Almost all of the final chapter (24) and in particular the narration of the apparitions.

As one can see, these are texts that connect Jesus to Jewish tradition and history and that give political meaning to his action. On the basis of information provided by Tertullian and substantially confirmed by Epiphanius, we know that Marcion reorganized the letters of Paul, which he called *Apostolikon*, per the following:

1. Compared to the canon subsequently adopted by the church, the later Pastoral Epistles (Timothy I and II, Titus) and the letter to the Hebrews (which is not Pauline) are missing.
2. Corinthians (I and II), Thessalonians (I and II), Colossians, Philippians, and Philemon were probably unchanged.
3. Galatians is missing the meeting with Peter, the division of tasks, and almost all of chapter 3 with its references to Mosaic law.
4. Romans is missing entire chapters, like 1, 9, 10 11, and 15.
5. Letter to the Laodiceans: according to Tertullian, it is to be identified with Ephesians of the Catholic canon.

The Fathers of the Church (Justin, Irenaeus of Lyon, Epiphanius of Salamis) agree with Tertullian's thesis that Marcion had modified the text of Luke to adapt it to his theses. Modern scholars (Ferdinand Christian Baur)[118] tend instead to speculate on a lost common source or that the

---

118. Ferdinand Christian Baur (21 June 1792–Dec. 1860) was a German Protestant theologian and founder and leader of the (new) Tübingen School of theology.

Gospel of Marcion is an older version (Albrecht Ritschl),[119] proffered to reduce the differences in the preaching of Peter and Paul, consistent with the content of the Acts of the Apostles, also attributed to Luke. Gilles Quispel[120] writes about Marcion's text: "The Greek text of Luke and Paul, on which Marcion made his version, was the standard text in Rome at the time when he began his revisions (about AD 144, when he was excommunicated from the congregation in the capital). This text was, of course, pre-Marcionite; it was also pre-western, and established before AD 144."[121]

## Quartodecimans

The issue of Quartodecimanism was also an important source of controversy in the early church. According to an ancient tradition, probably apostolic and connected by the bishops who were its custodians to the name of Saint John the Evangelist, in the eastern part of the Roman Empire, particularly in Syria, Mesopotamia, and some areas of Cilicia, there was the custom of celebrating Passover/Easter on Nisan 14,[122] like the Jews, whatever the day of the week. In this way, emphasis was placed on the passion, as is well understood by reading the Easter homily of Melito of Sardis (bishop of Sardis, passionate researcher of biblical texts), written between 166 and 180. In chapter 46, he writes: "What is the passover?

---

119. Albrecht Ritschl (25 Mar. 1822–20 Mar. 1889) was a German Protestant theologian.

120. Gilles Quispel (30 May 1916–2 Mar. 2006) was a Dutch theologian and historian of Christianity and Gnosticism.

121. Quispel, "Marcion and the Text," 359.

122. Jewish calendar and Gregorian calendar:
- Tishrei (thirty days): Sept.–Oct.
- Cheshvan (twenty-nine or thirty days): Oct.–Nov.
- Kislev (twenty-nine or thirty days): Nov.–Dec.
- Tevet (twenty-nine days): Dec.–Jan.
- Shevat (thirty days): Jan.–Feb/
- Adar I (twenty-nine days): additional month in leap years, Feb.–Mar.
- Adar (twenty-nine or thirty days): Feb.–Mar.
- Nisan (thirty days): Mar.–Apr.
- Iyar (twenty-nine days): Apr.–May
- Sivan (thirty days): May–June
- Tammuz (twenty-nine days): June–July
- Av (thirty days): July–Aug.
- Elul (twenty-nine days): Aug.–Sept.

Indeed its name is derived from that event—'to celebrate the passover' (to *paschein*) is derived from 'to suffer' (*tou pathein*)."[123] In fact, many Hellenistic authors between the second and third centuries based their adhesion to the quartodeciman rite on the belief that the term Pascha (πάσχα, paskha) is derived from the Greek verb πάσχειν (paskhein), which means precisely to suffer, even though, in reality, the term is derived from Pèsah (or Pàsach), which in Hebrew means passage and alludes to the passage of the angel, who according to the book of Exodus (12:29–34) struck the Egyptian firstborns.

Of course Melito is not the only witness, but there are others, both in favor of the quartodeciman use, like Apollinaris of Hierapolis,[124] who wrote in the same years, and against it, like Hippolytus of Rome (theologian and writer, first antipope), who lived between second and third century. The most authoritative proponent of this custom was Saint Polycarp of Smyrna,[125] most likely the last direct disciple of Saint John. He, during a trip to Rome, even tried to convince Pope Anicetus of the correctness of the quartodeciman tradition; he failed in his intent but, anyway, there were no schisms within the church.

The other Christian churches, headed by Rome and Alexandria of Egypt, celebrated Easter on the Sunday following Nisan 14, whatever the day of the month when the festival fell. Later, the celebration became closely linked to the spring equinox, which, for Jews, was only one of the factors that contributed to the definition of the date of Passover. This tradition is therefore linked to the idea of Easter as the passage of humanity. It is an anthropological festival, in which the protagonist is a man, thus taking up the allegorical concept of Philo of Alexandria,[126] according to which Christ, risen on Sunday, is the new Adam; according to Paul,[127] he is the source of a new eschatological creation, the New Jerusalem.[128] Easter Day, therefore, entails the possibility for one to be reborn in grace and becomes the privileged moment to impart baptism, the sacrament precisely with which one leaves the life of sin and is reborn in Christ. The

123. Melito of Sardis, "On the Passover."

124. Saint Apollinaris Claudius, otherwise Apollinaris of Hierapolis or Apollinaris the Apologist, was a Christian leader and writer of the second century.

125. Polycarp (69–155) was a Christian bishop of Smyrna.

126. Philo of Alexandria (c. 20 BC–c. AD 50), also called Philo Judaeus, was a Hellenistic Jewish philosopher who lived in Alexandria, in the Roman province of Egypt.

127. 1 Cor 15:45.

128. Rev 21.

passage of the Jews from slavery to freedom foreshadowed the one from the slavery of sin to the freedom of the children of God, which happened thanks to Christ.

Among the initiators of this interpretation, we find Clement of Alexandria, Father of the Church, who lived at the turn of the second to third century, the first Christian author in whose writings we find the concept of Easter as a passage. This concept was later reiterated by Origen, when, correcting the ancient error on the etymology of the word Easter, he wrote in his *De Pascha*: "Most brothers, not to say all, think that Easter is called by this name due of the Savior's passion. But in reality, among the Jews the aforementioned festival is not called *pascha*, but *phas*: it is these three letters of *phas*, plus the rough breathing which is more marked among them, which constitute the name of the festival, which translated means passage."[129]

Once the original meaning of the festival name was restored, many Christians began to accuse the Quartodecimans of being Judaizers, not respecting the prescriptions of the New Testament, because they continued to celebrate Passover with the Jews, while Jesus had abolished that Easter, establishing the real one. This inevitably led to a clash between the two factions. Moreover, the disagreement created a strong embarrassment in the face of pagan public opinion (keep in mind that at that time the Christian religion was a small minority in front of the great majority of the Roman one), who saw with amazement the fact that a religious community was divided on its most important celebration. According to Eusebius of Caesarea, starting from the end of the second century and throughout the third century, there were many synods that tried to resolve the issue, but, despite this, many Asian bishops, including Polycrates of Ephesus, continued to observe the quartodeciman practice. At this point, according to Eusebius, in 193 Pope Victor threatened to sever them from the community of the faithful, excommunicating all Christians who followed this practice, thereby excluding dissidents from the congregation. Many, however, including Saint Irenaeus of Lyon, exhorted him to peace, and thus the first schism was avoided. However Polycrates of Ephesus rose in defense of the quartodeciman tradition, tracing back the custom even to the apostles Philip and John. Due to protests from most Eastern bishops, the threat of excommunication was withdrawn, but the pope's decision to celebrate Easter on Sunday remained. According to most

---

129. Origen, *La Pasqua*, 1–2.

scholars, the quartodeciman observance declined and eventually disappeared before the Council of Nicea in 325.

## The Need for a Christian Canon and the Threat of Gnosticism

This widespread conflict that went from Italy to what is now called the Middle East and the quantity of Gospels, stories, memories, and testimonies that circulated in the times immediately after the death of Jesus and which, as we have seen, also resulted in open and violent conflicts, with different truths about Jesus thrown back to one another, baffled Christians. In fact, they saw themselves immersed in a quarrelsome world in which it became difficult to navigate, with the danger that the destruction and the antagonism that arose from it could lead to a dispersion and a drying up of the Christian movement.

### Irenaeus of Lyon

In this era of mutations, disturbances, and uncertainties, Irenaeus of Lyon was born. He is one of the greatest, most powerful, most decisive, and perhaps least known figures in the history of the church, to which he gave an impulse and direction that marked and marks still its course and life. Irenaeus was born in Izmir, a city in Asia Minor, around 130. He came from a Christian family and was a disciple of Polycarp, a great teacher, a pupil himself of Saint John the Evangelist. He received, therefore, a good education, and when the bishop of Lyon, Potinus, asked for help for his diocese, Polycarp sent Irenaeus. He was greatly appreciated by the Christian community of Lyon for his faith, teaching, wisdom, and balance, so much so, that when it came to sending a letter to Pope Eleuterius to clarify some doctrinal issues, Irenaeus was chosen. Upon his return, he found the community of Lyon decimated by the persecution of Christians by Marcus Aurelius, among whose victims there was also the elderly bishop Potinus. For the esteem and love he had gained, the faithful then elected Irenaeus bishop of Lyon and entire Gaul. Irenaeus, in his new responsibility, faced with determination that world, crossed by anxieties and protagonisms, and fought with all his strength the pitfalls that came from ever new interpretations of the figure of Jesus, the most widespread of which had become Gnosticism.

## Gnosticism and Notable Gnostics

We have already briefly mentioned Gnosticism, which is a subject of fundamental interest and which has opened debates, researches, adherents, and oppositions that have gone through history and are still present today. To the immense literature that it has created, I refer those who have an interest in deepening their knowledge. Here we will briefly recall its characteristics.

Gnosticism was known for a long time only through Christian authors who refuted its manifestations as heretical doctrines and in a few late period texts (fifth century); but in 1945, as we have seen, thirteen papyri of gnostic treatises in the Coptic language were found in Nag Hammadi, Egypt, which translated Greek texts from second century. A fundamental element of the gnostic soteriology (doctrine of salvation) is knowledge; that, not faith or deeds, is the only means of salvation. This image of a salvific knowledge in a religious sense was reached by different ways, ranging from the Greek philosophical tradition (for example, even Socrates said that he who knows, for this very reason cannot sin), to the revelations that were given to initiates, to mystery cults (do not forget that revelation is a fundamental component of Christianity itself). The object of this saving knowledge is the negativity of the worldly reality, expressed not so much through ethical-philosophical judgments, but through myths, all variations of a fundamental theme: the world was created by an evil being, in opposition to God and spiritual reality; humans are a part of spiritual reality imprisoned in the material world; in order to free them, God sends a celestial being to reveal this cosmo-anthropological situation; once knowledge, or gnosis, has been acquired, humans can behave adequately and, by refusing the world, restore themselves to the divine condition.

Gnostic ideology is above all concerned to rigorously separate gnosis, which is the only presence of spirituality in this material world, from any possible ethical-religious conception, however high it may be, intended to support human society; in fact, society must be destroyed and not supported. Even the idea of God is rejected: the true God is invisible, perfect, incomprehensible, and unnameable; one cannot have an idea of him. What we have is the idea of the Demiurge, of the Creator (often identified with the biblical God), that is, of that evil being who would like to impose his dominion over humanity. He is a material being like the world he created; he is ignorant (he does not even have knowledge of the divine reality, which he instinctively opposes), and he is blasphemous, in that he has proclaimed himself the only God. This subversion of traditional values generally involved, as in any mystical attitude, the renunciation of social life, asceticism, meditation, etc.; but it could also entail the conscious and programmatic violation of all moral laws in force, hence the accusation of libertinism that gnostics received from writers on the Christian side.

More or less legendary masters of gnosis were Simon Magus (from whom the adjective simoniac derives, to indicate someone trades sacred things, since Simon Magus wanted to buy from Peter his faculty to lay hands and was chased away by him), Menander his disciple (like Simon, a Samaritan), and Saturninus of Antioch. Of greater importance, both for the doctrine and for its effects, are Basilides, Carpocrates, and Valentinus, the most distinguished of all.

Valentinus was born in Phrebonis, on the Nile Delta, at an uncertain date but certainly prior to 135, the year in which we have the first news of his preaching. He moved at a young age to Alexandria in Egypt, then an important Christian center, and had as teacher Theudas, a mystery leader, who proclaimed himself a direct disciple of Paul of Tarsus and who claimed he had learned from Paul the secret revelations made by Jesus. These esoteric or initiatory teachings seem to have been later reported in the Gospel According to Philip, attributed to Valentinus himself. After completing his studies, Valentinus first taught in Alexandria in Egypt and then, around 140, moved to Rome, where he was deacon under Pope Hyginus,[130] and remained there until the pontificate of Anicetus.[131] Valentinus was endowed with a lively intelligence and a vast culture, so he made a breakthrough in the Christian community, where he began to play an increasingly important role until he competed in the elections as bishop of Rome (at that time the election of the bishop was made directly by the Christian congregation). Failure to be elected pushed Valentinus to abandon the church and decidedly embark on the path of Gnosticism, of which he became, with his bold theories, the most illustrious

---

130. Pope Hyginus was the bishop of Rome from c. 138 to his death in c. 142. Tradition holds that during his papacy he determined the various prerogatives of the clergy and defined the grades of the ecclesiastical hierarchy.

131. Pope Anicetus was the bishop of Rome from c. 157 to his death in Apr. 168. According to the Annuario Pontificio, the start of his papacy may have been 153. Anicetus actively opposed Gnosticism and Marcionism. He welcomed Polycarp of Smyrna to Rome, to discuss the controversy over the date for the celebration of Easter.

representative, also creating a following, the Valentinians, who continued his thought for a few centuries.

## Irenaeus and the Creation of a Canon against Heresies

Conscious of this reality, of the bewilderment it had created, and in which he himself lived, Irenaeus of Lyon strongly opposed all those conceptions that he considered wrong, branding them as heretics, and indicating, instead, those to follow and their sources. Irenaeus can be considered the first Christian theologian, in that he attempted to elaborate the first global synthesis of primitive Christianity. In fact, within a historical period marked by two cultural events of great depth—on the one hand, the onset of Gnosticism in the Christian sphere, as the first heresy in possession of a doctrinal system quite fascinating and captivating; and on the other, the diffusion in the pagan world of the philosophical current of Neoplatonism, which had many affinities with Christianity—Irenaeus, with his fundamental work (*Adversus Haereses* or *Against Heresies,* in five volumes) attempted to give a clear and precise answer against the alleged errors of Gnosticism. However, towards Neoplatonism, he opened up a certain dialogue, even accepting some general principles, subjecting them to a personal reflection.

The second-century church, in fact, was threatened, as we have seen, by the doctrine of gnosis, which stated that the faith taught by the church was just a collection of symbolisms, suitable only for the simplest and most ignorant, who were unable to understand the reality of difficult truths. The initiates, the intellectuals, or gnostics, as they called themselves, instead would have understood what was behind these symbols and thus would have formed an elitist, intellectualist, or gnostic Christianity. Obviously this new gnostic Christianity was increasingly fragmented into different currents, with thoughts that were often strange and extravagant, but also attractive to many. A common element of these different currents was dualism, which denied faith in the one God, the Father of all, Creator and Savior of humanity and the world, and affirmed, alongside the good God, the existence of a negative Principle, which had produced matter and all that derives from it. Firmly rooted in the biblical doctrine of creation, Irenaeus refuted both the dualism and the pessimism that devalued bodily realities. He decisively claimed the original goodness of matter, body, flesh, no less than spirit. His work goes far beyond the refutation of heresy, because he presents himself as the first great theologian of the early church, who created a systematic vision of theology, that is, of a theological system, fairly coherent among all the articles of faith.

At the heart of his reconstruction is the question of the rule of faith and its transmission. For Irenaeus the rule of faith coincides, in practice, with the Apostles' Creed,[132] which is the key to interpreting the gospel. The apostolic symbol, in fact, is a special synthesis of the gospel, which helps us understand both what it means and how we should read the gospel itself.

The gospel preached by Irenaeus, in fact, is what he received from Polycarp, bishop of Smyrna, who dates back to the apostle John. And so the true teaching is not the one invented by intellectuals beyond the simple faith of the church, but the one founded directly on the apostles, who communicated to the bishops in an uninterrupted chain forming the so-called tradition (from the Latin word *traditionem*, coming from verb *tradere*, to deliver, transmit, which translates the Greek παράδοσις, *paradosis*), which is one of the two sources of revelation.[133] The apostles taught a simple faith, which is based on the revelation of God. Thus—says Irenaeus—there is no secret doctrine behind the common creed of the church. There is no higher Christianity for intellectuals. The faith

---

132. I believe in God, the Father almighty,
creator of heaven and earth.
I believe in Jesus Christ, his only Son, our Lord.
He was conceived by the power of the Holy Spirit
and born of the virgin Mary.
He suffered under Pontius Pilate,
was crucified, died, and was buried.
He descended to the dead.
On the third day he rose again.
He ascended into heaven,
and is seated at the right hand of the Father.
He will come again to judge the living and the dead.
I believe in the Holy Spirit,
the holy catholic Church,
the communion of the saints,
the forgiveness of sins,
the resurrection of the body,
and the life everlasting. Amen.

"Apostles' Creed."

133. The sources of revelation are Scriptures and tradition.

publicly confessed by the church is the common faith of all. Only this faith is apostolic; it comes from the apostles, that is, from Jesus and God. By adhering to this faith publicly transmitted by the apostles to their successors, Christians must observe what the bishops say; they must especially consider the teaching of the church of Rome, paramount and very ancient. This church, because of its antiquity, has the greatest apostolicity, because it is derived directly from Peter and Paul, the columns of the apostolic college. All the local churches must agree with the church of Rome, recognizing in it the measure of the true apostolic tradition, of the one common faith of the church. Thus writes Irenaeus: "For it is a matter of necessity that every Church should agree with this Church, on account of its preeminent authority, that is, the faithful scattered everywhere, since in it the tradition of the apostles has always been preserved."[134] Apostolic succession, verified on the basis of communion with the church of Rome, constitutes the criterion of the permanence of the individual churches in the apostolic tradition. In fact, Irenaeus writes further: "In this order, and by this succession, the ecclesiastical tradition from the apostles, and the preaching of the truth, have come down to us. And this is most abundant proof that there is one and the same vivifying faith, which has been preserved in the Church from the apostles until now, and handed down in truth."[135] With these arguments, Irenaeus refutes the claims of the gnostics from the ground up. First of all, they do not possess a truth which would be superior to that of the common faith, because what they say is not of apostolic origin, but invented by them; secondly, truth and salvation are not the privilege and monopoly of a few, but everyone can achieve them, through the preaching of the successors of the apostles and above all of the bishop of Rome.

In particular—always arguing with the secret character of the gnostic tradition and noting its multiple and contradictory outcomes—Irenaeus takes care to illustrate the genuine concept of apostolic tradition, which can be summarized in three points:

1. Apostolic tradition is public, not private or secret. For Irenaeus, there is no doubt that the content of the faith transmitted by the church is the one received by the apostles and by Jesus, the Son of God. There is no other teaching than this. Therefore whoever wants to know the true doctrine suffices that he knows "the Tradition that

---

134. Irenaeus, *Contro le eresie (Against Heresies)*, bk 3, ch. 3, 2.
135. Irenaeus, *Contro le eresie (Against Heresies)*, bk 3, ch. 3, 3.

comes from the Apostles and the faith announced to men," tradition and faith that "have come down to us through the succession of Bishops."[136] Thus, the succession of bishops—personal principle—and apostolic tradition—doctrinal principle—coincide.

2. The apostolic tradition is unique. While in fact Gnosticism is divided into multiple sects, the tradition of the church is unique in its fundamental contents, which Irenaeus calls *regula fidei* or *regula veritatis*; it is so because it is unique, creating unity through different peoples and cultures; it is a common value, just like truth, despite the diversity of languages and cultures. There is a valuable passage by Saint Irenaeus in the first book of *Against Heresies*: "The Church, although scattered all over the world, carefully guards [the faith of the Apostles], as if it lived in a single house; in the same way the Church believes in these truths, as if she had one soul and the same heart; in full agreement these truths proclaim, teach and transmit, as if it had only one mouth. The languages of the world are different, but the power of Tradition is unique and the same: the Churches founded in Germany have not received or transmit a different faith, nor those founded in Spain or in the eastern regions or in Egypt or in Libya or in the center of the world."[137] We already see at this moment, around 200, the universality of the church, its catholicity, and the unifying force of truth, which unites these very different realities, from Germany to Spain, Italy, Egypt, and Libya, in the common truth revealed to us by Christ.

3. Finally, the apostolic tradition is pneumatic, that is, guided by the Holy Spirit (in Greek, spirit is called *pneuma*). It is not, in fact, a transmission entrusted to the ability of more or less learned men, but to the Spirit of God, which guarantees the faithfulness of such transmission. This is the life of the church, what makes the church always fresh and young, that is, fruitful of multiple charisms. Church and Spirit, for Irenaeus, are inseparable: 'We have received this faith and we keep it: faith, by the work of the Spirit of God, as a precious deposit kept in a valuable vessel always rejuvenates and it also rejuvenates the vessel that contains it .... Where the Church is,

---

136. Irenaeus, *Contro le eresie (Against Heresies)*, bk 3, ch. 3, 3–4.
137. Irenaeus, *Contro le eresie (Against Heresies)*, bk 1, ch. 10, 1–2.

there is the Spirit of God; and where the Spirit of God is, there is the Church and all grace."[138]

In conclusion, Irenaeus defines the concept of tradition as a reality internally animated by the Holy Spirit, which makes it alive and understandable by the church. The faith of the church must be transmitted in such a way that it appears as what it is, public, unique, pneumatic, and spiritual. From each of these characteristics, a fruitful discernment can be conducted of the authentic transmission of faith in the church today. In the doctrine of Irenaeus, the dignity of the human being, body and soul, stands out, firmly anchored in the divine creation, in the image of Christ, and in the permanent work of sanctification of the Spirit. This doctrine is like a main road to clarify, together with all people of good will, the object and boundaries of the dialogue on values and to give ever new impetus to the missionary action of the church, to the force of truth, which is the source of all true values in the world.

## The Christian Canon

With this mighty construction, Irenaeus frames the structure of the church and its hierarchical architecture as it will be over the centuries. He does not stop here but addresses the fundamental question of the sources and, to be even clearer, indicates the writings to which the Christians must refer; those and only those, because the others are heretical writings aimed at confusing and diverting the thought of Christians. Thus, among the Gospels that were born and circulated after the death of Jesus—and we saw how many there were—Irenaeus indicates the Gospels of Mark, Matthew, Luke, and John as the only ones which narrate the life, events, and teachings of Jesus in a correct and true way, and to which Christians should refer. He therefore excluded all the other Gospels, because they were compromised by gnostic values, and considered them heretical. He called the four Gospels the Quadrangular Gospel. He wrote, in fact, that in the four Gospels, today called canonical, a single spirit blows and that therefore it is a single tetramorph gospel, and that no more than four Gospels were needed, nor any Gospels other than these traditional four.

To reinforce this statement, he first introduced a comparison between biblical tetramorphs, the fourfold Gospel and four characteristics of Christ (regal as the lion; sacrificial victim and priest, such as the calf

---

138. Irenaeus, *Contro le eresie (Against Heresies)*, bk 3, ch. 24, 1.

sacrificed in Yom Kippur by the high priest; man because born of woman; and eagle because from heaven, he pours out his Holy Spirit on the church). The idea was taken up and modified by Saint Jerome, according to whom the tetramorph summarizes the totality of the Christian mystery: incarnation (the winged man), passion (the calf), resurrection (the lion), and ascension (the eagle). Therefore it symbolizes the four phases of the life of Christ: born as a man, he died as a sacrificial calf and was a lion in resurrection and an eagle in ascending (*fuit homo nascendo, vitulus moriendo, leo resurgendo, aquila ascendendo*). Irenaeus also first associated the four zoomorphic beings of the Apocalypse with the evangelists on the basis of the characteristics of the Gospels. Irenaeus's proposal, however, was modified by Saint Jerome, whose proposal is the one used today in religious iconography. Irenaeus, in fact, associated John with the lion and Mark with the eagle.

Today, however, we consider the way in which the Gospels begin their story:

- Matthew is depicted as a man (similar to an angel; all the figures are in fact winged). Matthew's Gospel begins with the earthly ancestry of Jesus and later narrates the childhood of the Son of Man, thus underscoring his human side.
- Mark is depicted as a lion. In the Gospel of Mark, the beginning of the story is dedicated to John the Baptist, whose *vox clamantis* in the desert "rises like a lion's roar" in the desert.
- Luke is depicted as an ox or a calf, a symbol of the sacrifice of Zechariah, which opens the Gospel of Luke.
- John is depicted as an eagle, since his Gospel in fact has a more spiritual and theological vision, turned towards the Absolute.

The correspondence between evangelists and the faces of the tetramorph determines the order in which the Gospels are found in ancient codes and in today's printed Bibles. The order followed, in fact, is that of Ezekiel:[139] man (Matthew), lion (Mark), ox (Luke), eagle (John). Among

---

139. The use of representing the evangelists with animals and winged characters dates back to the prophet Ezekiel, who lived between the end of seventh and the beginning of sixth century BC. When deported to Babylon, he had the opportunity to often observe depictions of mysterious beings in the Mesopotamian palaces and temples. The prophet speaks in his visions (Ezek. 1:5–14) of four creatures, with the appearance of man, lion, ox, and eagle.

the most important ancient codes, only the Codex Bezae from Lyon does not respect this order. Lyon is in fact the city of Irenaeus; therefore in the code, the position of Mark and John is exchanged.

Irenaeus does not limit himself to attesting to the canonicity[140] of the four Gospels, that is to say their divine inspiration, but also declares that these are canonical:

- The Acts of the Apostles
- The letters of Saint Paul
- Saint Peter's letter
- Saint John's letter
- The Apocalypse of Saint John

All of these then were incorporated, together with the Gospels, in the Christian canon of the Hippo Council-Synod of 393.

Irenaeus also turned his thoughts to Our Lady with a profound Marian doctrine, which always unites the Mother with the work of the Redeemer Son and is an important basis for the possible definition of the dogma of Mary Coredemptrix,[141] still under discussion. Irenaeus, cited not by chance in the eighth chapter of *Lumen gentium*,[142] recognized in fact the very special role of Mary in the history of salvation and, on the basis of the Pauline teaching of Christ as the new Adam, wrote: "The knot of Eve's disobedience was untied by the obedience of Mary; what the virgin Eve bound by her unbelief, the Virgin Mary loosed by her faith."[143] For this reason he attributed to Our Lady the title of advocate, which over the centuries would become very dear to the faithful. It is almost difficult to believe that a single person, just at the beginning of Christianity,

---

140. The books of the Bible were born not only from the initiative of human authors (who are tools) but also from an implicit intention and will of God. It is really Word of God (not a sort of summary) expressed in human words. God is the author of Scriptures.

141. Mary co-redemptrix is an as yet undefined dogma that has opened up a vast discussion in the church.

142. *Lumen gentium*, the Dogmatic Constitution on the Church, is one of the principal documents of the Second Vatican Council. An apostolic constitution (Latin: constitutio apostolica) is the most solemn form of legislation issued by the Pope. By their nature, apostolic constitutions are addressed to the public. The forms dogmatic constitution and pastoral constitution are titles sometimes used to be more descriptive as to the document's purpose.

143. Irenaeus, *Contro le eresie (Against Heresies)*, bk 3, ch. 22, 4.

had the ability to conceive such a complete and exhaustive doctrinal and organizational framework, which was and is the pillar of faith that the church professes and transmits unchanged. With him, however, every authoritative personal relationship with God disappears, as perhaps it was in the first assemblies, because the Christian must always refer to, learn, and obey the authority of the apostolic succession and in particular that of the church of Rome. Thus he establishes the primacy that still lasts.

Irenaeus recalls, as seen before, that "it would be too long to list the successors of the Apostles in all the Churches; [we do this, I say] by indicating that tradition derived from the apostles, of the very great, the very ancient, and universally known Church founded and organized at Rome by the two most glorious apostles, Peter and Paul; as also [by pointing out] the faith preached to men, which comes down to our time by means of the successions of the bishops. For it is a matter of necessity that every Church should agree with this Church, on account of its pre-eminent authority, that is, the faithful everywhere, inasmuch as the apostolical tradition has been preserved continuously by those [faithful men] who exist everywhere."[144]

In the furrow traced by Irenaeus, the church continued in the following centuries, even if the divisions between the various churches did not disappear.

## The Growth of Christianity, Further Divisions, and the Struggle for Unity

### Constantine: Religious Peace for Political Peace

In 313 the so-called Edict of Milan was issued (also known as the Edict of Constantine or Edict of Tolerance), which is the agreement signed in February 313 by the two *Augusti*[145] of the Roman Empire, Constantine for the West and Licinius for the East, in view of a religious policy common to both sides of the empire, which gave Christians the power and freedom to freely profess their religion. We dwell, albeit briefly, on one

---

144. Irenaeus, *Contro le eresie (Against Heresies)*, bk 3, ch. 3, 1–2.

145. In AD 284, Emperor Diocletian attempted to remedy the difficult situation of defending the empire, dividing it into four parts and establishing the tetrarchy or government of four people: two emperors called Augusti, helped by two vice-emperors, called Caesares. The tetrarchs, each ruling only one part of the empire, could have better defended it.

of the two signatories, Constantine, because his acts would influence the history of the Church and the world.

> *Cum feliciter tam ego [quam] Constantinus Augustus quam etiam ego Licinius Augustus apud Mediolanum convenissemus atque universa quae ad ostril et securitatem publicam pertinerent, in tractatu haberemus, haec inter cetera quae videbamus pluribus hominibus profutura, vel in primis ordinanda esse credidimus, quibus divinitatis ostriltn continebatur, ut daremus et Christianis et omnibus liberam potestatem sequendi religionem quam quisque voluisset, quod quicquid [est] divinitatis in sede caelesti, nobis atque omnibus qui sub potestate nostra sunt ostrilt, placatum ac propitium possit existere.*
>
> We therefore, Costantinus Augustus and Licinius Augustus, having met successfully in Milan and having discussed all the topics relating to public utility and safety, among the provisions that we saw useful to many people or to be implemented among the first, we placed these related to the cult of divinity, so that Christians and all others are allowed the freedom to follow the religion that everyone believes, so that the divinity that is in heaven, whatever it may be, gives us and all our subjects peace and prosperity.[146]

Few months had gone by since the Battle of Milvian Bridge, and since the *In Hoc Signo Vinces* that changed history and religion, even if it was never understood exactly what the sign was—a cross according to legend, a Christogram according to history, a meteorite or a conjunction of planets according to astronomers; religious integration, more likely, according to the first Christian emperor. Among the most ambitious rulers of Roman history, Constantine was born in 274 from the union of Constantius Chlorus and his concubine Elena and had grown up in the East at the court of Diocletian, during the tetrarchy that saw the empire administered by two Caesars and two Augusti. After the death of his father—Caesar, later Augustus of the West—in 306, Constantine had been acclaimed as his successor by his militias. Wars followed, which had

---

146. Constantine, cited in Lactantius, "De mortibus persecutorum," §48.

seen the pretender ally himself with Licinius[147] against Maxentius[148] and Maximinus Daia.[149]

Taking advantage of the power vacuum left by the two West Tetrarchs (who had chosen Trier and Milan as their capitals), General Maxentius had become the master of Rome, where only the Senate remained, but, after a series of battles, on 28 October 312, Constantine had definitively beaten him at Milvian Bridge, taking control of all Italy. According to tradition, when he was still in Turin, Constantine had turned in prayer to the "only God," and shortly after noon he had witnessed the appearance of a crossing of lights above the sun with the writing *en touto nika*, or "in this (sign) you win." The next night Christ appeared to him, ordering him to adopt the sign he had seen in heaven as his banner. In the following days Constantine called some Christian priests, in order to be educated in their religion, the content of which was still unknown to him.

In battle, Constantine therefore had his troops preceded by the imperial insignia with the monogram of Christ, formed by the letters XP (which are the first two Greek letters of the word *Christòs*) superimposed. Under these insignia the soldiers defeated their adversary. Maxentius, a pagan, drowned in the collapse of Milvian Bridge which he himself had built, and the new emperor converted to Christianity—at least according to tradition. In reality Constantine would be baptized only twenty-five years later, and throughout his life, he would maintain a certain religious ambiguity. What is sure, however, is that Constantine—on that occasion—had refused to consult the haruspices before battle, and when he

---

147. Licinius (Valerius Licinianus Licinius, c. 265–325) was Roman emperor from AD 308 to 324. For most of his reign he was the colleague and rival of Constantine I, with whom he co-authored the Edict of Milan (313) that granted official toleration to Christians in the Roman Empire. He was finally defeated at the Battle of Chrysopolis (324) and was later executed on the orders of Constantine I.

148. Maxentius (Marcus Aurelius Valerius Maxentius, c. 276–28 Oct. 312) was Roman emperor from 306 to 312. He was the son of former Emperor Maximian and the son-in-law of Emperor Galerius. The latter part of his reign was preoccupied with civil war, allying with Maximinus II against Licinius and Constantine. The latter defeated him at the Battle of the Milvian Bridge in 312, where Maxentius, with his army in flight, purportedly perished by drowning in the Tiber River.

149. Maximinus Daia or Daza (Galerius Valerius Maximinus, 20 Nov. c. 270–July or Aug. 313), also Maximinus II, was Roman emperor from 308 to 313. He became embroiled in the civil wars of the tetrarchy between rival claimants for control of the empire, in which he was defeated by Licinius. A committed pagan, he engaged in one of the last persecutions of Christians.

entered Rome in triumph, he avoided going up to the capitol, where the holiest temple of heathen gods was located.

Today there are the most disparate hypotheses regarding what the emperor saw in Turin (some hypothesized a conjuncture between planets called "the swan's cross") and what exactly was the meaning of that phrase passed into history in Latin, even if actually pronounced in Greek. Many argue that Constantine did not entrust the fate of the battle to Jesus Christ but to the sun god (whose symbol—a cross superimposed on an X with a circle in the center—looks very much like the monogram of Christ). But for him, Constantine, this didn't make much difference. The difference, for the emperor, lay rather between the Olympus of the gods and the unique and almighty God he had chosen to venerate. Constantine had stopped believing in Jupiter, Juno, Mars, and all the tales of Olympus for years. He had stopped participating in the sacrifices for Saturn and all the other gods. Just superstition, he thought. Nobody really believed in those stories, in the gossip about the gods. It was clear to everyone that that was a divine world made to measure for the human world, with lies, betrayals, rivalries, and wars. They were just stories to tell and simple sacrifices to ward off bad luck.

But the sun was a true god: he was completely different from the other gods and completely different from humans. He was there, on top of the sky. All humans could see it, and all humans experienced his power every day. Humanity owed him light and warmth. Without him, plants did not grow, animals were not born. Without him, humans were lost. The cold assailed them, and in the darkness they could not move; they could not defend themselves from dangers or see what surrounded them. The further away he was, the more difficult life was for humans. During the winter, he moved away, and the cold increased, the hours of light were shorter, and food was scarce.

He was a strange god, the most beautiful and powerful thing that could be admired in the sky. Yet, every day, he slowly went out, descended from the summit of heaven, fell under the earth, and died. And every day, he rose again, rising on the horizon to ascend his throne in the sky. A passion and glory that were renewed every day, every year. Every night, the moon was the bearer of hope for a new day; every day, the withering of light was the announcement of a night that would come. Each summer was spent in the heat and light, waiting with fear for the cold of winter. And every harsh winter had to be faced courageously in the certainty of a new summer.

Aurelian[150] had officially consecrated the *Sol Invictus* temple in AD 274, dedicating to the sun the feast of December 25 and making him the main deity of the Roman pantheon. With the passage of time, the young Constantine, born together with Sol Invictus, had become increasingly devoted to him. He loved to participate in the cults in the temple, to observe the songs and prayers that went up together with the smoke of the sacrifices, until, as they reached the sky, he would give thanks for the sun's giving humanity a new spring, new light, new warmth, new life, new hope. That it was the sign of Christ or the sign of the sun that gave him the victory at Milvian Bridge, then, changed very little. After all, Constantine did not see much difference. Christ, like the sun, cyclically lived a story made of glory, passion, death, and resurrection. And the God of Christians was unique, Father and omnipotent, exactly like the one whose protection he had invoked when going down to the Eternal City.

In the meantime, Emperor Galerius[151] had already issued, the previous year, an edict to end the fiercest and bloodiest persecution of Christians, initiated by Diocletian in 303. Diocletian had been a particularly conservative emperor from a religious point of view, even though it was Galerius himself, at the time his deputy, who instigated him against the Christians. At first the persecution had concerned only the heresy of the Manicheans, a foreign religion arrived from the East and accused of fomenting disorder and instability, while the persecution against Christianity as a whole had started on 17 November 303, with the torture and execution of the deacon Romanus of Caesarea,[152] guilty of refusing to per-

---

150. Aurelian was Roman emperor from AD 214 or 215 to 275. After becoming emperor, Aurelian devoted himself with admirable energy and ability to restoring order and security to imperial forces, defeating barbarians, rebels, and usurpers. In addition, he restored the state administration, harnessed the hostile senatorial party, and attributed to the imperial figure divine character, on the Asian model. Under his reign, the city of Rome was equipped with the mighty walls that take its name.

151. Galerius (Gaius Galerius Valerius Maximianus, c. 250–Apr. or May 311) was Roman emperor from AD 305 to 311. Although he was a staunch opponent of Christianity, Galerius ended the Diocletianic Persecution when he issued an Edict of Toleration in Serdica in 311.

152. Saint Romanus of Caesarea (also known as Romanus of Antioch) is venerated as a martyr. In 303 or 304, at the beginning of the Diocletianic Persecution, a deacon called Romanus of Caesarea in Palestine suffered martyrdom at Antioch. He was taken prisoner, condemned to death by fire, and bound to the stake; however, as Emperor Galerius was then in Antioch, Romanus was brought before him. At the emperor's command, Romanus's tongue was cut out. Tortured in various ways in prison, he was finally strangled.

form divinatory acts. Diocletian at first had thought of limiting himself to preventing Christians from holding political and military positions, but Galerius had convinced him of the need for a real extermination, if he wanted to ward off the wrath of the gods, outraged by the impiety of the new sect arrived from Palestine and increasingly widespread in Rome. The Christians, argued Galerius, had created a state within the state, which was governed by its own laws and magistrates, possessed a treasury, and maintained cohesio,n thanks to the work of the bishops, who directed the various congregations of the faithful to whom they were in charge through decrees which they obeyed blindly. Therefore, it was necessary to intervene before Christianity irreparably contaminated the ranks of the army. Power had to break down that counterpower that refused any assimilation. According to tradition, Apollo himself confirmed the need for drastic intervention, because the presence of ungodly men prevented him—according to the oracle—from providing his help.

On 23 February 303, in Nicomedia,[153] capital of the Eastern Empire, an edict was posted which ordered the burning of sacred books, the confiscation of church goods and their destruction, the prohibition for Christians to gather and attempt any kind of defense in legal actions, the loss of office and privileges for high-ranking Christians, the impossibility of achieving honors and jobs for Christians free-born and of obtaining freedom for Christian slaves, as well as arrest of some Christian state officials. After a couple of attacks suffered by Diocletian's residence, then, the persecution had become even more ferocious: arrests, torture, and executions had increased exponentially in the East and in Rome, whereas, in Britain, the father of Constantine had been much less intransigent. What is certain is that Diocletian's action failed miserably. Christianity had emerged strengthened by persecutions: the martyrs had become models of faith, still revered today, while the pagans themselves had ended up in solidarity with the victims of this religious cleansing. In 305, Diocletian—a unique case in the history of the Roman empire—resigned spontaneously, giving way to Galerius himself, who continued the persecutions, albeit intermittently, until 311, when he signed in Sofia[154] a

---

153. Nicomedia was an ancient Greek city in Turkey. In 286, Nicomedia became the eastern and most senior capital city of the Roman Empire (chosen by Diocletian, who assumed the title Augustus of the East), a status which the city maintained during the tetrarchy system (293–324).

154. The Edict of Serdica, also called the Edict of Toleration, was issued in 311 in Serdica (today Sofia, Bulgaria) by the Roman emperor Galerius, officially ending

surrender of sorts, with an edict on behalf of the whole tetrarchic college, published on April 30. It says:

"Considering our benevolence and the custom for which we are used to grant forgiveness to all, we have decided to extend our clemency to their chance, and without any delay, so that there are Christians again and the buildings in which they used to gather are reconstructed, on condition that they do not abandon themselves to actions contrary to the established order. With another document we will give instructions to the governors on what they will have to observe. Therefore, in accordance with our forgiveness, Christians will have to pray to their god for our health, that of the state, and of themselves, so that the integrity of the state is restored everywhere and they can lead a peaceful life in their homes."[155]

In reality, those instructions would never been issued because of Galerius's death. For this reason, in February 313, the two masters of the Empire met in Milan to discuss them and sign a joint document. Diocletian, who retired to a splendid villa in Split, at the same time had received an invitation to the wedding between Constantia, Constantine's sister, and Licinius, who succeeded Galerius as emperor of the Orient. Diocletian would die, significantly, on the eve of the Edict of Milan with which Constantine and Licinius formalized his defeat, officially and definitively clearing the Christian religion in the Roman Empire. It was especially Constantine who insisted on the rehabilitation of Christians; his sympathies for the church are certainly not a secret. Licinius, on the contrary, remained faithful to traditional religion but understood that religious peace was fundamental for the stability of the empire—the more in his part of the empire, which was where the persecutions were more ruthless and where the Christians were still subject to discrimination and forms of intolerance. His rival Maximinus Daia had restarted capital executions in the territories under his jurisdiction. Licinius, for his part, after defeating Maximinus in April, again allowed Christians to build places of worship and returned all confiscated property to them. If you can't beat them—both emperors thought—make them friends. The integration of Christians and their system of power within the empire could not be separated from their emancipation.

---

the Diocletianic Persecution of Christianity in the East. The edict implicitly granted Christianity the status of *religio licita*, a worship recognized and accepted by the Roman Empire. It was the first edict legalizing Christianity, preceding the Edict of Milan by two years.

155. Galerius, cited in Lactantius, "De mortibus persecutorum," §34.

More than the start of a Christianization of the empire, however, the Edict of Milan represents a model of integration. If in the text there was open talk of religious freedom for Christians, it was also added that the same had to be guaranteed to the faithful of any other creed, while religious reference was to a generic divinity—"whatever it is"—from whom protection is invoked. Constantine had no intention of changing the religious split of the empire, in which 90 percent of the population still followed traditional pagan cults. On the contrary, the emperor wanted to create a religious balance: he no longer wanted faith to be an element of tension, division, discrimination, and conflict. Roman peace passed through freedom and integration. And of this peace and integration was Constantine himself the guarantor. It is no coincidence that, while approaching ever more openly to Christianity, he held the position of Pontifex Maximus of traditional religion, had pagan temples built, and promoted the worship of the sun with ever greater force.

Paradoxically, while convening and presiding in Nicea over the first great Ecumenical Council, called to debate theological questions on the nature of Christ and to affirm a unique, clear, and definitive doctrine for the whole church by expelling the heretics, Constantine pursued a syncretism[156] that blended the cult of Christ, that of Mithras, and that of the sun in a single religion, in which all Roman citizens could recognize themselves. In particular, Constantine was interested in identifying Christ with the sun. It is not by chance that he chose the feast of Sol Invictus—December 25—as the date of Christmas and Sunday as the public holiday of the week, calling it Day of the Sun, while assigning the others six days to the old pagan deities: Moon, Mars, Mercury, Jupiter, Venus, and Saturn. On the other hand, the social crisis of the empire and the influence of Eastern spiritualities had put the ancient Roman religious system in crisis for some time, and a syncretism veined with monotheism had spread, which tended to see in the images of the traditional gods the expression of a single divine being. The religious model of Constantine, therefore, was that of a plurality of rites in the unity of God—a God who could take on different names, but who remained a Father, protective and omnipotent. In 316, during the war against Licinius to take control of the whole empire, Constantine would dedicate the coins "to Sol Invictus, minister of the Lord" even though, in the meantime, in some private

---

156. Religious syncretism is the blending of two or more religious belief systems into a new system, or the incorporation into a religious tradition of beliefs from unrelated traditions.

letters, he wrote of wanting to convert the whole world to Catholicism. More than a Christian then, Constantine—at least publicly—was a convinced monotheist and a great promoter of ecumenism, who tried to unify faiths related one to another and also foster respect for other ones.

The most sublime synthesis of Constantine's religious policy remains the column (made of porphyry from Heliopolis in Egypt, the city of the sun) erected in the new capital he founded, Constantinople. According to tradition, the palladium (the most important propitiatory simulacrum of the Roman religion) and some fragments of the cross of Christ found by Saint Helena in Palestine were buried under its base, while on the top there was a statue depicting the emperor, in dress of solar divinity with gaze turned to the rising sun, on the head a seven-rayed crown and on the right hand the globe with the cross. An inscription read "Constantine, who shines like the sun." Divine and devoted at the same time. Constantine, therefore, wanted peace, but the Christian communities were far from at peace. The divisions persisted, and indeed two disruptive cases arose against their unity. The first was Donatism.

## Donatism

Donatism was a Christian religious movement which arose in Africa in 311 from the ideas of the bishop of Numidia, Donatus of Casae Nigrae,[157] called Magnus for his remarkable eloquence. His doctrine began with an uncompromising criticism of those bishops who had not resisted the persecutions of Diocletian and had handed over the sacred books to Roman magistrates. According to Donatists, the sacraments administered by these bishops (called *traditores*, as they had performed a *traditio*, the surrender of sacred texts to the pagans) were not valid. This position presupposed therefore that the sacraments were not effective by themselves, but that their validity depended on the worthiness of those who administered them. The Catholic Church, instead, readmitted those sinners after the sacrament of penance; moreover, the mixture of good and bad had to be allowed, since not even the apostles, according to the Gospel parable (Matt 13:24–30), were allowed to separate the wheat from the chaff before the harvest. The two positions were irreconcilable and led

---

157. Donatus Magnus, also known as Donatus of Casae Nigrae, became leader of a schismatic sect known as the Donatists in North Africa. He is believed to have died in exile around 355. Little is known of his early life because of the complete loss of his correspondence and written works.

to a schism, which materialized as an official schism with the Council of Carthage (311), strongly advocated for by Donatus, which deposed the newly elected bishop of Carthage, the former *traditor* Caecilian.

On behalf of Emperor Constantine, who, as we have seen, intended to maintain peace in the Empire, the schism was judged in a council held in Rome on 2 September 313, with the participation of nineteen bishops presided over by Pope Miltiades.[158] The council declared the decision of the Council of Carthage invalid and confirmed the ordination of Caecilian, who was absent at that council and could not defend himself. Finally, Donatus was declared heretical.

The Donatists demanded a second trial, held outside the city of Rome, to review the cause. Constantine in 314 convened in Arles a new and more numerous council of bishops, which confirmed the sentence of the conference in Rome; but even that ruling of Arles was not accepted by the Donatists.

At this point, the emperor called the two competing bishops to appear before his court in Milan. There he decided in favor of Caecilian, then ordered that the churches occupied by the Donatists be seized and the penalty of exile and confiscation be applied to the schismatics. Not even these measures helped, though, and after five years of unrest and struggles, the emperor, having understood that even force was powerless to resolve questions of faith, decided to tolerate schismatics and convinced Catholics that the best thing to do was to wait for better times. Donatus was surprised in exile by death in 355, but his party remained alive and well, despite imperial proscriptions. Julian the Apostate,[159] meanwhile risen to the imperial throne, issued an edict in 362, allowing all exiled bishops to return to their seats. The Donatists also recovered their lost churches, with recourse to real massacres and barbaric retaliations, driven by thirst for revenge against the Catholics. Donatism was definitively condemned in the Council of Carthage in 411, but remained nonetheless present and well-rooted in northern Africa until the Arab conquest.

---

158. Pope Miltiades or Melchiades was bishop of Rome from 311 to his death on 10 or 11 Jan. 314. It was during his pontificate that Emperor Constantine the Great issued the Edict of Milan (313), giving Christianity legal status within the Roman Empire.

159. Julian (Flavius Claudius Julianus, 331–26 June 363) was Roman emperor from 361 to 363, as well as a notable philosopher and author in Greek. His rejection of Christianity and his promotion of Neoplatonic Hellenism in its place caused him to be remembered as Julian the Apostate by the Christian church.

The second, even more explosive disturbance, was Arianism.

## Arianism

Arianism is the name of a Christological doctrine, condemned in the first council of Nicea (325), elaborated by the presbyter, monk, and Christian theologian Arius.[160] He maintained that the divine nature of the Son was substantially inferior to that of God, that therefore there was a time when the Word of God did not exist, and that therefore it was only created later.

After the Constantinian edict of tolerance of 313, the Trinitarian controversy opened in Alexandria, Egypt, and the theses that the presbyter Arius had begun to spread extended to involve an increasing number of people (in reality, Arius did nothing more than organize theologically the interpretation of Christianity by previous thinkers, including Origen and Lucian of Antioch).[161] The bishop Alexander[162] condemned his positions as heretical in a synod composed of one hundred African bishops, held in 318, but Arius could count on a very large party of the faithful, which also included some bishops, both African and Eastern, including Eusebius of Caesarea and Eusebius of Nicomedia, who enjoyed a strong prestige even in the imperial court. The dispute opposed for years the Egyptian clergy to the Antiochene clergy (in particular Palestine and Bithynia),[163] attracting the attention of the emperor and the people. In an attempt to put an end to the question, which Constantine had initially underestimated, in 325 he called, also under pressure from his ecclesiastical advisers, who were very informed on the dispute, the Ecumenical Council of Nicea.

---

160. Arius (Libya, 256–Constantinople, 336) was a Christian priest and theologian. The Christian theological current that arose around his religious doctrines was condemned as heretical in the First Council of Nicaea and was later indicated with the name of Arianism. It spread mainly among Germanic peoples.

161. Saint Lucian of Antioch (c. 240–Jan. 7, 312), known as Lucian the Martyr, was a Christian presbyter, theologian, and martyr. Lucian is commonly credited with a critical recension of the text of the Septuagint and the Greek New Testament.

162. Alexander I of Alexandria, nineteenth pope and patriarch of Alexandria. During his patriarchate, he dealt with a number of issues facing the church in that day. He was the leader of the opposition to Arianism at the First Council of Nicaea. He also is remembered for being the mentor of the man who would be his successor, Athanasius of Alexandria, who would become one of the leading Church Fathers.

163. Bithynia was an ancient region, kingdom, and Roman province in the northwest of Asia Minor, adjoining the Sea of Marmara, the Bosporus, and the Black Sea.

The convocation of the council was not, however, of only religious importance. The emperor, as we have seen, was, above all, concerned with the stability of the state. Theological questions, with the unrest and disputes that ensued, constituted a political problem that had to be resolved with the defeat of either of the two factions. In fact, Constantine had no theological convictions that made him lean particularly towards one or the other party in conflict. At the council, Arius and Eusebius of Caesarea did not convince the assembly. Their argument was as follows: if the Son of God was not equal to the Father, then he was not even divine, or at least not as much as the Father. This was not acceptable to the orthodox. The thesis that "there was a time when the Son was not there" horrified the council fathers, who placed in the minority and definitively condemned Arius's ideas. The council elaborated a symbol, that is, a dogmatic definition relating to faith in God, in which appears, attributed to Christ, the term *homooùsios* (translated from Latin as consubstantial [with the Father], but in Greek of equal essence), which constitutes the dogmatic basis of historical Christianity. In the absence of the bishop of Rome, Sylvester I[164] (who sent his legates), Bishop Hosius of Cordoba[165] presided over the assembly. He was a favorite of the emperor (present at all the sessions), and his influence on the emperor himself made an easy game of swaying the sovereign to the cause of orthodoxy. The heretics were threatened with exile, and Arius was banished and sent to Illyria.[166]

The lack of solidity of Constantine's theological convictions is however demonstrated by the fact that, in just three years, his positions towards Arianism had become absolutely indulgent and tolerant. At the suggestion of his sister Constantia and at the insistence of Eusebius of Nicomedia, the exile for Arian bishops was revoked. Arius himself was later recalled (in 331 or 334) and introduced to the court, where he managed to convince the emperor of the goodness of his opinions, although

---

164. Sylvester I (also Silvester, died 31 Dec. 335) was bishop of Rome from 314 until his death. He is regarded as the thirty-third pope of the Catholic Church.

165. Hosius of Corduba (c. 256–359), also known as Osius or Ossius, was bishop of Corduba (now Córdoba, Spain) and an important and prominent advocate for Homoousion Christianity in the Arian controversy that divided early Christianity. He likely presided at the First Council of Nicaea and also presided at the Council of Serdica. He was a close Christian advisor to Emperor Constantine the Great.

166. In classical antiquity, Illyria was a region in the western part of the Balkan Peninsula. The Roman province of Illyricum stretched from modern Albania to Istria (Croatia) in the west and to the Sava River (Bosnia and Herzegovina) in the north. Salona (near modern Split in Croatia) functioned as its capital.

they were heretical, so that Constantine himself restored him and sentenced to exile bishop Athanasius of Alexandria, who had been among the most acrimonious opponents of Arius. The Arian Eusebius of Nicomedia replaced Hosius of Cordoba in the role of imperial ecclesiastical adviser, eventually baptizing the emperor on his deathbed.

The Nicene affirmation that defined that Son as much God as the Father, however, posed at least three major questions in the Arian but also in the orthodox environment:

1. Can God generate a Son?
2. Can God separate himself?
3. Can God die (on the cross or in any other way)?

The followers of Arius brought to the extreme the answers to these three questions, which had in common the conclusion that the Son was not divine in nature but, as a creature of God, was an intermediary or medium between divinity and humanity.

Arianism is the Christian heresy which, more than any other, had the serious possibility of becoming the official doctrine of the church. From the fourth to the seventh century, it was adopted by bishops, emperors, local churches, and entire nations and had millions of followers. Arianism, in fact, was particularly successful under the emperors Constantius II[167] (son of Constantine I, 337–61 AD), Valens[168] (364–78 AD) and in the last phase of the Roman Empire. Constantius, unlike his brothers Constans[169] and Constantine II,[170] was of Arian tendency. Following the fratricidal wars and his definitive supremacy (350), Constantius was able to devote himself, in the last decade of his reign, to the resolution of Christological questions. During this period, in fact, Constantius convened many provincial councils appointed to define the Christian

---

167. Constantius II (Flavius Julius Constantius, 7 Aug. 317–3 Nov. 361) was Roman emperor from AD 337 to 361.

168. Flavius Valens (328–9 Aug. 378) was Eastern Roman emperor from AD 364 to 378. He was given the eastern half of the empire by his brother Valentinian I after the latter's accession to the throne. Valens was defeated and killed in the Battle of Adrianople, which marked the beginning of the collapse of the Western Roman Empire.

169. Constans (Flavius Julius Constans, 320–350) or Constans I was Roman emperor from AD 337 to 350.

170. Constantine II (Flavius Claudius Constantinus, Feb. 316–340) was Roman emperor from AD 337 to 340.

Creed: Sirmium[171] (351), Arles (353), Milan (355), Sirmium II (357), Rimini[172] (359), and finally Constantinople (360). The most important, due to the effects it caused in the West, however, was Sirmium II of 357, in which only bishops from the East (mainly Arians) participated and which banned terms such as ousìa[173] and consubstantiality. The bishops of the West (closer to the church in Rome and therefore faithful to the Nicene Creed), expressed their dissent. Pope Liberius and Hosius of Corduba were imprisoned and forced to submit to the decisions of Sirmium, whereas in the council of Rimini (or Ariminum, according to the Latin toponym) of 359, Sirmium was overruled and condemned. Constantius eventually tried to find a compromise formula in the Council of Seleucia in 359, which instead saw the triumph of Arian positions, reaffirmed by the Council of Constantinople the following year. Unrest and violence occurred in several other circumstances, such as on the occasion of the succession to Bishop Alexander of Constantinople;[174] the Arian Macedonius[175] obtained the episcopal see only by force and military intervention, after his rival Paul, closer to the church of Rome, was kidnapped, exiled, and murdered. The popular uprisings that followed Macedonius's settlement were stifled in blood. The same bishop felt authorized by the imperial authority of Constantius, who protected him and had favored his appointment, to impose his ministry also with torture and the force of arms. Even in the Nicene West there were repercussions on appointment of bishops. In Milan, Dionysius[176] was exiled by the emperor and the Arian Auxentius[177] imposed as his successor.

---

171. Sirmium was a city in the Roman province of Pannonia, located on the Sava River, on the site of modern Sremska Mitrovica in northern Serbia.

172. Rimini (Latin: Ariminum) is a city in the Emilia-Romagna region of northern Italy, on the Adriatic Sea.

173. In Christian theology, the concept of θεία ουσία (*Theia ousia*, divine essence), is one of the most important doctrinal concepts, central to the development of trinitarian doctrine.

174. Alexander of Constantinople (c. 237/240–c. 340) was bishop of Byzantium and the first archbishop of Constantinople (the city was renamed during his episcopacy), a strong opponent of Arianism.

175. Macedonius (d. after 360) was a Greek bishop of Constantinople from 342 up to 346 and from 351 until 360.

176. Dionysius was bishop of Milan from 349 to 355. He is honored as a saint in the Catholic and Eastern Orthodox Churches.

177. Auxentius of Milan or of Cappadocia (c. 355–374) was an Arian theologian and bishop of Milan. Because of his Arian faith, Auxentius is considered by the

Julian, openly pro-pagan, revoked all those beneficiary laws that his immediate predecessors had promulgated towards Christians. In his opinion, Christianity had to weaken more and more, through the flourishing of the theological disputes silenced a few years earlier by Constantius, and for this reason the new emperor had Christians of Nicene faith recalled from exile.

After the short reign of Jovian,[178] the empire returned to be divided into two sections: the *Pars Occidentalis* was entrusted to Valentinian I,[179] the *Pars Orientalis* to Valens. If Valentinian, a Christian like Jovian, maintained a tolerant policy towards all religious faiths, his younger brother Valens was a fanatic supporter of Arianism and restored the ecclesiastical dispositions of Constantius. The climate of terror and oppression that Valens established in the eastern area of the empire ended with his defeat and killing in the great battle of Adrianople (378), fought against the Goths.

## The Defeat of Arianism and the Definition of Catholic Doctrine: The Creed

In 380, under the influence of the bishop of Milan, Ambrose,[180] the edict of Thessalonica was issued by Theodosius I[181] and Gratian,[182] which defined the Nicene Creed (and therefore orthodoxy) as a state religion.

---

Catholic Church as an intruder, and he is not included in the Catholic lists of the bishops of Milan such as that engraved in the Cathedral of Milan.

178. Jovian (Flavius Jovianus, 331–17 Feb. 364) was Roman emperor from AD June 363 to Feb. 364.

179. Valentinian I (Flavius Valentinianus, 3 July 321–17 Nov. 375), also known as Valentinian the Great, was Roman emperor from AD 364 to 375. Upon becoming emperor, he made his brother Valens his co-emperor, giving him rule of the eastern provinces while Valentinian retained the west.

180. Aurelius Ambrosius (c. 340–397), better known in English as Ambrose, was bishop of Milan, a theologian, and one of the most influential ecclesiastical figures of the fourth century.

181. Theodosius I (11 Jan. 347–17 Jan. 395), also known as Theodosius the Great, was Roman emperor from AD 379 to 395. Theodosius is considered a saint by the Armenian Apostolic Church and Eastern Orthodox Church.

182. Gratian (18 April/23 May 359–25 Aug. 383) was Roman emperor from AD 367 to 383.

*IMPPP. GR(ATI)ANUS, VAL(ENTINI)ANUS ET THE(O)D(OSIUS) AAA. EDICTUM AD POPULUM VRB(IS) CONSTANTINOP(OLITANAE).*

*Cunctos ostril, quos clementiae nostrae regit temperamentum, in tali volumus religione versari, quam divinum Petrum apostolum tradidisse Romanis religio usque ad nunc ab ipso ostrilt ostrilt quamque pontificem Damasum sequi claret et Petrum Aleksandriae episcopum virum apostolicae sanctitatis, hoc est, ut secundum apostolicam disciplinam evangelicamque doctrinam patris et filii et spiritus sancti unam deitatem sub pari maiestate et sub pia trinitate credamus. Hanc legem sequentes Christianorum catholicorum nomen iubemus amplecti, reliquos vero dementes vesanosque iudicantes haeretici dogmatis infamiam sustinere 'nec conciliabula eorum ecclesiarum nomen accipere', divina primum vindicta, post etiam motus ostril, quem ex caelesti arbitro sumpserimus, ultione plectendos.*

*DAT. III Kal. Mar. THESSAL(ONICAE) GR(ATI)ANO A. V ET THEOD(OSIO) A. I CONSS.*

*EMPERORS GRATIAN, VALENTINIAN AND THEODOSIUS AUGUSTI. EDICT TO THE PEOPLE OF CONSTANTINOPLE*

*We want all the peoples we deign to keep under our rule to follow the religion that St. Peter the Apostle taught the Romans, today professed by Pope Damasus[183] and Peter,[184] bishop of Alexandria, a man of apostolic holiness; that is, in accordance with apostolic teaching and gospel doctrine, three equal persons are believed in the one divinity of the Father, the Son and the Holy Spirit. Those who follow this rule will be called Catholic Christians, while others will be considered foolish heretics; we will not attribute the name of church to their meetings. They will be condemned first of all by divine punishment, then by our authority, which comes to us from the Heavenly Judge.*

---

183. Pope Damasus I (c. 305–11 Dec. 384) was bishop of Rome from Oct. 366 to his death. He presided over the Council of Rome of 382 that determined the canon or official list of sacred Scripture. He is recognized as a saint by the Catholic Church and the Eastern Orthodox Church.

184. Pope Peter I of Alexandria (died 311) was the seventeenth pope and patriarch of Alexandria. He is revered as a saint by the Coptic Orthodox Church, the Eastern Orthodox Church, and the Catholic Church.

GIVEN IN THESSALONICA ON THE THIRD DAY FROM THE CALENDS OF MARCH, DURING THE FIFTH CONSULATE OF GRATIAN AUGUSTUS AND FIRST OF THEODOSIUS AUGUSTUS.

In addition to the affirmation of the Nicene formula, which therefore removed the Arian doctrines, the edict defined for the first time the church which professed the Nicene Creed as catholic (from the Greek *katholikòs*, universal) and orthodox (from the Greek *orthos-doxa*, of right doctrine), marking all the other Christian groups as heretics and as such subject to punishment. It was, in fact, a bloodless anti-Arian persecution, in which bishops were removed and all the churches entrusted to the control of Catholics, excluding Arians from any place of worship even where, as in Constantinople, their community was by far more numerous.

Right in the capital of the empire, Emperor Theodosius himself replaced Bishop Demophilus[185] with Gregory Nazianzen,[186] bringing him almost in triumph through the streets of the city and protecting his position with a department of armed imperial guards. The bishop deplored having to be protected by weapons, among people who looked at him angrily and considered him an enemy; it seemed more like the entrance by a barbarian invader into a conquered city. No less passionate and violent was the dispute that took place in the West between Ambrose, bishop of Milan, and the Arian empress Justina,[187] mother and regent of the future emperor Valentinian II.[188] The condemnation of Arianism was then reiterated in 381 during the first council of Constantinople, right in the city which, despite the edict, had somehow managed to preserve a populous Arian colony that housed all the heretics of various denominations. In the

---

185. Demophilus (died 386) was an Arian bishop of Berea and an archbishop of Constantinople from 370 until he was expelled in 380.

186. Gregory of Nazianzus (c. 329-25 Jan. 390), also known as Gregory the Theologian or Gregory Nazianzen, was a fourth-century archbishop of Constantinople and a theologian. Gregory made a significant impact on the shape of Trinitarian theology among both Greek- and Latin-speaking theologians, and he is remembered as the Trinitarian Theologian. Gregory is a saint in both Eastern and Western Christianity. In the Catholic Church, he is numbered among the Doctors of the Church; in the Eastern Orthodox Church and the Eastern Catholic Churches, he is revered as one of the Three Holy Hierarchs, along with Basil the Great and John Chrysostom.

187. Justina (c. 340-c. 388) was the second wife of the Roman Emperor Valentinian I (reigned AD 364 to 375) and the mother of Valentinian II, Galla, Grata, and Justa.

188. Valentinian II (Flavius Valentinianus Augustus, 371-15 May 392) was Roman emperor from AD 375 to 392.

following years, Theodosius reiterated with a series of edicts his persecution against the Arian heresy, which provided for the prohibition of worship meetings, the dismissal and imposition of strong fines on bishops and priests, the exclusion from honorable and lucrative professions, and (since the Arians separated the nature of the Father from that of the Son) inhibition of the ability of testamentary bequests. In some cases, even capital sentences were pronounced, although rarely carried out, because Theodosius was actually more inclined to correction than to punishment. By entrusting the execution of his edicts to a host of officials, the emperor basically created the seed of an inquisition office. The Edict of Thessalonica is considered important by historians, as it initiated a process according to which "for the first time a doctrinal truth was imposed as state law and, consequently, religious dissidence was juridically transformed into *crimen publicum*: now heretics could and should be persecuted as public danger and enemies of the state."[189] It should also be noted that throughout the Roman Empire and even during the Exarchate of Italy[190] (which lasted until 752), the church did not have civil or judicial power, which remained the monopoly of the state.

The creed, in Catholic liturgy and devotion, is the profession of faith that the community of the faithful makes in liturgical moments, mainly in the Eucharistic celebrations of Sundays and liturgical solemnities. The liturgy proposes two formulas for the creed:

- The Apostolic Symbol: it is a second-century text, born in the liturgy of baptism.
- The Nicene-Constantinopolitan Symbol: it is a development of the previous one, enriched with the Christological affirmations defined in the Council of Nicea and with the pneumatological affirmations of faith defined in the First Council of Constantinople.

In the rite of baptism, the mode in the form of questions and answers is preferred. To the questions of the presbyter or the bishop on the three articles of faith of the Apostolic Symbol, the cathecumens respond together, "Yes, I believe." After that, they are baptized. This method can also be used in the Eucharistic celebration and is mandatory in the liturgy

---

189. Filoramo, *La croce e il potere*, xii.

190. The Exarchate of Ravenna or of Italy was a lordship of the Eastern Roman Empire (today referred to by some as the Byzantine Empire) in Italy from 584 to 751, when the last exarch was put to death by the Lombards.

of the Easter Vigil. Although the creed is recited as if it were a prayer, it is not in its own way, but it is precisely a solemn declaration of the main articles of the faith, that is, a summary of the main dogmas.

The Nicene-Constantinopolitan symbol has been a source of controversy between the Catholic Church and the Orthodox Church, over the question of the *filioque* clause. This was an expression added by the Latin Church to the Nicene-Constantinopolitan Creed to better explain the procession of the Holy Spirit—*qui ex Patre Filioque procedit*. It was one of the main causes of dissent and separation between the Greek and Latin churches and also one of the most controversial points at the Council of Florence (1439), which however ended up accepting it, considering it had been added "lawfully and reasonably."

The Nicene-Constantinopolitan symbol used in the liturgy of the Roman rite mass can be replaced by the Symbol of the Apostles, also called the baptismal symbol of the Roman Church, in particular during Lent and Easter.

This is the Nicene Symbol:

> We believe in one God, the Father Almighty, Maker of all things visible and invisible.
>
> And in one Lord Jesus Christ, the Son of God, begotten of the Father the only-begotten; that is, of the essence of the Father, God of God, Light of Light, very God of very God, begotten, not made, being of one substance (ὁμοούσιον, homooùsion) with the Father; by whom all things were made both in heaven and on earth; who for us men, and for our salvation, came down and was incarnate and was made man; he suffered, and the third day he rose again, ascended into heaven; from thence he shall come to judge the living and the dead.
>
> And in the Holy Ghost.
>
> But those who say: "There was a time when he was not;" and "He was not before he was made;" and "He was made out of nothing," or "He is of another substance" or "essence," or "The Son of God is created," or "changeable," or "alterable"—they are condemned by the holy catholic and apostolic Church.

The differences between this text of the Council of 325, which anathematizes the typical statements of the Arians, and that of the Council of Constantinople of 381 are indicated in italics below.

This is the Nicene-Constantinopolitan symbol:

> I believe in one God, the Father Almighty, Maker *of heaven and earth, and* of all things visible and invisible.
>
> I believe in one Lord Jesus Christ, the only-begotten Son of God, begotten of the Father *before all worlds (æons)*, Light of Light, very God of very God, begotten, not made, being of one substance with the Father; by whom all things were made; who for us men, and for our salvation, came down *from heaven*, and was incarnate *by the Holy Ghost of the Virgin Mary*, and was made man; *he was crucified for us under Pontius Pilate*, and suffered, *and was buried*, and the third day he rose again, *according to the Scriptures*, and ascended into heaven, *and sitteth on the right hand of the Father*; from thence he shall come again, *with glory*, to judge the quick and the dead; *whose kingdom shall have no end*.
>
> And in the Holy Ghost, *the Lord and Giver of life, who proceedeth from the Father, who with the Father and the Son together is worshiped and glorified, who spake by the prophets. In one holy catholic and apostolic Church; we acknowledge one baptism for the remission of sins; we look for the resurrection of the dead, and the life of the world to come. Amen.*

The term symbol is derived from the Greek *symbolon*, which initially had the sense of identification card or sign. Two people broke a terracotta tile or a piece of wood, and each kept one of the two parts, so that, at a later time, the perfect matching of the two parts put together would prove the identity of the people or their respective delegates. Thus the symbol of faith is the card or sign of recognition among the Christian faithful. In the church of the early centuries there was a rite called *Traditio Symboli* (Delivery of the Symbol or Creed) with which the church metaphorically put together (as in the meaning of the Greek word *symbolon*) and delivered to catechumens a sort of synthesis of the truths in which one believes. Only around 1024, within the tensions of the time, did Emperor Henry II require the Pope to insert the creed into the liturgy of the Mass, which is still in use today.

The symbol, which still represents a central point of Christian celebrations, explicitly established the doctrine of *homooùsion*, that is, of the consubstantiality of the Father and the Son. It denies that the Son is created (*genitum, non factum*—begotten, not made), and that his existence is posterior to the Father (*ante omnia saecula*—before all worlds). In this way, Arianism is denied in all its aspects. Furthermore, the incarnation, death, and resurrection of Christ is repeated, in contrast to the gnostic doctrines that came to deny the crucifixion. The virginal birth of Jesus is declared (born of the Virgin Mary—see Matt 1:18, 25; Luke 1:34–35). And the supporters of certain Arian affirmations are anathematized ("those who say: "There was a time when [Jesus] was not [there]").

Adding to the indications of Irenaeus, the symbol thus completes the framework of Catholic religion, as it still presents itself today.

# 3

# Faith and Hope

## The Relationship between Humanity and Religion

AT THIS POINT, IT is convenient to summarize our narrative.

We have seen how humans, in their journey, has always been accompanied by a search for what is metaphysical, which has materialized in the presence of thousands of gods, different and with different characteristics depending on places and times, to which they turned for protection, favors, and mitigation of fears. In what has been defined as natural religion, therefore, humans see in the forces of nature the presence of the divinity, of Someone who is superior. Through the beauty of nature, in its unstoppable succession of seasons, in the wonder in the renewal of life, but also in its display of power, to which we often struggle to give an explanation, is the sign of a mysterious existence. The rising of the sun and its setting, which leaves room for darkness, the onset of thunderstorms, volcanic eruptions, the immensity of the sea and so on, are interpreted as signs of something huge that cannot be regulated by us. Thus, there is, in prehistory, a first religious experience, which, as we have seen, will later be developed in ancient religions, essentially linked to nature and characterized by two aspects:

- One, very positive, linked to life and amazement in the face of beauty
- A second, more ambiguous, linked to fear in the face of forces that can harm life, even destroying it

The gradations of religious forms are infinite, between negative and positive. But there is neither an entirely negative or an entirely positive form. And the positive element, essential to religiosity, leads the human spirit to progressively elaborate the concept of the transcendent being, towards which he orients himself with all the theoretical and practical needs and from which he moves to think and direct his own life. Elaboration historically manifests itself as an ever greater (increasingly logical) spiritualization of the transcendent. The transcendent is already a person, to whom humans can address their propitiatory prayers, even when present in materialistically natural forms; but, in the most advanced religions, it reflects the ever deeper awareness of one's freedom, which the spirit is acquiring. God is always conceived, more or less coherently, as a person, because a person is and always remains the human, who represents this transcendent as being infinite, and therefore cannot deny him what is most positive that one finds in oneself, without stripping him of the infinity a person attributes to him as essential. God cannot be less than human.

Another principle is immanent, though not always explicitly developed and consciously affirmed, in religious thought: that of the immortality of the soul, that is, of the subject who puts oneself in relationship with God. For, if in one sense, religious sentiment is the denial of the being of the subject, for the other, this feeling, in its positive attitude (bringing humanity back to God and resolving the subject in the absolute object), can no longer see the first if not in the second: participating in that divine life which is proper to this, infinite, and therefore immortal.

This absolute necessity of a relationship between the two concepts, of humanity and of God, is the source of the universality of religion, so that there is no people or individual who is completely devoid of any concept of the divine and of every feeling that we refer to this concept. Humans, who cannot conceive of themselves without conceiving God, are not seen from the outside, as one of the infinite objects of thought, defined and classified in their relations with all the others; instead, it is the human who carries out the experience of humanity, realizing, in the personal spiritual life, that self-awareness in which each one, in fact, distinguishes himself or herself from things. The distinction is in one's own being or realization as a human; and the concept with which we are dealing is therefore nothing foreign to being human. A human is one who acquires an ever deeper awareness of himself or herself, and in this awareness acquires the concept of what he or she actually, in concrete terms, is. This religion and this feeling, linked to nature, has been, as we have seen, with humanity for hundreds of centuries until the emergence of revealed religions.

## What Is Faith?

A revealed religion is a religious experience whose origin depends only on God who, by his free initiative, reveals himself and makes himself known to humans. It is the experience of Abraham, who encounters God and begins a path of salvation; it is the experience of the encounter with God, who enters history and communicates with humanity. This religious form has God and humans as its protagonists; it is characterized by the love of God and human faith, which is the trustful response to God. Faith is generally the assent of intellect, motivated by the value of a testimony. In everyday life, we proceed largely with this form of knowledge, which is not absent in the scientific field either. It includes intelligence, because nobody wants to trust those who don't deserve it; it includes volitional elements, because there is no authority that can force the intellect, as a mathematical or philosophical demonstration forces it; and it includes feelings, as they can affect acceptance of one doctrine rather than another.

According to Catholic doctrine, faith is the assent of reason to the truths revealed by God, which we must accept because of the authority of those who reveal them. As for its object, it embraces all the truths and precepts that are contained in the deposit of revelation, in that they fall under the testimony and truthfulness of God; subjectively, it is an act of intelligence motivated by the reasons that make it wise and dutiful, determined by the will, which remains free in that acceptance, and even more highly justified by an intimate impulse of the grace that induces the act.

As an act of intelligence, faith demands that man makes sure of the historical fact of divine revelation, that he becomes aware of the internal and external reasons which make his assent prudent and dutiful. Prophecy, insofar as it includes a prediction of a future beyond any human possibility, and miracle, as a fact that transcends the forces of nature and therefore manifests the intervention of the first cause, in connection with a doctrine and with a testimony that presents itself as divine, are the best arguments to which the revelator par excellence, Jesus Christ, has appealed.

In the face of the affirmations and proofs that Jesus Christ brought to demonstrate his divine mission, many believed and believe, many others did not and do not. The fact has an explanation in the intrinsic darkness of the content of faith and in the bad disposition of the human will, which remains free to believe, due to the supernaturality of the mystery. Although the argument of divine testimony is the strongest of all, in itself and for humans, the freedom of assent however remains, and, if the will is ill-disposed, the intellect remains restless and suspended. The reconciliation of freedom of faith with the reasonableness of assent to revelation is explained by the fact that the demonstration insists on the credibility of the divine testimony, with a corresponding duty to accept it, but does not give evidence of the revealed truth. The extrinsic evidence that is proper to the knowledge of faith makes doubt illogical but does not force consent; that is, it does not remove the possibility of a suspension of judgment. Therefore, moral reasons must be granted their right value, but it is not scientific to overlook the intellectual reasons for faith in revelation.

Moral provisions are not enough, though. An act of supernatural faith requires that intimate energy which is called grace. To the extrinsic causes that induce faith, we must add this internal cause, which illuminates intelligence, reinvigorates the will, and puts proportion between human intellect and the supernatural object, which is intelligently and freely accepted. If faith were the necessary conclusion of human reasoning, it would belong to philosophy and have nothing supernatural. If there were no signs and arguments to justify the adhesion of our intellect, it would not be the *rationabile obsequium* of Saint Paul, it would not be the substance (foundation) of the things hoped for, and it would not be the subject of what cannot be seen. When the martyr dies for his faith, he does not justify his heroic act with the apologetic science that he may have acquired but mainly with this intimate gift, which is supernatural as a source, nature, and object. The definition of Saint Thomas is perfect: "The act of believing is an act of the intellect assenting to the Divine truth at the command of the will moved by the grace of God, so that it is subject to the free-will in relation to God."[1]

The church is not the source of faith, but her mission is to safeguard the deposit of revealed truth, take care of its exact formulation, defend it from counterfeiting, extend its knowledge to all peoples, and live it in a coherence of holiness. The definitions of the councils and theological progress develop the knowledge of dogma and make explicit what was implicitly contained in the Bible and tradition, but they cannot create new truths, much less make them occur as revealed. The universal church, in

---

1. Aquinas, *Summa Theologiae,* II-II, question 2, article 9.

its dual mission of magisterium and sanctifying ministry, constitutes an event which historically fulfills Christian prophecies and constitutes a new reason for faith in the divine nature of the Christian religion.

In Protestant doctrine, faith was conceived as the trust that sins are forgiven and the merits of Christ are attributed to us, even without good personal deeds. Modernist Catholics are inclined to believe in a moral faith, almost a religious sense, a beneficial experience of the truths that the church teaches, regardless of the intrinsic truth of the same. This was a derivation of the Kantian concepts according to which we believe in the existence of God, the immortality of the soul, and the other life, not for philosophical demonstrations or for the authority of a divine revelation, but for the need of practical reason, which needs those truths in order to establish a moral system.

So, is it all right? Not at all!

## Faith and Reason

Faith and reason have sparked bitter debates, antagonisms, controversies—that still persist—between thinkers and writers of all centuries, about the supremacy of one over the other or the dependence of one on the other. The relationship between these two realities has varied over the centuries, sometimes in deep harmony, sometimes in open contrast. Christian thought, based on faith in the incarnate Word of God, on Jesus Christ in particular, and on the entire Bible (Old Testament and New Testament) in general, was immediately confronted by the Greek thought of the great philosophers, in particular Plato and Aristotle,[2] who are the columns of Greek philosophy. Philosophy, unlike faith, does not start from a divine revelation, but from the human search for truth. The true father of philosophy is, in fact, Socrates, master of Plato and Aristotle, who spent his days in the square of Athens (the *Agora*) talking to people, because he

---

2. Aristotle (384–22 BC) was a Greek philosopher and polymath during the classical period in ancient Greece. Taught by Plato, he was the founder of the Lyceum, the Peripatetic school of philosophy, and the Aristotelian tradition. His writings cover many subjects, including physics, biology, zoology, metaphysics, logic, ethics, aesthetics, poetry, theater, music, rhetoric, psychology, linguistics, economics, politics, and government. Aristotle provided a complex synthesis of the various philosophies existing prior to him. It was above all from his teachings that the West inherited its intellectual lexicon, as well as problems and methods of inquiry. As a result, his philosophy has exerted a unique influence on almost every form of knowledge in the West, and it continues to be a subject of contemporary philosophical discussion.

was convinced that truth lived within them, in their conscience, so it had to be patiently investigated and discovered.

## Saint Augustine

The first great Christian thinker who knew how to admirably unite the faith arising from the word of God with philosophy, fruit of the rational research of humans, was Saint Augustine of Hippo,[3] who lived between the fourth and fifth centuries (354–430), towards the end of the Western Roman Empire (which would happen in 476).

Augustine preferred to address Plato's thought, closer to theology, precisely because of his philosophical thought (the real world is the spiritual world of ideas, whereas the material world is only a pale reflection of it). For Augustine, faith must be distinguished from opinion, which is an uncertain assent, while faith is a certain assent to certain things. Thus, there are truths that, if believed, can be demonstrated and truths that instead should be only believed and possibly demonstrated. Faith illuminates and indicates the object of human search, which is God. Augustine maintains that there is an agreement between reason and faith and that reason cannot establish itself without the light of faith.

For Augustine, the Holy Scriptures are also very important or, better to say, their interpretation is; they must be read carefully and must be interpreted well, because they express testimony of an event that has happened but also express further truths about humanity, God, and their relationship. Augustine elaborates the doctrine of knowledge, stressing that it occurs by enlightenment. That is, the truth is already within humans, enlightenment is used by them to discover the truth, and that light is precisely faith. In his words: "*Credo ut intelligam, intelligo ut credam*" (I believe so that I may understand, I understand so that I may believe).

---

3. Augustine of Hippo (13 Nov. 354–28 Aug. 430), also known as Saint Augustine, was a theologian, philosopher, and tbishop of Hippo Regius in Numidia, Roman North Africa. His writings influenced the development of Western philosophy and Western Christianity, and he is viewed as one of the most important Church Fathers of the Latin church in the patristic period.

## Saint Anselm of Canterbury, Peter Abelard, and William of Ockham

In later times, starting from the eleventh century, the use of dialectics in the explanation of religious dogmas caused concern in those who feared that the firmness of the truths of faith could be weakened by philosophical arguments. In this context, contrast developed between dialectic philosophers, who advocated the use of reason to understand the truths of faith, and antidialectic ones, who denied reason any value in understanding the mysteries of faith. In the twelfth century, a discussion on the relationship between faith and reason developed among the major proponents of the various groups, especially Anselm of Canterbury[4] and Peter Abelard.[5]

For Anselm, faith constitutes the guide for rational research; this does not stray far from the idea of Saint Augustine. Augustine's phrase is abbreviated by Anselm and becomes "I believe to understand"—that is, to understand the truth, it is necessary to believe; without faith, nothing can be understood. Anselm does not exclude reason. On the contrary, reason clarifies and determines the truth of faith, and faith seeks the intellect. All mysteries of faith can never be clarified, because they go beyond the human intellect. The human intellect uses reason not to acquire faith but to realize the greatness of the things that are believed. Anselm also presents us with the figure of the insipient, who, unable to prove that God exists, says he does not exist. Given that the believer can be weakened by the insipient, the believer must continuously strengthen faith with rational research and must help the insipient understand that not everything can be explained. Anselm also supports the existence of God by not resorting to creation: when one thinks of God, one thinks of him as a superior, omnipotent, perfect being, who does not lack anything; therefore he must necessarily exist, otherwise he would lack something.

According to Peter Abelard, however, a conflict between reason and faith cannot exist, because they are both gifts from God. In Abelard's thought, the *credo ut intelligam* of Anselm and Augustine is reversed

---

4. Saint Anselm of Canterbury (1033/4–1109), also called Anselm of Aosta after his birthplace and Anselm of Bec after his monastery, was an Italian Benedictine monk, abbot, philosopher, and theologian of the Catholic Church, who held the office of Archbishop of Canterbury from 1093 to 1109. After his death, he was canonized as a saint.

5. Peter Abelard (c. 1079–21 Apr. 1142) was a medieval French scholastic philosopher, theologian, and preeminent logician. His love for and affair with Héloïse d'Argenteuil has become legendary.

in "I understand to believe," which means that, before being believed, something must be understood; if something is not understood, it cannot be believed. Rational research precedes faith therefore, according to Abelard. Divine truths cannot be logically understood by man. Rational research manages to give us the idea of divine truths through analogical language, that is, similar to the logical, to the true.

A couple of centuries later, William of Ockham[6] addressed again the topic. For William there is no harmony between philosophy and theology, given that reason and faith are two distinct tools of knowledge, even if not in contrast. According to him, truths of faith are neither evident nor demonstrable, nor can they be the object of rational demonstration, otherwise the revelation would be useless. God revealed to us the truths of faith, because he knew that we would never have been able to grasp them only through our own means (intellect). The truths of faith cannot be demonstrated, but nor can they be denied. For example, immortality of the soul can be neither demonstrated nor denied.

This great medieval synthesis between faith and reason, the Augustinian intellectual synthesis, centered on the grace of God (and therefore on faith), dominated Christian thought up to Saint Thomas Aquinas.[7]

## Saint Thomas Aquinas

Saint Thomas, who lived in the thirteenth century—a century characterized by great transformations and a new human initiative (the birth of the bourgeoisie and the prevalence of commercial activities)—preferred to combine Christian thought with that of Aristotle, who, until then, had remained in the background. This thought, we would say today, was more materialistic than spiritualistic, more centered on concrete reality than on

---

6. William of Ockham (c. 1287–1347) was an English Franciscan friar, scholastic philosopher, and theologian, who is believed to have been born in Ockham, a small village in Surrey. He is considered to be one of the major figures of medieval thought and was at the center of the major intellectual and political controversies of the fourteenth century. He is commonly known for Ockham's razor, the methodological principle that bears his name, and also produced significant works on logic, physics, and theology.

7. Thomas Aquinas (1225–7 Mar. 1274) was an Italian Dominican friar, philosopher, Catholic priest, and Doctor of the Church. An immensely influential philosopher, theologian, and jurist in the tradition of scholasticism, Aquinas is considered one of the Catholic Church's greatest theologians and philosophers. His influence on Western thought is considerable, and much of modern philosophy developed or opposed his ideas, particularly in the areas of ethics, natural law, metaphysics, and political theory.

the world of ideas, on the concrete *reason* of man. Thomas (and with him many other philosophers and theologians of the latter phase of the Middle Ages, when humanism was already beginning to appear), thanks to Aristotle's philosophy, was able to elaborate a great synthesis between faith and reason, like two entities that recall and support each other. This philosophical-theological current that would dominate Christian thought for many centuries was called Scholastic philosophy. According to Thomas's thought, faith needs reason to become understandable ("faith that seeks intelligence"); but at the same time, reason also needs faith to expand its capacity for understanding ("reason that seeks faith"). In other words, according to these great Christian philosophers and theologians of Scholasticism (in addition to the aforementioned extraordinary minds, were Duns Scotus,[8] Roger Bacon,[9] Albertus Magnus,[10] Scotus Eriugena[11]), man should have believed (had faith) to understand (understand with reason), and at the same time have understood (understood with reason) to believe (have faith). In this great synthesis between faith and reason, faith occupied the main place anyway and reason acted as *ancilla* (handmaid), that is, it was at the service of faith. This was a kind of summary of all medieval thought. The main work of Thomas would be, in fact, called *Theological Summa* (the summary of all theology). Thomism, as the thought system of Thomas would be called, would remain the official thought of the Catholic Church until the Second Vatican Council.

This great medieval synthesis cracked at the beginning of the modern era, for several reasons. First of all, with the Protestant reform (Martin Luther),[12] there was a comeback of Augustinian thought, much

---

8. John Duns (c. 1266–8 Nov. 1308), commonly called Duns Scotus, was a Scottish Catholic priest, Franciscan friar, university professor, philosopher, and theologian. He is one of the three most important philosopher-theologians of Western Europe in the High Middle Ages, together with Thomas Aquinas and William of Ockham.

9. Roger Bacon (c. 1219/20–c. 1292), also known by the scholastic accolade Doctor Mirabilis, was a medieval English philosopher and Franciscan friar who placed considerable emphasis on the study of nature through empiricism.

10. Albertus Magnus (before 1200–Nov. 15, 1280), also known as Saint Albert the Great and Albert of Cologne, was a German Catholic Dominican friar and bishop. Later canonized as a Catholic saint, he was known during his lifetime as doctor universalis and doctor expertus and, late in his life, the sobriquet Magnus was appended to his name. The Catholic Church distinguishes him as one of the thirty-six Doctors of the Church.

11. John Scotus Eriugena or Johannes Scotus Erigena (c. 815–c. 877) was an Irish theologian, neoplatonist philosopher, and poet.

12. Martin Luther (10 Nov. 1483–18 Feb. 1546) was a German professor of

more based on the resources of faith (man is saved only by grace) than on that of reason (human possibilities for his own salvation). Secondly, there was the birth of scientific thought, rigorously based on the rational and experimental method (Galileo Galilei),[13] which was perceived by the church as a displacement of the primacy of theology and a threat to faith.

Galileo Galilei, as a man of deep Catholic faith, had perfectly understood that the results of the scientific method (which he had invented) could not conflict with the Bible, since the author of the Bible (God) was the same author of nature (the Bible itself affirmed God as Creator of nature). The contrasts therefore, according to him, were only apparent. He would push to try to better understand both science and the Bible itself, which had to be interpreted correctly and not read literally. But Galileo was not understood and was condemned by the ecclesiastical hierarchies of the time, causing a fracture between faith and scientific reason. Thus, while the church continued to propose its medieval synthesis, in the modern era grew the awareness of the autonomy of human reason, increasingly detached from religious questions.

## Descartes and Pascal

The extraordinary dispute that arose between Descartes's ideas and Pascal's, from two of the most prodigious minds of the time, was emblematic.

*"Cogito ergo sum"* (I think, therefore I am) is the synthesis of Cartesian thought; *"Credo ergo sum"* (I believe, therefore I am) is the synthesis of Pascalian thought.

Descartes[14] was both a philosopher and a sincere believer, an almost naïve believer, if one keeps in mind that he made the vow to go to

---

theology, composer, priest, Augustinian monk, and seminal figure in the Protestant Reformation. Within fifty years from 1517, the year in which he affixed the famous ninety-five theses to the door of the church of Wittenberg, to 1563, the ending year of the Council of Trent, Luther changed the religious face of Europe and, in perspective, of the whole Christian West.

13. Galileo di Vincenzo Bonaulti de Galilei (15 Feb. 1564–8 Jan. 1642) was an Italian astronomer, physicist, and engineer, sometimes described as a polymath, from Pisa. Galileo is considered the father of the scientific method and the father of modern science.

14. René Descartes (31 Mar. 1596–11 Feb. 1650) was a French philosopher, mathematician, and scientist. Descartes has often been called the father of modern philosophy and is largely seen as responsible for the increased attention given to epistemology in the seventeenth century. Descartes's influence in mathematics is equally apparent;

the sanctuary of Loreto[15] for having discovered the method from which modern atheism would stem. With Descartes and his *cogito*, reason acquires an autonomy that is both gnoseological and ontological.[16] It is true that Descartes rationally demonstrated the existence of God, in a geometrizing way, but he did it in order to seek a stable point on which to base the certainty of the *cogito*. He looked for a God who had a systematic value and therefore, as Pascal[17] would say, his is the God of philosophers. Descartes thematized finiteness to reach infinity, but that was accomplished only in speculative and logical terms. To delineate it clearly, is the Cartesian God, a God to whom one who can pray and therefore relate as to a person?

Pascal was already answering this question in a negative way, and the polarity between Descartes and Pascal is the origin of modernity and the two different paths it has followed. This alternative lies entirely in the different interpretation of the relationship between the finite and the infinite. Pascal also thematized man's finiteness, not in logical terms but with an existential gesture. He wanted to keep the finite and the infinite together, even at the cost of launching an attack on reason. In his eyes, the finiteness that Descartes scrutinized is a logical fiction, dramatically denied by the principle of the *cogito*, by which finiteness expands out of all proportion. In Pascal, finiteness is pushed so far as to include reason itself and to put the alleged autonomy of the *cogito* in check. The necessity of faith, in Pascal, is not an anti-philosophical instance, but rather the landing place of a different philosophical approach. It is the other face of

---

the Cartesian coordinate system was named after him, and he is credited as the father of analytical geometry.

15. The Basilica della Santa Casa (Basilica of the Holy House) is a shrine of Marian pilgrimage in Loreto, Italy. The basilica is known for enshrining the house in which the Blessed Virgin Mary is believed by some Catholics to have lived.

16. Gnoseology is the philosophical study of knowledge; ontology is the philosophical study of being.

17. Blaise Pascal (19 June 1623–19 Aug. 1662) was a French mathematician, physicist, inventor, writer, and Catholic theologian. A child prodigy, he made important contributions to the study of fluids and geometry and started some pioneering work on calculating machines. Pascal's development of probability theory was his most influential contribution to mathematics. Originally applied to gambling, today it is extremely important in economics, especially in actuarial science. His literary work is best remembered for its strong opposition to the rationalism of René Descartes and simultaneous assertion that the main countervailing philosophy, empiricism, was also insufficient for determining major truths.

modernity—a face that does not absolutize reason but preaches its limits and sees in this a possible relationship with transcendence.

There is no escape from this polarity between Descartes and Pascal. The history of modern thought is the history of this polarity, even though, in modern rationalism, the Cartesian line would tend to prevail.

Descartes's biographers attest that he prayed, although the God he discovered in philosophy was certainly not such as to whom could be prayed. There is such a radical dichotomy between Descartes's consciousness and his philosophy that he could not even perceive it; but Pascal did perceive it and, precisely by virtue of this, led philosophy to take a step back, to remove itself from the space that must be that of faith.

Pascal endeavored in every way to free himself from the God of philosophers and from the proofs that philosophers have provided of his existence, which, albeit logically flawless, lead to a supreme and necessary being who is not the God of Abraham, Isaac, and Jacob. This Pascalian delimitation of philosophy in favor of faith is, of course, a philosophical act itself. However, an imperfect symmetry can be identified in this polarity, because, unlike Descartes, Pascal knew that dichotomy, did not evade it, but decided existentially for one of the two alternatives. Thus, Descartes prayed as a man but not as a philosopher; in order to pray as a man, Pascal had to lead philosophy to the awareness of its own limits.

Both men assumed the estrangement between philosophy and prayer but in different ways. In fact, this is seen, in Descartes, as the impossibility of praying to the God discovered with reason; in Pascal, as the explicit refusal of that God, in the name of another God who is unreachable by reason. It is at the beginning of modern philosophy that the principle of immanence inaugurated by the *cogito*, implied by the God of the philosophers, already atheism in essence, is affirmed in human thought. He is a God who has nothing to offer to humanity and with whom it makes no sense to try to establish a relationship. Such a God is not only compatible with a sort of creeping atheism, but perhaps he somehow requires it. This is precisely what takes away every meaning and foundation from prayer. Following this line, prayer could represent the abdication of the centrality of humanity or the abdication of human freedom. What else is the Cartesian *cogito*, if not a clear rejection of the possibility that its foundation is external? With Descartes, the subject assumes full autonomy and therefore no longer needs to look for a foundation that is other than oneself.

## The Prevalence of Reason and Its Consequences

In the following currents (deism,[18] empiricism,[19] etc.) this will be the winning line, always carrying—implicitly or thematically—a denial of the meaning of prayer or, as in the case of Spinoza, its acceptance at the naïve level "of women and children." In the opposite case of idealism,[20] it is the consciousness itself that becomes absolute and therefore seeks nothing else outside of itself, so that idealism is also the son of the Cartesian *cogito*.

With the advent of the Enlightenment,[21] during the eighteenth century, reason was increasingly considered as the only source of the light of knowledge, hence the very name of Enlightenment. By contrast, faith was increasingly relegated to the realm of the irrational. The endless wars of religion that devastated Europe in the sixteenth and seventeenth centuries had greatly influenced this profound transformation. The military, political, and civil clashes that followed one another after the confessional splits that took place following the Protestant Reformation (1517–1555) and the Anglican Schism (1534) had religion as a trigger, which turned into widespread extreme ideology and a reason for heated intolerance, even in the lower strata of the European population. Instead of uniting people in the name of a higher truth, religion ended up preventing them from sharing the same values. The idea that only human reason could illuminate the path of modern humanity and create a universally recognized common base made headway on this ground. In many philosophers, scientists, and intellectuals, the contrast between faith and reason became more radical.

If the eighteenth century was the century of the Enlightenment with the deification of reason (the Goddess Reason of the French revolutionaries), the nineteenth century would be the century of the birth and the

---

18. Deism is the philosophical position that rejects revelation as a source of religious knowledge and asserts that reason and observation of the natural world are sufficient to establish the existence of a Supreme Being or creator of the universe.

19. In philosophy, empiricism is a theory that states that knowledge comes only or primarily from sensory experience. Empiricism emphasizes the role of empirical evidence in the formation of ideas, rather than innate ideas or traditions.

20. In philosophy, idealism is a diverse group of metaphysical views which all assert that reality is in some way indistinguishable or inseparable from human perception and/or understanding, that it is in some sense mentally constituted, or that it is otherwise closely connected to ideas.

21. The Age of Enlightenment (also known as the Age of Reason or simply the Enlightenment) was an intellectual and philosophical movement that dominated the world of ideas in Europe during the seventeenth to nineteenth centuries.

affirmation of atheism (Feuerbach,[22] Marx,[23] Nietzsche,[24] Freud,[25] etc.) and the radical affirmation of reason that denies faith. The church, faced with this progressive departure from religion by the world of modern European thought and culture (the process of secularization) was tempted to entrench itself and place barriers to defend itself against modernity. This attitude lasted roughly until the great event of Council Vatican II, celebrated in Rome (at the Vatican, hence the name) from 1962 to 1965, promoted by John XXIII and continued by Paul VI. The Council constituted an epochal event for the topics addressed and debated, among which the relationship between faith and reason had a predominant place. This eventually led, by the will of John Paul II, to the rehabilitation of the great scientist and man of faith Galileo Galilei. John Paul II dedicated an entire encyclical to the relationship between faith and reason (*Fides et Ratio*, 1998), which begins with the poetic metaphor of the two wings, faith and reason, with which the human spirit takes flight towards the search for truth.

However, the discussion remains suspended, because even the most profound arguments do not reconcile the two sides. Instead relativism is becoming more and more widespread as a form of thought, about which

---

22. Ludwig Andreas von Feuerbach (28 July 1804–13 Sept. 1872) was a German philosopher and anthropologist best known for his book *The Essence of Christianity*, which provided a critique of Christianity that strongly influenced generations of later thinkers, including Charles Darwin, Karl Marx, Sigmund Freud, Friedrich Engels, Richard Wagner, and Friedrich Nietzsche.

23. Karl Heinrich Marx (5 May 1818–14 Mar. 1883) was a German philosopher, economist, historian, sociologist, political theorist, journalist, and socialist revolutionary. His political and philosophical thought had enormous influence on subsequent intellectual, economic, and political history.

24. Friedrich Wilhelm Nietzsche (15 Oct. 1844–25 Aug. 1900) was a German philosopher, cultural critic, composer, poet, and philologist whose work has exerted a profound influence on modern intellectual history. In his works coexist a violent destructive criticism of the past (the philosophical, moral, and religious tradition of the West, from Socrates onwards) and a passionate appeal to the future, to the creation of a new man capable of facing the tragedy of life without the need for philosophical or religious certainties.

25. Sigmund Freud (6 May 1856–23 Sept. 1939) was an Austrian neurologist and the founder of psychoanalysis, a clinical method for treating psychopathology through dialogue between a patient and a psychoanalyst. Freud's work has suffused contemporary Western thought, popular culture, and psychoanalysis. Although debated, it remains influential within psychology, psychiatry, and psychotherapy and across the humanities.

it can be said, in the words of Cardinal Newman:[26] "There never was a device of the Enemy so cleverly framed and with such promise of success."[27]

## Relativism

Relativism is a philosophical conception that denies the existence of absolute truths or critically questions the possibility of reaching their absolute definition. Relativism maintains that an absolute truth does not exist or, even if it exists, it is not knowable or expressible, or, alternatively, it is only partially known (relatively known). Individuals can therefore obtain only relative knowledge, as each statement refers to particular factors and is true only in reference to them. The subject to which the judgments are related can be understood either as this or that individual or as the universal subject. Relativism therefore does not connote a real doctrine or a nucleus of thought but rather a heterogeneous set of conceptions and attitudes that vary, even a lot, depending on the historical and conceptual framework of reference.

Thus, it can be noted that there are at least five different general meanings of relativism, which have intertwined and merged throughout the history of Western philosophical and scientific thought, and a series of other secondary connotations, which depend on the particular conceptual framework of reference:

1. In general, relativist conceptions deny the existence of absolute principles, of a universal subject, of subjects always identical to themselves, or of an entity that acts as the foundation of being and knowing. Sometimes, therefore, relativism can be understood as the absence of a single and absolute foundation of knowledge.

2. A second way of understanding relativism is logically connected with the first. Denying a single and absolute foundation does not entail the logical need to deny that knowledge can be based on a plurality of principles, placed in mutual relationship. So, relativism can be understood as the relational determination of truth.

---

26. John Henry Newman (21 Feb. 1801–11 Aug. 1890) was an English theologian and poet, first an Anglican priest and later a Catholic priest and cardinal, who was an important and controversial figure in the religious history of England in the nineteenth century. He was known nationally by the mid-1830s, and was canonized as a saint in the Catholic Church in 2019.

27. Newman, *Speech*, 9–10.

# Faith and Hope

3. The term relativism has sometimes been used to indicate the impossibility or inability to determine any truth objectively and interpersonally, given that each representation of it is modified by an unknowable multiplicity of subjective and objective factors. So, relativism is sometimes understood as radical skepticism, to mean the absolute impotence of thought.

4. In particular contexts, the term relativism can indicate the conjectural and provisional nature of any knowledge, taking place by successive approximations, and therefore as a relationship of the part with the whole. The finite part of an infinite or indefinite process, which is the potential totality of knowledge, is relative.

5. A further meaning of relativism, which in part contains elements of the previous ones, may concern a theory of knowledge focused on the activity of signification or interpretation of the world by various subjects, which however are in turn interpreted or modified from the perspectives present in the cultures of which they are part. This, too, is a form of relationalism similar to that indicated in point 2; but in this case, the cognitive relationship does not take place between elements, but between perspectives, or horizons of meanings, which mutually change and merge together in the hermeneutic[28] circle that is established between the subject and the object.

In this case, relativism indicates:

a. the plurality of horizons of meaning, none of which is truer than any other

b. the perspective is relative to the subject, no less than the subject is relative to the perspective (horizon)

c. the fusion of horizons and perspectives leads to an indefinite increase in knowledge of the world, but in such a way that it is not possible to indicate a destination or a way to go

d. this hermeneutic circle is the only way to establish from time to time what is considered Truth

e. this perspective relativism has nothing to do with solipsistic[29] subjectivism or radical and agnostic skepticism

---

28. Hermeneutics is the theory and methodology of interpretation, especially the interpretation of biblical texts, wisdom literature, and philosophical texts.

29. Solipsism is the philosophical idea that only one's mind is sure to exist. As

As a philosophical orientation, relativism can be traced back to Protagoras,[30] who underscored with his famous formula "man is the measure of all things" the inevitable role of opinion in human knowledge, denying the possibility of achieving objective and unchanging knowledge. In both Protagoras and Sophistic,[31] relativism affects not only the field of knowledge but also that of ethics, where it is characterized by the denial of the existence of absolutely valid judgments and moral principles. In modern thought, relativism occurs above all in connection with skepticism,[32] as in the case of Montaigne,[33] who, influenced by the radical changes that had taken place in scientific knowledge and the recent geographical discoveries, highlighted on one hand the substantial precariousness and historical relativity of absolute truths, as were once conceived; on the other hand, the lack of real objectivity of the judgments on the barbaric cultures of the New World, based on an illegitimate absolutization of the evaluation canons in force in European culture.

For philosopher Nicola Abbagnano,[34] ancient Sophistic, skepticism, empiricism, and critical philosophy[35] are manifestations of a relativism

---

an epistemological position, solipsism holds that knowledge of anything outside one's own mind is unsure; the external world and other minds cannot be known and might not exist outside the mind.

30. Protagoras (c. 490–c. 420 BC) was a pre-Socratic Greek philosopher. He is numbered as one of the sophists by Plato. In his dialogues, Plato credits him with inventing the role of the professional sophist. Protagoras also is believed to have created a major controversy during ancient times through his statement that "man is the measure of all things," interpreted by Plato to mean that there is no objective truth. Whatever individuals deem to be the truth is true.

31. Sophistic was a philosophical current that developed in ancient Greece, in Athens in particular, starting from the second half of the fifth century BC. It rejected any metaphysical research, established the principle of subjectivity of knowledge, identified in practical convenience the only criterion of the truth of a statement, and for this purpose practiced and taught rhetoric, considered the only effective means of conviction and persuasion.

32. Skepticism is generally a questioning attitude or doubt towards one or more putative instances of knowledge, which are asserted to be mere belief or dogma.

33. Michel Eyquem de Montaigne (28 Feb. 1533–13 Sept. 1592) was one of the most significant philosophers of the French Renaissance, known for popularizing the essay as a literary genre. His work is noted for its merging of casual anecdotes and autobiography with intellectual insight and skeptical attitude.

34. Nicola Abbagnano (15 July 1901–9 Sept. 1990) was an Italian existential philosopher.

35. The critical philosophy movement, attributed to Immanuel Kant (1724–1802), sees the primary task of philosophy as criticism rather than justification of knowledge.

that tries to create a background of tradition. But in reality, that current, for Abbagnano, was born as a modern phenomenon, linked to the culture of the nineteenth century.

A consequent and systematic relativism developed from the end of the nineteenth century, within the current of thought known as historicism. The historical relativization of each cultural manifestation and the multiplicity of worldviews represent the most significant outcomes of the historicism of Wilhelm Dilthey,[36] who thus intended to restore every single form of life, value system, religion, and philosophy to that historical dimension (partial and determined) within which they arise and run out. These outcomes would be radicalized by Oswald Spengler,[37] for whom every culture is a living organism and, as such, subjected to a life cycle going from birth to maturity to decadence. As he writes in his book *The Decline of the West*, where he affirms the relativity of all the values of life in relation to historical eras, considered as organic entities, each of which grows, develops, and dies without relationship with the other: "Each culture has its own criterion, whose validity begins and ends with it. There is no universal human morality."[38] To some extent, Max Weber[39] himself falls within the perspective of historicist relativism, when, while theorizing the objectivity of historical knowledge through the delineation of positivism-derived[40] epistemological[41] criteria, he nevertheless recognizes the inevitable relativity or polytheism of values.

---

Criticism, for Kant, meant judging as to the possibilities of knowledge before advancing to knowledge itself.

36. Wilhelm Dilthey (19 Nov. 1833–1 Oct. 1911) was a German historian, psychologist, sociologist, and hermeneutic philosopher.

37. Oswald Arnold Gottfried Spengler (29 May 1880–8 May 1936) was a German historian and philosopher of history whose interests included mathematics, science, and art and their relation to his cyclical theory of history. He is best known for his book *The Decline of the West* (*Der Untergang des Abendlandes*), published in 1918 and 1922, covering all of world history. Spengler's model of history postulates that any culture is a superorganism with a limited and predictable lifespan.

38. Spengler, *Untergang des Abendlandes*, I, 55.

39. Maximilian Karl Emil Weber (21 Apr. 1864–14 June 1920) was a German sociologist, philosopher, jurist, and political economist, who is regarded today as one of the most important theorists on the development of modern Western society.

40. Positivism is a philosophical theory stating that certain (positive) knowledge is based on natural phenomena and their properties and relations. Thus, information derived from sensory experience, interpreted through reason and logic, forms the exclusive source of all certain knowledge.

41. Epistemology is the branch of philosophy concerned with knowledge.

After the experience of historicism ended, relativism affected other cultural sectors of the twentieth century, such as sociology, analytical philosophy, and philosophy of science. In Karl Mannheim's[42] sociology of knowledge, relativism presents itself in the form of historical and social conditioning of the cognitive discourse itself. Ludwig Wittgenstein's[43] reflections on dependence on the conventions, social practices, and forms of life of the various language games that preside over communication, interindividual relationships, cognitive procedures, and rationality criteria, can also be considered relativistic. Partly influenced by Wittgenstein, but not entirely unrelated to the sociology of knowledge and historicism, are the theses supported by Thomas Kuhn[44] who, relativizing scientific knowledge to the cultural and historically changing contexts dominated by paradigms,[45] came to an image of the history of science, in which each era has its own metaphysical presuppositions, cognitive criteria, verification procedures, and truths.

A lively debate has characterized the more recent philosophy of science and language, and the relativism of paradigms, conceptual frameworks, and life forms has been contested by Karl Popper,[46] Willard

---

42. Karl Mannheim (27 Mar. 1893–9 Jan. 1947) was an influential German sociologist during the first half of the twentieth century. He is a key figure in classical sociology, as well as one of the founders of the sociology of knowledge.

43. Ludwig Josef Johann Wittgenstein (26 Apr. 1889–29 Apr. 1951) was an Austrian-British philosopher who worked primarily in logic, the philosophy of mathematics, the philosophy of mind, and the philosophy of language.

44. Thomas Samuel Kuhn (July 18, 1922–June 17, 1996) was an American philosopher of science whose 1962 book *The Structure of Scientific Revolutions* was influential in both academic and popular circles.

45. "Universally recognized scientific achievements that, for a time, provide model problems and solutions for a community of practitioners" (Kuhn, *Structure of Scientific Revolutions*, 10).

46. Sir Karl Raimund Popper (28 July 1902–17 Sept. 1994) was an Austrian-born British philosopher, academic, and social commentator. One of the twentieth century's most influential philosophers of science, Popper is known for his rejection of the classical inductivist views on the scientific method in favor of empirical falsification. According to Popper, a theory in the empirical sciences can never be proven, but it can be falsified, meaning that it can (and should) be scrutinized with decisive experiments.

Quine,[47] Donald Davidson,[48] and Henry Putnam,[49] who underscored in various ways its self-confuting character, which, while asserting the relativity of all knowledge, assumptions, and values, nevertheless assumes the objectivity and unconditional validity of its own point of view. In the wider anthropological sector, there is mention of cultural relativism regarding the orientations developed by the school of Franz Boas,[50] which contrast the analysis of individual cultures, historically and spatially determined, with their comparative analysis, aimed at identifying the existence of common principles. The recognition of cultural multiplicity and differences results in a recognition of the importance of customs (or culture) in the organization of human life and society. At the basis of relativism, there is a deep diffidence towards the universality of psychic or mental structures of a natural order, which all peoples would have in common. Relativism does not deny that such structures exist. It believes, however, that they represent a minority component, so to speak, in the human organization: the cultural dimension, with its inevitable variability, is more important. Therefore what distinguishes humans in their true essence would be precisely this variability rather than the uniformity of laws or natural structures. The ways in which one may choose to enter the cultural universes can be very different and respond to even opposite methodological criteria; but, in general, relativism would tend to make its own, as when the anthropologist Bronislaw Malinowski,[51] with regard

---

47. Willard Van Orman Quine (June 25, 1908–Dec. 25, 2000) was an American philosopher and logician in the analytic tradition, considered one of the most influential philosophers of the twentieth century.

48. Donald Herbert Davidson (Mar. 6, 1917–Aug. 30, 2003) was an American philosopher.

49. Hilary Whitehall Putnam (July 31, 1926–Mar. 13, 2016) was an American philosopher, mathematician, and computer scientist and a major figure in analytic philosophy in the second half of the twentieth century.

50. Franz Uri Boas (1858–1942) was a German-born American anthropologist and a pioneer of modern anthropology. His work is associated with the movements known as historical particularism and cultural relativism.

51. Bronisław Kasper Malinowski (7 Apr. 1884–16 May 1942) was a Polish-born British anthropologist whose writings on ethnography, social theory, and field research had a lasting influence on the discipline of anthropology.

to the native of the Trobriand islands,[52] said that it is necessary to grasp "his vision of his world."[53]

The acquisition of a vision from within—however this is then pursued—represents the most productive point of relativism, the one for which it is not reduced only to an attitude of detection of multiplicity and respect for cultural diversity, but translates to a cognitive effort brought into the depths of otherness. The propensity to enhance a vision from within, elaborated through particular and unrepeatable principles and categories, specific to a specific society, bonds cultural relativism with linguistic relativism. From Boas to Edward Sapir[54] and to Benjamin Whorf,[55] there re-emerges, in the anthropological and linguistic culture of the twentieth century, a tradition of thought that goes back to Herder[56] and especially to Friedrich von Humboldt.[57] For Humboldt, language on the one hand is "the formative organ of thought" and at the same time of humanity; on the other hand, it can result only in an indefinite series of particular languages, each of which expresses "not a diversity of sounds and of signs, but a diversity of worldviews." In such formulations it is possible to trace a combination of two principles: that of linguistic relativity, expressed in the formula "there is no limit to the structural diversity of languages," and that of linguistic determinism, expressed in the formula "language determines thought."[58] It is the second principle that manages to transform relativism from a simple observation of structural diversity and irreducible multiplicity into an attitude of global research.

---

52. The Trobriand Islands are a 450-square-km (174-square-mile) archipelago of coral atolls off the east coast of New Guinea.

53. Malinowksi, "Argonauts of the Western Pacific," 25.

54. Edward Sapir (Jan. 26, 1884–Feb. 4, 1939) was an American anthropologist-linguist, widely considered to be one of the most important figures in the early development of the discipline of linguistics.

55. Benjamin Lee Whorf (Apr. 24, 1897–July 26, 1941) was an American linguist and fire prevention engineer. Whorf is widely known as an advocate for the idea that differences between the structures of different languages shape how their speakers perceive and conceptualize the world.

56. Johann Gottfried (after 1802, von) Herder (25 Aug. 1744–18 Dec. 1803) was a German philosopher, theologian, poet, and literary critic.

57. Friedrich Wilhelm Christian Karl Ferdinand von Humboldt (22 June 1767–8 Apr. 1835) was a Prussian philosopher, linguist, government functionary, diplomat, and founder of the Humboldt University of Berlin, which was named after him in 1949 (and also after his younger brother, Alexander von Humboldt, a naturalist).

58 Humboldt, *La diversità delle lingue*, 42.

## Faith and Hope

The debate on relativism has always been a rather heated and animated one, opposing two sides: that of relativists, for whom the admission of multiplicity and the recognition of differences entail an opening towards the most diverse forms that humanity can take, not perceiving this as a danger, but rather as an enrichment; and that of the anti-relativists, for whom the thesis of multiplicity is configured instead as a threat brought towards the sense of unity as humans: if human beings were so culturally different, and if cultural diversity were such as to affect human beings so deeply, would not the possibility of understanding and dialogue between individuals, groups, and societies be questioned? Ian Jarvie,[59] a philosopher trained under the leadership of Popper, said that nihilism can be glimpsed behind relativism. It is easy to understand how this stance appears to Clifford Geertz,[60] one of the staunchest supporters of relativism, as a completely unfounded evocation of an unproven ghost, of unjustified fear. Yet, it is undeniable that relativism can take on disturbing aspects, showing how this movement of thought does not present a single face but can shift to multiple uses and interpretations.

Even the knowledge of contemporary civilization, in which science makes amazing progress, such as to make men so little aware of their limits, can be questioned. There is no single truth that can hold up to a refined form of skepticism, as Descartes well demonstrated with hyperbolic doubt: it can never be excluded that "a bad genius, shrewd and mendacious as powerful" uses his superhuman power to fool and to deceive men. Indeed, each one can say only of oneself that I exist. Many philosophers blame the presumption of men to know everything, but here I want to remember only one poet, Calderón de la Barca,[61] who in his most famous work sings: "What is life? Delirium. What is life? An illusion, a shadow, a fairy tale, and the greatest of goods is a trifle: because all life is a dream, and dreams are nothing but dreams."[62]

---

59. Ian Charles Jarvie (born 8 July 1937) is a philosopher trained in England, a long resident in Canada. Jarvie studied at the London School of Economics under Karl Popper.

60. Clifford James Geertz (Aug. 23, 1926–Oct. 30, 2006) was an American anthropologist who is remembered mostly for his strong support for and influence on the practice of symbolic anthropology.

61. Don Pedro Calderón de la Barca y Barreda González de Henao Ruiz de Blasco y Riaño (17 Jan. 1600–25 May 1681), usually referred as Pedro Calderón de la Barca, was a dramatist, poet, writer, and a knight of the Order of Santiago, as well as a soldier and a Roman Catholic priest.

62. Calderón, *La vita è sogno,* closing of act 2.

## Relativism versus Catholicism

Gnoseological relativism, brought to its most extreme consequences, offers a dramatic image of humanity: humans are like perfect and self-sufficient spaceships traveling in the universe, each of which, having lost memory of other spaceships and even of the universe in which it is moving, imagines being in its own virtual reality; even if communications between the various spaceships were possible, they would be useless, since there are no common criteria for judging things. The only form of coherent relativism is the one that denies any absolute truth in the field of knowledge and every immutable principle in the moral sphere.

Therefore, of course, the most intense clash occurs with the Catholic religion. Relativism applied to religions means considering any belief as on the same level of any other belief, therefore putting all beliefs on the same level: one equals the other, because there is no absolute truth. The truth is what is true for me; what I personally believe is true, this is the truth for me. These cultural forms can contrast, but in relation to the objects to which they refer, they all have equal value. They are different ways, culturally and historically limited, to allude, in a very imperfect way, to certain realities that cannot be known. Ultimately, none of the conceptual or religious systems has, in any sense, an absolute value of truth. All is related to the historical moment and the cultural context; from this is derived their diversity and also their opposition. Within this relativity, all is equally valid, as different and complementary ways to approach the same reality, which substantially remains hidden.

What are the reasons for this attitude? It is indisputable that today's culture lives more and more in the perception of a non-cognitivism, in a non-possibility of accessing definitive basic truths regarding essential problems. Consequently, the centers of reference, the undisputed instances for a rational foundation of affirmations, are lacking. Culture is experiencing a profound intellectual and practical loss. Now, all this finds its mirror in and has a consequent effect on the religious world. The world of religions cannot be expected to remain excluded from this total corrosion of values and ideals. In this situation, values have become more like sensations that we project onto the world, while the very concept of reality and truth has shattered, as a glass shatters into a thousand pieces.

Therefore today there is a relativist interpretation of religion, currently known as a theology of religious pluralism. This theological theory affirms that pluralism of religions is not only a factual reality but a reality of law: God deliberately considers non-Christian religions as different ways through which men unite with him and receive salvation, regardless of Christ. Christ, at best, holds a position of particular importance but is only one of the possible ways and, of course, neither exclusive or inclusive with respect to the others. All religions would be partial ways; all could learn something of the truth about God from the others; all (or many of them) would contain an authentic divine revelation, with a consequent re-evaluation of polytheism with respect to monotheism.

The obvious consequence of all this is religious syncretism: since there are no guarantees for an absolute truth, an acceptable puzzle must be built on the ruins of modern consciousness. It might be an artificial montage of small truths, but it is a religious response in line with postmodern culture. Syncretism is the fusion of elements taken from different and non-converging religious forms. That is, syncretistic belief is generally based on an interpretation of systems of thought and religious currents, which in some cases tends to minimize, eliminate, or underscore these systems' affinities. In other cases, it combines and mixes completely irreconcilable and incompatible elements. In practice, syncretism takes elements from various realities, puts them together, and creates a new philosophical, religious, or whatever conception. In this way, syncretism is a reductive attitude towards the original doctrinal forms from which it draws the elements, because it reduces them, empties them of meaning, in order to create a new meaning. This position rests on the assumption of the essential historical and cultural relativity of the saving action of God in Christ. The universal salvific action of the divinity takes place through different limited forms, depending on the diversity of peoples and cultures, without fully identifying with any of them. The absolute truth about God could not have an adequate and sufficient expression in the history and language of humanity, always limited and relative. The actions and words of Christ are subjected to this relativity, more or less like the actions and words of any other great religious figure of history. The figure of Christ does not have an absolute and universal value. Nothing that appears in history can have this value. Consequently, there is no permanent truth, for the simple reason that there are only opinions. We choose the most useful ones for today. A theory does not hold whether it is true or not, but whether it works or not for a purpose, until a more useful one is found. This means that—today—only experimental science can tell us something about reality, whereas metaphysical, ethical, and religious truths have to do exclusively with subjectivity, privacy, aesthetics, fiction, and personal feelings. They can no longer say anything about reality. The lack of a religious reference makes ethics subjective, and therefore, the only mortal sin is to distinguish between true and false, between good and evil, between vice and virtue. Only descriptive, non-evaluative speeches can exist. In fact, any evaluation already implies discrimination; it is offensive. No one can say, for example, that traditional (heterosexual and monogamous) marriage is today superior or better than the formulas equated to it or to any future ones. Indeed, heterosexual marriage is a cultural choice among others . . . No one can say that euthanasia should be prohibited, if the person concerned finds the consent of another person; everyone can choose when and how to die without suffering, provided that one finds consent (if one cannot do it oneself).

## Political Correctness

The insidious offspring of this relativism is the so-called political correctness which, born with the idea of countering negative behaviors by changing language, has turned into real forms of censorship of thought. Political correctness is a liberal- and radical-inspired movement of ideas born in American universities in the late eighties, which proposed, in the recognition of multiculturalism, the reduction of some linguistic habits judged as discriminatory and offensive towards any given minority. It then turned into a real ideology which, in an unthinkable contrast with its own original ideas, admits no difference from the ideas it professes and spreads.

Apparently, it advocates an increasingly pressing need to change language so that it is more respectful of the various possible sensitivities, for example:

- Afro-Americans or, better, African Americans, replaces blacks, niggers, negros, etc.
- Gay replaces sodomite, faggot, etc.

In reality, however, it is a subtle attempt to alter language to shape a mentality, imposing the crumbling of an idea of coexistence based on shared principles. The reiterated axiom is that everything is relative and, therefore, nothing is given for sure and shareable. The idea of a heritage of certain values falters. The paradox is that, in the allegedly cleared freedom to define everything and everyone from time to time, one certainty has become absolute: the contrast between the obscurantism of those who resist these logics and the enlightenment of the most zealous followers of political correctness. The contrast that emerges is nothing short of dogmatic: relativism becomes absolute.

Old ideologies were based on the dialectical conception of history and politics. Instead, political correctness rejects dialectic, because it attributes to relativism the ability to ensure a coexistence without conflict. Therefore, those who continue not to accept the dogmas and precepts of the new religion cannot have citizenship in the discussion and must be excommunicated, because they are insane or pretend to be.

As Nietzsche put it: "No shepherd and one flock! Everyone wants the same things, everyone is the same: those who hear differently go to the asylum by themselves."[63] With these words, written in *Thus Spoke Zarathustra*, the philosopher painted the homologous spirit of a humanity with no God anymore.

Political correctness corrodes freedom of expression. It becomes a rhizome that expands in every direction, mad cells binding people up, breaking down the pillars of freedom of thought and expression, proud achievements of European thought. It goes even further, since it reconfigures words not only in the meanings but, above all, in the judgments they contain, with some imposed expressions and others prohibited. Political correctness, therefore, becomes an anti-culture that denies citizenship to what it does not recognize based on its a priori understanding, a radical relativism based on the idea of equality declined as uniformity, a denial of differences masked by fake non-evaluativeness. The founding core of political correctness is the adherence to a bigotry of qualitative equivalence of ideas, people, civilizations, religions, and principles, a grey nihilism in ethical sauce, certain of its superiority, as the only truth is the identical. Political correctness, judging by a priori criteria, devalues and denies. It is a form of obscurantism, oriented to the replacement of words and meanings, to prohibition, to the ethical expulsion from universities and libraries (therefore from the common horizon) of books, ideas, and authors, based on a grotesque preventive interdict that does not spare

---

63. Nietzsche, *Thus Spoke Zarathustra*, 10.

Shakespeare,[64] Kant,[65] Dante,[66] and the Bible itself, removed from the shelves of a university in Wales. Its fierce totalitarian drive is no different from that of Caliph Omar[67] allegedly saying, in front of the library of Alexandria, the melting pot of ancient culture: "In those books there are either things already present in the Koran, or there are things that are not part of it: in the first case they are useless, in the other they are harmful and must be destroyed."[68]

It is a mechanism that imposes a discreet, disguised censorship, which does not say its name and does not physically punish, but sanctions with isolation in the name of a supposed and never really defined correctness. To a large extent, it is a modern inquisition that leads to silence.

The diagnosis is made; the prognosis, in a society dominated by political correctness, is unfavorable, due to the nihilism it spreads and the intrinsic weakness of those who can only deny. There is no qualitative difference between people, their ideas, their civilizations; everything is the same; there is no good and bad, except for that initial negation.

Political correctness, in fact, leads to expressing oneself not as one really thinks but, dragged by frivolity, cowardice, and opportunism, aligning one's opinions with the more conformist ones. It is a lack of sincerity and authenticity that transforms political, social, and cultural life into a caricature, into something forced, a systematic falsity in which genuine convictions cannot be expressed, but only platitudes, poses, commonplaces. Raised in universities, it leads to their radical denial, since it closes knowledge in a suffocating enclosure where the mind, half-educated, becomes most inclined towards utopias and new fanaticisms.

---

64. William Shakespeare (bapt. 26 Apr. 1564–23 Apr. 1616) was an English playwright, poet, and actor, widely regarded as the greatest writer in the English language and the world's greatest dramatist

65. Immanuel Kant (22 Apr. 1724–12 Feb. 1804) was an influential German philosopher in the Age of Enlightenment, who had a profound influence on Western thought.

66. Dante Alighieri (often referred to simply as Dante, c.1265–1321), was an Italian poet. His *Divine Comedy*, originally called *Comedia* and later christened *Divina* by Giovanni Boccaccio, is widely considered the most important poem of the Middle Ages and the greatest literary work in the Italian language.

67. Omar, also spelled Umar (Umar ibn al-Khaṭṭāb, c. 584–3 Nov. 644), was one of the most powerful and influential Muslim caliphs in history. He was a senior companion of the Islamic prophet Muhammad.

68. al-Qifṭī, cited in "Destruction of the Library."

The deviant act—pronouncing certain words, expressing certain judgments—produces a social reaction, as the dominant culture postulates and imposes a negative (pre)judgment on it. Cultural relativism becomes the strong point: the new politically incorrect deviant is labeled as evil, guilty in his own feelings expressed with words, a different one, to be isolated in a world of the identical. A kind of society is advancing that proscribes any dissidence in the name of the comfort of any minority, in which free thinking cannot exist if the comparison of ideas is compressed and declassified to an inventory of offensive or morally reprehensible words.

The list of follies is now endless. On the campuses of some Anglo-Saxon universities, places have been created, called safe spaces, where each student can express himself or herself freely, that is, according to the supporters of the experiment, without fear of not feeling comfortable or unsafe about his or her sex, race, ethnicity, sexual orientation, gender, biography, cultural background, religion, age, or physical and mental identity. Faceless beings and identities participate in debates in which applause is not allowed, as clapping could be aggressive for some spectators. Applause is replaced by a movement of raised hands, called "jazz hands."[69] Gender neutral bathrooms are built in various public spaces so as not to offend transgender people.

It is the dream of a world without homelands, properties, and faiths, devoted only to the satisfaction of the individual's instant emotion. It is the one who takes the place of God and who paradoxically nullifies oneself by reducing oneself to a bundle of drives. Without its own statute, it is a totally manipulable entity. Or, perhaps, replaceable. What political correctness does not understand, is that religion is not the same as veganism, astrology, or cheering for a sports team. Religion is at the origin of humanity and satisfies the transcendent needs of many human beings, the search for answers that are not rational (from a strictly philosophical point of view), something immeasurable in its power and dimension in which to be—or feel—lost.

## Faith and Reason Today

We have seen (lived) the immeasurable throughout our journey from prehistory to today, and it has left us with the antinomy between faith

---

69. Jazz hands in performance dance is the extension of a performer's hands with palms toward the audience and fingers splayed.

and reason, never really reconciled. In fact, faith and reason still seem to be like two parallel lines that never meet. As in a fictional or cinematographic representation of the famous Schroedinger's cat,[70] who experiences multiple lives and deaths in parallel worlds but knows only what it is, what it does, in each of those worlds and cannot move with a megagalactic acrobatic jump from one world to another—something analogous to the "infinite possible worlds of the divine intellect" which the philosopher Leibnitz[71] describes in his *Theodicy*.[72]

Not *fides et ratio* (faith and reason), then, but *fides aut ratio* (faith or reason)?

No.

Faith is legitimate if it does not change lanes, as it has too often done, especially in the West; does not swerve; does not cross paths to clash with reason; does not demand, from the top of the divine bench, to lay down law on reason and science. On the other hand, it is necessary to ensure that science is not transformed into dogma, into a system of absolute and undoubted truths, alternative to religious ones. As explained by Popper and Peirce,[73] the two great twentieth-century philosophers of science, the key to scientific research is fallibilism, the methodology of "try and try again," the awareness that history of science is an alternation of errors and correction of errors ("you learn by mistake," the primary school teachers once recommended to their young pupils).

The reason that ascends to Goddess Reason betrays itself, is no longer reason, critical and relative, that is, fallible, but it self-posits itself as absolute. And, as an absolute, it must be rejected. How? With reason itself, which is the enemy of any absolute, including the absolutization of itself. Therefore Reason, or Word, deified Logos, perhaps incarnate, crucified and

---

70. Schroedinger's cat is a thought experiment, sometimes described as a paradox, devised by Austrian physicist Erwin Schroedinger in 1935, during the course of discussions with Albert Einstein. It illustrates what Schroedinger saw as the problem of the Copenhagen interpretation of quantum mechanics applied to everyday objects. The scenario presents a hypothetical cat that may be simultaneously alive and dead, a state known as a quantum superposition, as a result of being linked to a random subatomic event that may or may not occur.

71. Gottfried Wilhelm (von) Leibniz (also spelled Leibnitz, 1 July 1646–14 Nov. 1716) was a prominent German polymath and one of the most important logicians, mathematicians, and natural philosophers of the Enlightenment.

72. Leibniz, *Theodicy*, 147.

73. Charles Sanders Peirce (10 Sept. 1839–19 Apr. 1914) was an American philosopher, logician, mathematician, and scientist.

risen, is not a figure, a sign, a symbol of reason, but of faith. Foreign and incomprehensible to reason. Reason, science, is not only fallible, but also limited. It cannot know everything. On the contrary, it does not even know what everything is (in reality, another term, synonymous, to indicate the absolute); its search is endless. However, the unfathomability of the mystery that surrounds us remains, which scientific knowledge cannot definitively thin out, incapable as it is of crossing the boundaries of experience.

The big questions remain (where from, why, where to, is there a meaning, and which), which are inherent in humanity, in our imperfection, finiteness, and contingency, but to which we cannot give a definitive rational answer. This is the terrain of religiosity, not of statutory religions, as Kant would call them, which are historical, dogmatic, and doctrinaire. Indeed, it is the philosopher of Koenigsberg who indicates to us in the *Critique of Judgment* a concept of faith that should perhaps still be explored: doubtful faith (*Zweifelglaube*): "Faith is the moral way of thinking of reason, in adhering to what is unattainable by theoretical knowledge."[74] To combine faith with doubt, with the uncertain, with the fallible, which is the distinctive sign of reason. Or rather, combine it with not knowing. With knowing not to know and never to be able to know, neither everything nor incontrovertibly. A skeptical faith. Without dogmas. An agnostic faith, which turns to a God, whom nobody knows if he exists or not. And who, if there is one, is unknowable to us: a hidden *Deus absconditus*.[75] It is the paradox of Nicolaus Cusanus:[76] "*Quia ignoro, adoro*" ("I believe, because I ignore"; it is the beginning of one of his famous written brochures in 1444–45, which reports an imaginary dialogue between a Catholic and a pagan). Obviously, in the same way—but this the believer Cardinal Cusanus does not say, even if he could have said it—for the unbeliever the symmetrically opposite consequence holds: *Quia ignoro, non adoro*; precisely because I ignore, I do not believe. And so, if intrinsic obscurity, doubt, an ill-disposed will, the impossibility of reaching a

---

74. Kant, *Kritik der Urtheilskraft (Critique of Judgment)*, 472.

75. The hidden God (Latin: *Deus absconditus*) refers to the Christian idea of the fundamental unknowability of the essence of God. The name comes from the Bible, specifically Isa 45:15: "Indeed, you are a hidden God, you God of Israel, the Savior."

76. Nicholas of Cusa (1401–11 Aug 1464), also referred to as Nicholas of Kues and Nicolaus Cusanus, was a German philosopher, theologian, jurist, and astronomer. One of the first German proponents of Renaissance humanism, he made spiritual and political contributions in European history.

conciliation, can undermine the faith, it helps then, as also suggested by Juergen Moltmann,[77] to turn to hope.

## Hope

What is hope above all?

Hope is the tension towards our best future way of existing, as if our soul grasped its legitimacy, its credibility, in the temporal trajectory stretched towards the future, magically getting rid of the waste of the past. Hope is a state of mind that creates a prolonged emotional state, which determines our inner disposition towards what we are about to do. Hope anticipates the future and determines how we feel in the present. Mental and emotional states in turn affect the consequent behavior in the present. All of this, by reflex, can influence the way one sees oneself. Having hope makes thinking more flexible, more inclined to explore new situations; improves school, sports, professional performance; increases well-being; makes one feel more self-effective, happy; elevates self-esteem, induces one to take care of oneself; helps one to better tolerate pain; makes one more socially collaborative, grateful, joyful; decreases the fear of death; and makes the immune system more efficient. Since hope is directed towards the expectation of positive results, it seems to unconsciously determine our behavior towards concrete and constructive actions in the direction of achieving proposed objectives. On the other hand, those who have little hope tend to choose only tasks they already know how to do; avoid putting themselves to the test; and when they fail, give up continuing. They believe very little in their ability to achieve the desired future. The way hopeful people cope with uncomfortable situations differs from the way of those who have little hope. Even if the present condition is tiring, such people nourish the thought of a better future, capable by itself of reducing tensions. This makes them feel adaptable, able to face the situation, and reassures them that there will be better moments. Having hope also goes hand in hand with an infinite positive version of the future. Hopeful and optimistic people, thus,

---

77. Juergen Moltmann (born 8 Apr. 1926) is a German Reformed theologian who is professor emeritus of systematic theology at the University of Tübingen. Moltmann developed a form of liberation theology predicated on the view that God suffers with humanity, while also promising humanity a better future through the hope of the Resurrection, which he has labeled a theology of hope.

## Faith and Hope

manage to justify the negativities of the present, while pessimistic ones remain in resentment and concern.

The etymology of the Latin noun for hope, *spes*, derives from the Sanskrit root *spa*, which means striving for a goal. In the Spanish language, hoping and waiting both translate with *esperar*, as if one could only wait for what one hopes. I believe that our thinking is made of hope, because we evaluate our future every minute, even if only for the next minute, and we want it to be a positive future. Now, since no one wants evil for himself, hope, since ancient times, means tending towards good, so we can say that hoping is almost a biological necessity for the individual, close to the imperative of survival.

For Goethe: "Those who do not hope for another life are always dead to this one."[78]

For Gandhi: "Take hope, and live in its light."[79]

For Hesiod, at the bottom of Pandora's box, which had caused all the evils of the world, there was hope.

For Thales: "Hope is the only good that is common to all men, and even those who have nothing more, still possess it."[80]

For Heraclitus: "Without hope it is impossible to find the unexpected."[81]

---

78. Goethe, cited in Eckermann, "Conversations with Goethe." 86. Johann Wolfgang von Goethe (28 Aug. 1749–22 Mar. 1832) was a German writer and statesman. He is considered the greatest German literary figure of the modern era.

79. Gandhi, cited in Cinelli Colombini, "Happy Easter." Mohandas Karamchand Gandhi (2 Oct. 1869–30 Jan. 1948) was an Indian lawyer, anti-colonial nationalist, and political ethicist, who employed nonviolent resistance to lead the successful campaign for India's independence from British rule and in turn inspired movements for civil rights and freedom across the world. The honorific *Mahatma* (Sanskrit: great-souled, venerable), first applied to him in 1914 in South Africa, is now used throughout the world.

80. Thales, cited in Edwards, *Dictionary of Thoughts*, 234. Thales of Miletus (c. 624/623–c. 548/545 BC) was a Greek mathematician, astronomer, and pre-Socratic philosopher from Miletus in Ionia, Asia Minor. He was one of the Seven Sages of Greece. Many, most notably Aristotle, regarded him as the first philosopher in the Greek tradition, and he is otherwise historically recognized as the first individual in Western civilization known to have entertained and engaged in scientific philosophy.

81. Heraclitus, Fragment 18. Heraclitus of Ephesus (c. 535–c. 475 BC) was a pre-Socratic Ionian Greek philosopher and a native of the city of Ephesus, in modern-day Turkey and then part of the Persian Empire.

For Gilbert Keith Chesterton: "There is one thing which gives radiance to everything. It is the idea of something around the corner."[82]

## Christian Hope

What about Christian hope? This hope of which we have talked until now, as Moltmann notes, is however entirely intramundane, therefore absolutely incapable of facing death. In front of death, hope is shattered. Only Christian hope, placing the accent on an ultramundane and transcendent reality, can overcome death. So not Marxism (as Bloch[83] believed) but Christianity, with its hope in God, must be considered as the "learned hope" (Bloch), which inherits the hopes of the past and keeps the prospect of a future of justice alive among the oppressed. The hope of Christianity is therefore resurrection: resurrection of Christ and all the dead, without which nothing makes sense.

"Remember our brothers who fell asleep in the hope of the resurrection," we ask God at Mass. The perception that contemporary society has of death seems to oscillate between removal (of one's own death) and spectacularization (of the death of others). The removal relegates death to a private, anonymous fact (death is only for those who die, and for the few who are in some way affected by it) and reduces it to a purely biological moment, devoid of every spiritual and communal dimension. Spectacularization introduces death into our life with media images. Salvatore Natoli[84] spoke of the "epic of the macabre," where death—between advertising a product to be tasted and a beautiful girl to be looked at—is exhibited in the blatantly exposed corpses, in the massacres and ethnic cleansing persistently shown. Death, precisely because exhibited with no respect, ends up losing its character of a tremendous reality, to become simply ruthless.

This reality then is seen and considered without the pity that, far from being superficial emotion and elusive feeling, allows one to take upon oneself the pain of the other, to share it to the end, to carry the other

---

82. Chesterton, cited in introduction of Oddie, *Chesterton* (no page number available). Gilbert Keith Chesterton (29 May 1874–14 June 1936) was an English writer, philosopher, lay theologian, and literary and art critic. He has been referred to as the prince of paradox.

83. Ernst Bloch (8 July 1885–4 Aug. 1977) was a German Marxist philosopher. Bloch's work focuses on the thesis that in a humanistic world where oppression and exploitation have been eliminated, there will always be a truly revolutionary force.

84. Salvatore Natoli (18 Sept. 1942) is an Italian philosopher.

on one's shoulders, as Sirach[85] recommends: "Give graciously to all the living; do not withhold kindness even from the dead. Do not avoid those who weep, but mourn with those who mourn."[86]

Or, as the Virgilian Aeneas[87] does, towards his father: "Come then, dear father, mount upon my neck; on my own shoulders I will support you, and this task will not weigh me down. However things may fall, we two will have one common peril, one salvation."[88]

A death shown in the spectacular way, even if it manages to move one, does so for only a few moments, because it is quickly and easily forgotten. Suspicion may arise that such an epic of the macabre could be a singular and refined way to exorcise death: death is always there, but it is always of others, it is far away, and therefore it can be visible, tolerable. If, however, it is mine, if it touches me, then it is good that it disappear as soon as possible, perhaps with the justification that science and technology are in a position to manage it much better than human pity can do.

Death frightens, but Christian hope says that, even at the end of your life, you are in the penultimate chapter. The last is the promise: presence, closeness, sonship by an infinitely good God who, in order to remove all fear of the present and the future, passed himself first through solitude, overcoming it with the cry of hope that saved the world: "In your hands I entrust my spirit."

Hope does not need legitimation and therefore does not collide with reason, as faith may do, but it flows from the heart, intimate and personal, sees the invisible, touches the intangible, reaches the impossible, and brings with it, hidden, the seed of faith itself, which can bloom suddenly and unexpectedly, like a flower.

---

85. The Book of the All-Virtuous Wisdom of Yeshua ben Sira, commonly called the Wisdom of Sirach or simply Sirach, and also known as the book of Ecclesiasticus or Ben Sira, is a work of ethical teachings from approximately 200 to 175 BC, written by the Jewish scribe Ben Sira of Jerusalem, on the inspiration of his father Joshua son of Sirach, sometimes called Jesus son of Sirach or Yeshua ben Eliezer ben Sira. Sirach is accepted as part of the canon by Catholics, Eastern Orthodox, and most of Oriental Orthodoxy, but is not in the Jewish Canon.

86. Sirach 7:33.

87. In Greco-Roman mythology, Aeneas was a Trojan hero, the son of the prince Anchises and the goddess Aphrodite (Venus). He is a character in Greek mythology and is mentioned in Homer's *Iliad*. Aeneas receives full treatment in Roman mythology, most extensively in Virgil's *Aeneid*, where he is cast as an ancestor of Romulus and Remus. He became the first true hero of Rome.

88. Virgil, *Aeneid*, bk 2, lines 707–10.

And so with Saint Augustine, we can say: "May your hope be the Lord your God. Do not hope for anything else from the Lord God, but let him be your hope." We can also listen to the words of Pope Francis:[89] "May the Lord, who is the hope of glory, who is the center, who is the whole, help us on this path: to give hope, to have a passion for hope. And, as I said, it is not always optimism, but it is what Our Lady, in her heart, had in the greatest darkness: on the evening of Friday until the first morning of Sunday. That hope: she had it. And that hope has redone everything. May the Lord give us this grace."[90]

## The Modernity of Hope: *Spe Salvi*

Pope Benedict XVI;[91] in his encyclical *Spe salvi* (30 Nov. 2007), opens us to an extraordinary journey on the path of hope: "This Encyclical starts, in order to understand what is hope in Christianity, from the first part of the verse 24 of one of the fundamental chapters of the whole New Testament: 'In hope we are saved.'"[92]

And if we have been saved, says Pope Benedict, it is because, right now, hope helps us face the arduous present, the hard path to that goal of which we can be sure, a goal "so great as to justify" all the difficulties necessary to achieve it.[93]

Then he asks himself: what kind of hope is this ever, if only its being in us already makes us redeemed, that is, if already "hope is redemption"?[94] In fact, he says a little earlier, Christianity does not consist only in giving good news, in communicating things to know, but "in a communication that produces facts and changes life," which opens up "the dark door of

---

89. Pope Francis (born Jorge Mario Bergoglio, 17 Dec. 1936) is the head of the Catholic Church and sovereign of the Vatican City State. Francis is the first Jesuit pope, the first from the Americas, the first from the Southern Hemisphere, and the first pope from outside Europe since the Syrian Gregory III, who reigned in the eighth century.

90. Morning Mass Homily, Santa Marta Chapel, Sept. 9, 2013.

91. Pope Benedict XVI (born Joseph Aloisius Ratzinger, 16 Apr. 1927) is a retired prelate of the Catholic Church who served as head of the Church and sovereign of the Vatican City State from 2005 until his resignation in 2013. Benedict's election as pope occurred in the 2005 papal conclave that followed the death of Pope John Paul II. Benedict chose to be known by the title pope emeritus upon his resignation.

92. Rom 8:24

93. Benedict XVI, *Spe Salvi*, 1.

94. Benedict XVI, *Spe Salvi*, 3.

time and future."[95] If we must consider ourselves already redeemed, then, it is not only because this hope transforms us from now on, but also because already, with its very being, it makes us certain about what has yet to happen. So the next question that needs to be asked is: "What kind of certainty is it?"[96] In the last letter he writes, Paul says he is convinced that the one in whom he believed will give him enough strength to keep his "deposit[97] until that day."[98]

By virtue of what comes from God, those who hope can every time regain unspeakable forces, put on "wings like eagles."[99]

To hope, in Christianity, is to live in the light of a truth that is a gift to be preserved, in view of a goal towards which we perpetually strive. Whoever stops having before him or her the day when our Lord will come, stops believing and therefore hoping according to that deposit passed on from generation to generation. The true desperate is a very peaceful person, and the worst despair is the unconscious one, as Kierkegaard[100] knew well, that of one who is satisfied without awaiting anything more from the future.

Even Thomas Aquinas considered sloth the greatest despair, the boring tedium of living. The opposite of hope would therefore not be despair but indifference: God can die before our yawns. The true hope, that which comes to us from Christ, is instead restlessness, expectation, a cry. In this way, Christ lived it himself, sinking into the abysses of the *kenosis* (Greek word that means emptying): "Adopt the same attitude as that of Christ Jesus, who, existing in the form of God, did not consider equality with God as something to be exploited. Instead he emptied himself by assuming the form of a servant, taking on the likeness of humanity."[101] This famous passage from Paul opens us to that mystery of Christ which,

---

95. Benedict XVI, *Spe Salvi*, 2.

96. Benedict XVI, *Spe Salvi*, 1.

97. The sacred deposit of the faith (*depositum fidei*) refers to the teachings of the Catholic Church that are believed to be handed down since the time of the apostles— namely the Bible and apostolic tradition. Saint Paul uses the Greek word *paratheke* (deposit) meaning something precious entrusted to a depositary for safekeeping.

98. 2 Tim 1:12.

99. Isa 40:31.

100. Søren Aabye Kierkegaard (5 May 1813–11 Nov. 1855) was a Danish philosopher, theologian, poet, social critic, and religious author who is widely considered to be the first existentialist philosopher.

101. Phil 2:5–7.

from a theological and biblical point of view, goes by the name of *kenosis*. The Son of God decides, with a free act, to empty himself of himself, that is, to estrange himself from his divine form and take human nature, that is, as a servant, since such is our nature from God's point of view. There, where hope and despair have come to touch, the question shouted from the cross still tells us today that God remains faithful to his promises, especially towards the desperate of every generation of human history. Hope is not generic optimism in the face of the concerns of living but is waiting for the impossible. It is not difficult to hope that a pregnant woman will give birth to a healthy baby, just as it is not difficult to hope that a freshly sown field will end up yielding a good harvest. When hope comes into play, it is always because there are margins of uncertainty, but the expectations are reasonable here: easily this will happen, because after all, this has usually happened. What is repetitive and foreseeable—therefore predictable—basically provides a lot of security and quiet, even in hope. Reducing the complexity of things, such as giving—perhaps cheap—answers to everything, renouncing the effort of invoking the question, makes us feel safe, certainly, albeit far from the truth and from those who do not have what we have. But when it comes to the impossible, to that "great hope that must overcome everything else," that "can only be God who embraces the universe, and offer us, and give us what we cannot achieve by ourselves,"[102] when it comes to hope that goes even against those laws of nature considered eternal, when it comes to resurrection of the dead, then things get really difficult, to the point that every reasonable and common-sense person could say, in the end, what Spinoza[103] said: "The more we try to live under the guidance of reason, the more we try not to depend on hope."[104]

Only those who do not know how things really go, say the philosophers, can hope for the impossible. Hope is for the weak, the unconscious, the ignorant, those who delude themselves, those who fail either to know or accept reality. Woe to him who wants to change the least thing

---

102. Benedict XVI, *Spe Salvi*, 31.

103. Baruch (de) Spinoza, anglicized to Benedict de Spinoza (24 Nov. 1632–21 Feb. 1677) was a Dutch philosopher of Portuguese Sephardi origin. One of the early thinkers of the Enlightenment and modern biblical criticism, including modern conceptions of the self and the universe, he came to be considered one of the great rationalists of seventeenth-century philosophy.

104. Spinoza, *Ethics* 4, prop. 47, note.

# Faith and Hope

in the perfect harmony of the cosmos, say the Hellenes;[105] everything has always been and always will be so, everything is regulated by a supreme reason. The wise man does not allow himself to be seized by the desire for something other than this reasonable universal harmony, which moves and envelops everything. There is no escape therefore; the true sage is "the one who knows how to live without hope and without fear,"[106] says Seneca,[107] philosopher, poet, minister of Nero, and contemporary of Christ. Stoicism[108] had great influence in ancient Christianity. Apathy soothes and calms, whereas it is really hard to follow the pathos of a God who cries and dies in pain. But that—not another—is the God of Christ, the God who promises to resurrect the dead. Resignation, then, is a sister to destiny and fate. Whoever believes in those is there to tell us: for what do you hope, if the future has already been written all along, and if you can already read it in the eternal movement of the stars? And then, what is this idea that death is the great ultimate enemy and whoever dies must also rise? How does a pagan not laugh at hearing such things? What could be more natural than the fact that a man gets old and dies at some point? Poor, truly poor is he who does not resign himself to dying.

And yet, against any resigned adaptation to cosmic harmonies and fate, Christian hope awaits a final outcome, a break. The one who hopes is the one who, at a certain point, opens the heart and begins to believe, disposing oneself to the will of God, just as Mary did when the angel said to her: "Nothing is impossible for God."[109] If there is continuity without crisis between the history of this world and the kingdom, if there is preparation for that, through political, technical, scientific action, then we are dealing with an object God, immobile, a God who is no longer an agent but an ornament that is placed in a corner. So wait for us, and let us do it.

---

105. Other name for Greeks.

106. Seneca, *De Constantia Sapientis*, 9:2.

107. Lucius Annaeus Seneca (c. 4 BC–65 AD), also known as Seneca the Younger, was a Roman Stoic philosopher, statesman, dramatist, and—in one work—satirist from the Silver Age of Latin literature.

108. Stoicism is a school of Hellenistic philosophy founded by Zeno of Citium in Athens in the early third century BC. It is a philosophy of personal ethics informed by its system of logic and its views on the natural world. According to its teachings, as social beings, the path to *eudaimonia* (happiness, or blessedness) is found in accepting the moment as it presents itself, by not allowing oneself to be controlled by the desire for pleasure or fear of pain, by using one's mind to understand the world and to do one's part in nature's plan, and by working together and treating others fairly and justly.

109. Luke 1:37.

The book of Revelation is linked to the thought of a God who intervenes in a story, who decides himself, acting as sovereign, and creating with his omnipotent word the world he wants, while his ardent approach makes the mountains melt and shake the humans and their works. It is a matter of taking the living God seriously. Now, hope is precisely this work that urges this living God to come and reveal himself no longer in privacy, weakness, and humiliation, but also in glory. Unless the glory of God expressed Revelation is hoped for, there is no hope, as Jacques Ellul[110] maintained in his *Hope in Time of Abandonment*. But, on this same point, the theologian Ratzinger, more than thirty years ago, treating eschatology as a basic theme of preaching, was explicit: "The apocalyptic epoch in which we live, has guided thoughts of Christianity, again and more forcefully, towards the eschatological message of the New Testament, which draws its specific strength and vitality from the powerful tension towards the final event." And this is precisely because it is "a book of hope that looks forward, towards the future, towards the end which is the true principle."[111] "Now in this hope we were saved, but hope that is seen is not hope, because who hopes for what he sees? Now if we hope for what we do not see, we eagerly wait for it with patience."[112]

Hope is directed towards what is not seen, what is not yet there. Redemption has indeed begun, but it has yet to be accomplished, and hope has to do, above all, with the expectation of this accomplishment. But what is it that the Christian still does not see? What is he awaiting with perseverance, if not events that will happen when the one who has promised to come, and to come soon, does come? Is this not the true hard struggle of the believer today, surrounded, as perhaps never before, by mocking ridiculers, who sarcastically whisper in his ear? "They will say: Where is this coming he promised? Ever since our ancestors died, everything goes on as it has since the beginning of creation"[113]—as if to

---

110. Jacques Ellul (6 Jan. 1912–19 May 1994) was a French philosopher, sociologist, lay theologian, and professor who was a noted Christian anarchist. His writings are frequently concerned with the emergence of a technological tyranny over humanity. As a philosopher and theologian, he further explored the religiosity of the technological society.

111. Ratzinger, *Dogma und Verkündigung*, cited in Garota, "Tra Caparra e Compimento," 132.

112. Rom 8:24–25.

113. 2 Pet 3:4.

say, what are you still hoping for? Can't you see that death has always given the final blow to every living thing?

"The great hope based on God's promises"[114] is the hope of redemption, as unique as the God who promised it, a hope that comes to us from millenary biblical roots and from the church that has continued to transmit it to us. A hope made their own especially by the little ones and the humble ones of Israel,[115] by those who cried out in pain, just as Christ cried out in pain on the cross. A hope that arose with great force since the time of the Maccabees, which is still possible to find, albeit distorted, in the anxieties and expectations of modernity.

Is it not from this hope and this hunger for justice that the great revolutions of the last centuries have sprung up, from scientific and industrial ones to Marxist ones? Are not certain revolutionaries the ones who have listened to the cries of the poor and oppressed, in years when the ears of too many people of the church had gone deaf? Redemption is ultimately the resurrection of the dead, the heavens and earth become new—events that no technique and no social revolution can ever achieve. Redemption is the event impossible for men, yet possible for God, an event so unheard of, that in front of it, hope is not only put to the test but could even become vain. Paul on this point was even more explicit: "For if the dead are not raised, then Christ has not been raised either. And if Christ has not been raised, your faith is futile; you are still in your sins. Then those also who have fallen asleep in Christ are lost. If only for this life we have hope in Christ, we are of all people most to be pitied."[116]

We hope because a historical fact has already happened. Here is the foundation of our hope: faith in the risen Christ, two thousand years ago. But if the second fact, the resurrection of the dead, does not follow, the first fact remains meaningless: "If the dead are not raised, let us eat and drink, for tomorrow we die."[117]

With the coming of Christ, the future of hope does not stop, as if everything has already been accomplished. Christ rises, then ascends to heaven, but not to remain there. Those who believe in him know that he will come again in glory, to judge the living and the dead. The Christian faith, so to speak, relaunches hope towards the future, towards the

---

114. Benedict XVI, *Spe Salvi*, 35.

115. "But I will leave within you the meek and humble. The remnant of Israel will trust in the name of the LORD" (Zeph 3:12).

116. 1 Cor 15:16–19.

117. 1 Cor 15:32.

*parousia*,[118] towards the second coming of Christ. One must be vigilant in waiting, then. The center of Christian hope will not be the afterlife of souls without concreteness and timelessness, but the future redemption of the world, which will happen in the blink of an eye, just when no one expects it anymore. Christianity never expresses an escape from the world, nor even the quiet of an eternal present, but an intense desire for the future, for the salvation of this world. "The souls of the righteous are in the hands of God, no torment will touch them." It is their hope to be "full of immortality," since they "will shine" and "like sparks in the stubble, they will run here and there" only "on the day of judgment."[119]

Of course, as Pope Benedict says, love can "reach to the afterlife," allowing us to remain "tied to each other with bonds of affection beyond the border of death," because truly "our lives are in deep communion with each other,"[120] but this cannot change the fundamental fact that redemption must remain a liberation to await. Hoping for redemption means believing in the promise that God has made, that one day we will be definitively freed from the forces of evil and death. What did God say to Moses when he revealed himself in the fiery bush? That he listens to us, that he is close to us in pain, and that he will do incredible things for us in the future, in order to free us from all that now afflicts and oppresses us. There is a great charge towards future and action, in that mysterious name which means, according to exegetes, "I am who I will be," "I am now and I will always be there," "Who I am you will see from what I will do."[121] The God of the bush is the same that Revelation also reveals to us three times as "he who is, who was, and who is to come."[122]

The Jewish-Christian God is the God of history, the one who stands at the beginning of everything and who, in the end, will redeem the whole creation that now "groans and suffers" in anticipation, since "it nourishes the hope of being also freed from the slavery of corruption."[123] In the memory of what has been and in fidelity to a promise, the believer is such because he or she believes and hopes, waiting for what will come from

---

118. The word *parousia* is an ancient Greek word meaning presence, arrival, or official visit. It is used in Christian theology mainly to refer to the second coming of Christ.

119. Wisdom 3:1–7.

120. Benedict XVI, *Spe Salvi*, 48.

121. Exod 3:14.

122. Rev 1:4, 1:8, 4:8.

123. Rom 8:20–23.

the future. The church teaches the believer to say: "I await the resurrection of the dead and the life of the world to come." No, it is not the souls who ascend to heaven on the day of our death that really concern our hope, but the New Jerusalem that will come down from heaven to be "God's dwelling place with men." Yes, there God will wipe the tears from our eyes, and we will be comforted forever, because "there will be no more death."

## Is It Possible to Hope Today?

Hence the question that, even when reading this encyclical, arises: is it possible to continue to hope in this way? Of course, he who wrote it is aware of being a shepherd of many sheep who are always on the verge of getting out of the sheepfold; it is to be believed that he does not delude himself too much by seeing the enthusiasm of those who run around him, smiling and waving flags. Pope Benedict knows well that the increasingly empty churches are matched by increasingly full malls and business centers, by young people who choose less and less to marry at the altar and by parents who no longer have an interest in baptizing their children, or in seeing how the key to eternal life can be found in faith. Indeed, the Pope says again, the very words eternal life frighten us, arousing in us the idea of the interminable.[124] Not to mention the emptiness of the knowledge of Christ even where, in a more or less habitual and slavish manner, one continues to participate in the Sunday liturgies. It is true, there is in the world the great mass of the poor, who await words of consolation and bread on which to feed, but the real challenge, for faith, is the rich opulent North of the world. Benedict XVI knows this. It's there where sheep are seduced and dragged away by mass hedonism and indifference, as the masters of the Frankfurt School, among others, had also well understood.

It is from this awareness, perhaps, that Pope Benedict, and a part of the church with him, shows that sort of fear of continuing to open the doors to the world as his predecessors had done since the years of the last council. It is from the fear that everything may get out of hand, perhaps, that spurs the tightening of ranks, the calling to order, the saying to everyone: look, the church is continuing to announce to you a sure and reasonable hope. The church is the only one left, after not only Marx and his companions but also the advocates of science and technology have long since failed or reached impassable limits.

---

124. Benedict XVI, *Spe Salvi*, 12.

It is not easy to work on rubble, though. The fresh hope of the early days of the church is not easy to recover. Here, perhaps it is precisely by starting again from the awareness of defeats, of the betrayals that arose, first of all, from within the church, that at least something can be recovered of that hope that burned bright in the heart of the first Christian communities. We must not be afraid to say that Peter, the cornerstone, shamelessly betrayed his Lord, just when he should have been closer to him who was begging for help and closeness. In Gethsemane, those who had to be on watch were asleep, the Evangelists are not ashamed to tell us, because this is how truth is said and preached, perceiving oneself as a useless sinner. It is from poverty and from below that the true path of hope can begin, believing in and waiting for those things which are impossible to us, possible only to God.

To say that it is love that saves the world, not science and technology, is not enough, if then one is forced to use, like everyone else, what science and technology have been able to achieve for addressing health and human life problems, managing to build not only the megabomb, but also the airplane and operating room—instruments that contribute a great deal "to the humanization of the world and humanity."[125] It is true, faith in progress has replaced faith in God, and "it can also destroy man and the world, if it is not oriented by forces that are outside of it." The church cannot face this dilemma. It can neither go back, though, because no one can renounce progress, nor delude oneself that things can be solved with the "growth of the inner man" or with "progress in the ethical formation of man" to pair with the ever faster progress of technical discoveries. There are too many things that ethics alone cannot tackle, things in the face of which it is perhaps more necessary than ever to rediscover the radicality of evangelical faith, that naked and humble invoking, just when one feels like a useless servant, after having done all that was to be done.[126]

Hope in Greek is *elpis*, which also means forecast or legitimate expectation, on the basis of very precise data available, a sort of calculation that has nothing to do with effects but with the critical prudence of those who try to have everything under control. Unlike this kind of hope, Christian hope is beyond measure, that is, it concerns the impossible, the incredible, the never before seen, what goes beyond the laws of

---

125. Benedict XVI, *Spe Salvi*, 25.
126. Luke 17:10.

nature, what "is in fight against evidence"—Lev Shestov[127] would say—and, therefore, *contra spem*. In Hebrew, hope is *tiqwah*, a word that also means thread. Hope, in the Jewish way of feeling it, is a tightrope between pain and the expected consolation, between humanity and God. Job, who is indescribably troubled, perceives the fading of the thread of hope that still inhabits him.[128] Not only when the thread breaks but also when it comes loose, hope fails.

The decisive question then is: what kind of hope can come from a past that has seen God die? What kind of redemption has been promised for the future by this God who died and then rose again? Is it not in fact in the tightrope between deposit and fulfillment, in the radical passage between cross and resurrection, that the redemption of the world is played out? Are not heaven and earth, are not all the dead waiting for the Lord who promised to come on the last day to redeem and judge history? Was this not the living hope, which beat in the heart of the early church, which appeared scandalous not only to the philosophers of Athens but also to the religious power of Jerusalem? Hard, really hard, was to see "the Son of God die like a failure, exposed to ridicule, among the criminals."[129]

Christian hope trusts in the Lord who will come to annihilate, with the "breath of his mouth," the unjust, "the son of perdition," and all the "lying wonders" of which he is capable.[130] Christian hope yearns for the redemption of the world and never adapts to makeshift solutions or unanimous climbs to heaven, similar to those of the times of Babel.[131] Despite his tenderness and mercy leading him to slow down the hands of the clock of universal judgment each time he finds himself faced, in every generation, with those hidden "thirty-six righteous"[132] mentioned by Jewish tradition, God himself, immediately afterwards, can only speed them up, upon realizing how much those righteous ones are forced to

---

127. Lev Isaakovich Shestov (1866–1938), born Yehuda Leib Shvartsman, was a Russian existentialist philosopher known for his philosophy of despair.

128. Job 7:6.

129. Benedict XVI, *Spe salvi*, 50.

130. 2 Thess 2:3–9.

131. Gen 11:1–9.

132. Mystical Hasidic Judaism as well as other segments of Judaism believe that there exist thirty-six righteous people *(Tzadikim Nistarim)*, whose role in life is to justify the purpose of humankind in the eyes of God. Jewish tradition holds that their identities are unknown to each other and that, if one of them comes to a realization of his or her true purpose, he or she would never admit it.

suffer in the world. The end time also depends, like that of the beginning, at the time of the flood, on the painful alternation of justice and compassion[133] in divine intimacy: "The judgment of God is hope, both because it is justice and because it is grace."[134]

Therefore, it seems right to us that Benedict XVI recalls that "a self-critique of modernity is needed in dialogue with Christianity and its concept of hope," while inviting Christians to "learn anew in what their hope truly consists, what they have to offer to the world and what they cannot offer," learning to understand themselves "starting from their roots" and without falling into the clutches of that "faith in progress" that can lead, in all its ambiguity, "from the sling to the atom bomb" and can offer "new possibilities for good, but . . . also open[ing] up appalling possibilities for evil—possibilities that formerly did not exist."[135] And it seems right to us to recall how modern Christianity, faced with "the progressive structuring of the world," ended up restricting "the horizon of its hope."[136] Secularization has eliminated from Christian hope the expectation of the impossible. It has already fallen even lower. The really big problem today is that nothing is taken seriously anymore, and that nobody cares about being saved anymore. A sea of indifference is reigning. True hope is an unknown thing, and its unknown being is, at the same time, the cause of all desperation, as well as of all positive and destructive impulses towards the authentic world and the authentic man. "We are asleep, full of semi-erased images of lost Eden," said Léon Bloy, "blind beggars on the threshold of a sublime palace, whose door is closed."[137]

---

133. Gen 6:6.
134. Benedict XVI, *Spe Salvi*, 47.
135. Benedict XVI, *Spe Salvi*, 22.
136. Benedict XVI, *Spe Salvi*, 25.
137. Bloy, *Dans les ténèbres*, cited in Garota, "Tra Caparra e Compimento," 146. Léon Bloy (11 July 1846–3 Nov. 1917) was a French novelist, essayist, pamphleteer, and poet known additionally for his eventual, passionate defense of Roman Catholicism and influence within French Catholic circles.

## Christian Hope as the Ultimate Beacon in Today's World

So the church in her liturgy, as well as through this encyclical by Benedict XVI, has managed to safeguard, albeit wearily, the decisive points of the Jewish-Christian hope, those that concern the ultimate things (the redemption of the world, the judgment on history, the resurrection of the dead).

Of course, the resurrection of the dead is among the most difficult hopes to believe, for its absurdity. It is not for nothing, in fact, that so often we are tempted to make it a symbol of something else. But, even more than to believe, it is a difficult hope for which to live in wait. Waiting means being tense towards that event, wanting it to happen as soon as possible, in our day. So it was, anyway, for the church at its origins. To believe that the individual soul is immortal, that whoever dies continues to live for eternity, is not very difficult at all. To hope and wait for the dead in flesh and blood to rise, that the past will be recovered, judged, redeemed together with the whole creation, which groans and suffers together with us in waiting[138]—now this is bordering on the impossible, this is hoping against any reasonable hope, just as it happened to Abraham when he was heading towards Moriah with the knife in his hand. But isn't it really through the reverberations of such an incredible path out, that this hope has definitely marked our world with its idea of progress? In short, it is doubtful that airplane and operating room would have existed without Abraham's faith, without the defeated and yet victorious love of the crucified Christ, and without the Christianity that followed.

This is where Christian hope really takes root, where it never turns back except to await a future deliverance from past things. Redemption looks ahead, waiting for what must come to redeem the past. God, according to Qohelet, puts "the notion of eternity in our hearts," so that all our past is not swallowed by oblivion but handed over to the memory of God, "who seeks what has already passed" to redeem it. This means that someday, even if we could build a perfect society, without wars or diseases, a society in which we could all live very long, this society, said the Russian Fyodorov,[139] would be the most unjust of all societies that

---

138. Rom 8:19–23.

139. Fyodorov, cited in Garota, "Tra Caparra e Compimento," 148. Nikolai Fyodorovich Fyodorov (surname also anglicized as Fedorov, 9 June 1829–28 Dec. 1903)

inhabited the earth, because it would forget and abandon all generations of the past in injustice and death. We also want to add the intuitions of another modern Jewish thinker, Walter Benjamin, who, in his second "Theses on the Philosophy of History," talks about the "mysterious appointment between the generations that have been and ours," as if we were "expected on earth," so that a "weak messianic force to which the past has a right" could be given to us "as to every generation before us."[140]

Looking at today's society, two great structural anxieties of man emerge, which nowadays, more than ever, take the form of an unhappy mass consciousness, a depressive pandemic: the perception of being lost and abandoned in a hostile, cruel, and senseless universe; and the loss of awareness of human dignity, of the abysmal difference between human consciousness and animal life. Cosmological nihilism on the one hand, which would like to reduce the whole creation and the human being to banal accidents of a random process intrinsic with matter; and on the other hand, the progressive depersonalization and disintegration of the subject, in turn reduced to the fragmentation of the its biological or psychological components—and therefore entirely determined by social or environmental influences—are two intrinsically connected traits of contemporary nihilism. All the dominant culture is imbued with this sneaky and creeping nihilism that weakens the human being, reducing us to meek consumers, with no destiny and wno vocation, ready, therefore, for all the *diktats* of propaganda and perhaps of some other totalitarian political power in the future.

No.

The human being is no longer "hopeless and without God in the world."[141] The universe and my life do not depend on the ruthless "elements of the world."[142] Ultimately, and beyond all the contrary appear-

---

was a Russian Orthodox Christian philosopher who was part of the Russian cosmism movement and a precursor of transhumanism. Fyodorov advocated radical life extension, physical immortality, and even resurrection of the dead, using scientific methods.

140. Benjamin, *Illuminations*, 253–54. Walter Bendix Schönflies Benjamin (15 July 1892–26 Sept. 1940) was a German Jewish philosopher, cultural critic, and essayist. An eclectic thinker, combining elements of German idealism, Romanticism, Western Marxism, and Jewish mysticism, Benjamin made enduring and influential contributions to aesthetic theory, literary criticism, and historical materialism.

141. Eph 2:12.

142. Col 2:8.

ances of the moment, everything is wanted and regulated by "reason, will, love—a Person."[143]

Evil, death, and all their enslaving derivatives, however, are not wanted by this Absolute Person, by this God who is light, undisputedly free of darkness,[144] but they are precisely the effect of going against his will, that is, the effects of a fall, a lack of listening, a catastrophic disobedience, which is radically healed only in Christ. This means that we are not slaves to the universe, to its laws, but we are free.

This is the first great hope: we human beings are not corruptible products of matter, but we are spirits, free people, who come from God, from the Absolute Power, who is always present in us and who loves us. We are embodied spirits and not just meat ready to rot, destined to go bad anyway. Jesus Christ has shown us, once and for all, that the destructive powers of the universe cannot overwhelm nor destroy the freedom and power of the Son of God. Neither death nor satanic hatred nor the destruction of the physical body can prevail over the incorruptible beauty of the Risen Body, of the true divine-human body, to which each of us is already grafted, as a branch of the luxuriant vine.

So the second great hope, which the Christian faith feeds, tells us that each of us is a son in the Son, each of us is a unique being, and firmly anchored in the heart of the Eternal, because "life in its totality is a relationship with him who is the source of life. If we are in relation with him who does not die, who is Life itself and Love itself, then we are in life. Then we *live*."[145]

This is the dignity of man: our eternal destiny.

This is our hope: our eternal destination.

We will not die and become nothing, but we will be transformed on the basis of what we have accomplished in this life, because "evildoers, in the end, do not sit at table at the eternal banquet beside their victims without distinction, as though nothing had happened."[146] This perspective of justice fills us with hope, because it tells us that human history is not a joke without consequences, nor a useless game of massacre, nor a tragedy without meaning.

---

143. Benedict XVI, *Spe Salvi*, 5.
144. 1 John 1:5.
145. Benedict XVI, *Spe Salvi*, 27.
146. Benedict XVI, *Spe Salvi*, 44.

No. In the end, all accounts are made, and each one will be given according to what he has done or not done in life on earth. In short, there is a greater justice than human justice. Moreover, only an ultramundane perspective can make us seriously hope in the justice of things, in a serious and concrete redemption for all victims, as Benedict reminds us again: "Justice cannot be, without resurrection of the dead."[147]

In other words, we must not be afraid of purifying ourselves of all that, in our Christian history, has defaced and distorted, often suffocated, our message of hope. Only this historical and structural purification can once again release, in the daily fabric of earthly affairs, the strength of our hope in the Eternal, as John Paul II again indicated in 1994, when he maintained that the church "cannot cross the threshold of the new millennium without encouraging her children to purify themselves, through repentance, of past errors and instances of infidelity, inconsistency, and slowness to act. Acknowledging the weaknesses of the past is an act of honesty and courage which helps us to strengthen our faith, which alerts us to face today's temptations and challenges and prepares us to meet them."[148] But even modern cultures should have the courage to understand their one-sidedness, their presumptions, their catastrophic errors. This mutual purification and correction between two great strands of the modern West, the Catholic Church and secularized scientific and political cultures, is a long and arduous process, through which we are rediscovering at a new level that only one who is freed in the inner depths can build truly liberating forms of life and coexistence on earth. Likewise, the freedom of the Spirit, and therefore an authentic life of faith and hope, can only translate into liberation practices for others, such as the Second Vatican Council reminded us. "Man's social nature makes it evident that the progress of the human person and the advance of society itself hinge on one another."[149] Then our hope in the Eternal becomes today, in this

---

147. Benedict XVI, *Spe Salvi*, 42.

148. John Paul II, *Tertio millennio adveniente*, 33. *Tertio millennio adveniente* (as the third millennium approaches) is an apostolic letter of Pope John Paul II, promulgated on 10 Nov. 1994, concerning preparation for the Great Jubilee of 2000.

149. Second Vatican Council, *Gaudium et spes*, 25. *Gaudium et spes* (joy and hope), the Pastoral Constitution on the Church in the Modern World, was one of the four constitutions resulting from the Second Vatican Council in 1964. Together, the Dogmatic Constitution on the Church (*Lumen Gentium* [LG]) and the Pastoral Constitution on the Church in the Modern World (GS) stand as the two pillars of the Second Vatican Council. The Dogmatic Constitution treats the nature of the church in itself; the Pastoral Constitution treats its mission in the world.

singular and—in many respects—unique situation in history; also hope in the birth of a new culture, able to combine the hope of the kingdom with all hopes of justice and earthly freedom, forcefully investing our life, freed in the Spirit, in the processes of concrete liberation of other human beings from all the structures of physical and moral enslavement that still loom over our hearts. Mind you, this may even be also God's hope.

## Conclusion

I would like to end with a story by an unknown author and two short poems of mine.

The story is called "The Four Candles."

The four candles burned slowly.

They shone so softly you could hear them speak.

The first candle said, "I am Peace, but these days, nobody wants to keep me lit."

Then Peace's flame slowly diminished and went out completely.

The second candle said, "I am Faith, but these days, people believe they no longer need me."

Then Faith's flame slowly diminished and went out completely.

Sadly, the third candle spoke, "I am Love, and I haven't the strength to stay lit any longer. People put me aside and don't understand my importance. Sometimes they even forget to love those who are nearest to them." And waiting no longer, Love went out completely.

A child entered the room and saw the three candles no longer burning.

The child asked, "Why are you not burning? You are supposed to stay lit forever and ever."

Then the fourth candle spoke gently to the little boy, "Don't be afraid, for I am Hope, and while I still burn, we can re-light the other candles."

With shining eyes, the child took the candle of Hope and lit the other three candles.

And so we never let the flame of Hope go out.

With Hope in our lives, Peace, Faith, and Love may shine brightly once again.

In this small cove of pebbles
I listen to the voice of the waves
And narrowing my eyes
I seem to hear Yours

I am weary, Lord
and I am lonely
and I have no
more prayers to offer
now it is all up
to You

# Bibliography

*I vangeli apocrifi* (*The Apocryphal Gospels*). Edited by Marcello Craveri. Torino: Einaudi, 2014.
"Apostles' Creed." https://en.wikipedia.org/wiki/Apostles%27_Creed.
Aquinas, Thomas. *Summa Theologiae*. 5 vols. Translated by V. Cairoli and F. Fiorentino. Rome: Città Nuova, 2018.
Benedict XVI, Pope. *Spe Salvi*.Vatican City: Libreria Editrice Vaticana, 2007.
Benjamin, Walter. *Illuminations*. Edited by Hannah Arendt. Translated by Harry Zohn. New York: Shocken, 1969.
*Bhagavadgita*. Edited by A. M. Esnoul, translated by B. Candian. Milan: Adelphi, 1991.
Brezzi, Francesca. *Dizionario delle Religioni*. Rome: Editori Riuniti, 1997.
Calderón, Pedro. *La vita è sogno* (*La Vida es Sueño*). Edited by D. Puccini. Milan: Garzanti, 2011.
Campbell, Joseph. *Primitive Mythology*. The Masks of God 1. New York: Penguin, 1991.
Ching, Julia and Hans Küng. *Christianity and Chinese Religions*. New York: Doubleday, 1989.
Cinelli Colombini, Donatella. "Happy Easter." Apr. 4, 2021. https://www.cinellicolombini.it/en/farm-experiences/happy-easter-2021/#.
"Destruction of the Library of Alexandria by the Arabs: The Account of the Arab Historian al-Qifti." Discorsus Boles on Coptic Nationalism Oct. 5, 2017. https://copticliterature.wordpress.com/2017/10/05/the-account-of-the-arab-historian-al-qifti-on-the-destruction-of-the-library-of-alexandria/.
Eckermann, Johann Peter. "Conversations with Goethe in the Last Years of His Life." http://www.kouroo.info/kouroo/transclusions/18/39/1839_MargaretFuller_Goethe.pdf.
Edwards, Tyron. *A Dictionary of Thoughts*. https://books.google.com/books/about/A_Dictionary_of_Thoughts.html?id=JIQcAAAAMAAJ.
Ellul, Jacques. *La speranza dimenticata* (*Hope in Times of Abandonment*). Translated by A. Zarri. Brescia: Queriniana, 1975.
*Enciclopedia Garzanti di Filosofia*. Milan: Garzanti, 1990.
Epiphanius of Salamis. *Panarion*. 3 vols. Edited and translated by G. Pini. Brescia: Morcelliana, 2016.
Fabris, Rinaldo. *Le Prime Comunità Cristiane e lo Straniero*. Bologna: EMI, 2004.
Filoramo, Giovanni. *La croce e il potere. I cristiani da martiri a persecutori*. Laterza: Bari-Roma, 2011.

Garcia, José Miguel. *Il Protagonista della Storia* (*Los Orígenes Históricos del Cristianismo*). Translated by E. Z. Merlo. Milan: Rizzoli, 2008.

Garota, Daniele. "Tra Caparra e Compimento." In *Salvati nella Speranza: Commento e guida alla lettura dell'enciclica Spe salvi di Benedetto XVI*, 121–50. Milan: Paoline, 2008.

Guzzi, Marco. "Sperare nell'Eterno per Trasformare la Storia." In *Salvati nella Speranza: Commento e guida alla lettura dell'enciclica Spe salvi di Benedetto XVI*, 66–93. Milan: Paoline, 2008.

Harnack, Adolf von. *Marcione: Il Vangelo del Dio straniero* (*Marcion: The Gospel of the Alien God*). Edited by F. Dal Bo. Milan: Marietti, 2007.

Humboldt, Wilhelm von. *La diversità delle lingue*. Edited by D. Di Cesare. Rome: Laterza, 1991.

Irenaeus of Lyon. *Contro le eresie* (*Against Heresies*). 2 vols. Edited by V. Della Giacoma. Siena: Cantagalli, 2005.

John Paul II, Pope. *Tertio Millennio Adveniente*. Vatican City: Libreria Editrice Vaticana, 1994.

Kant, Immanuel. *Kritik der Urtheilskraft* (*Critique of Judgment*). https://korpora.zim.uni-duisburg-essen.de/kant/aa05/.

Kuhn, Thomas S. *The Structure of Scientific Revolutions*. 3rd ed. Chicago: University of Chicago Press, 1996.

Lactantius. "De mortibus persecutorum." http://www.thelatinlibrary.com/lactantius/demort.shtml.

Leibniz, Gottfried Wilhelm von. *Theodicy: Essays on the Goodness of God, the Freedom of Man and the Origin of Evil*. Translated by E. M. Hubbard. https://gutenberg.org/files/17147/17147-H/17147-h.htm.

Malinowski, Bronislaw. "Argonauts of the Western Pacific." https://archive.org/details/argonautsoftheweo32976mbp/page/n63/mode/2up.

Melito of Sardis. "On the Passover." https://www.kerux.com/doc/0401A1.asp.

Moltmann, Juergen. *Teologia della speranza: Ricerche sui fondamenti e sulle implicazioni di una escatologia cristiana* (*Theology of Hope: On the Ground and the Implications of a Christian Eschatology*). Translated by A. Comba. Brescia: Queriniana, 1970.

Newman, John H. *Speech of His Eminence Cardinal Newman on the Reception of the "Biglietto" at Cardinal Howard's Palace on the 12th of May 1879*. Rome: Spithoever, 1879.

Nietzsche, Friederich. *Thus Spoke Zarathustra: A Book for All and None*. Edited by Adrian del Caro and Robert B. Pippin. Translated by Adrian del Caro. Cambridge, UK: Cambridge University Press, 2006.

Nikaya, Samyutta. "In a Rosewood Forest." https://suttacentral.net/sn56.31/en/sujato.

Oddie, William. *Chesterton and the Romance of Orthodoxy: The Making of Gilbert Keith Chesterton, 1874–1908*. Oxford: Oxford University Press, 2008.

Origen. *La Pasqua*. Edited and translated by Roberto Spataro. Rome: Città Nuova, 2011.

Pagels, Elaine. *Il vangelo segreto di Tommaso: Indagine sul libro più scandaloso del cristianesimo delle origini* (*Beyond Belief: The Secret Gospel of Thomas*). Translated by C. Lazzari. Milan: Mondadori, 2005.

———. *I Vangeli Gnostici* (*The Gnostic Gospels*). Translated by M. Parizzi. Edited by L. Moraldi. Milan: Oscar Mondadori, 1981.

Quispel, Gilles. "Marcion and the Text of the New Testament." *Vigiliae Christianae* 52 no. 4 (Jan. 1988) 349–60.
*Relativismo*. In *Enciclopedia Italiana Treccani*. https://www.treccani.it/enciclopedia/relativismo/.
Ribichini, Sergio. "Credenze e Vita Religiosa." In *I Fenici*, edited by Sabatino Moscati, 104–25. Milano: Bompiani, 1988.
*Samyutta Nikaya*. Translated and edited by V. Talamo. Rome: Ubaldini, 1998.
Second Vatican Council. *Pastoral Constitution Gaudium et Spes (Church in the Modern World)*. Vatican City: Libreria Editrice Vaticana, 1965.
Seneca, Lucius Annaeus. *De Constantia Sapientis*. Edited by N. Lanzarone. Milan: Rizzoli, 2001.
Sordi, Marta. *I Cristiani e l'Impero Romano*. Milan: Jaca, 2020.
———. *Il Cristianesimo e Roma*. Bologna: Cappelli, 1965.
Spengler, Oswald. *Il Tramonto dell'Occidente (Der Untergang des Abendlandes)*. Edited by R. Calabrese Conte, M. Cottone, and F. Jesi. Translated by J. Evola. Milan: Longanesi, 1957.
Spinoza, Baruch. *Ethica More Geometrico Demonstrata*. Edited by G. Radetti. Translated by G. Durante. Milan: Bompiani, 2019.
Tertullian. "Tertulliani adversus Marcionem Liber Quartus." www.thelatinlibrary.com/tertullian/tertullian.marcionem4.shtml.
Virgil. *Eclogues. Georgics. Aeneid: Books 1–6*. Translated by H. Rushton Fairclough. Revised by G. P. Goold. Loeb Classical Library 63. Cambridge, MA: Harvard University Press, 1916.